LIBRARY OF MONEY AND BANKING HISTORY

THE QUANTITY THEORY OF MONEY

THE QUANTITY THEORY OF MONEY

A CRITICAL STUDY OF ITS HISTORICAL DEVELOPMENT AND INTERPRETATION AND A RESTATEMENT

BY

HUGO HEGELAND

REPRINTS OF ECONOMIC CLASSICS

AUGUSTUS M. KELLEY · PUBLISHERS
NEW YORK 1969

First edition 1951
(Göteborg 1951)

Reprinted 1969 by
Augustus M. Kelley • Publishers
New York, New York 10010

FROM A COPY IN THE COLLECTIONS OF
THE NEW YORK PUBLIC LIBRARY
ASTOR, LENOX AND TILDEN FOUNDATIONS

SBN 678 00500 1

Library of Congress Catalogue Card Number
68-55731

PRINTED IN THE UNITED STATES OF AMERICA
by SENTRY PRESS, NEW YORK, N. Y. 10019

To the Memory of

Emma

CONTENTS

PREFACE

Hardly any theory in economics has been so long debated as the quantity theory of money. Yet, no thorough analysis of its original content and purpose, of its historical development, and of all its numerous misinterpretations has been undertaken. Thus, there is still no unanimity as to the formulation and interpretation of the quantity theory. Almost every economist has written something about the quantity theory, but only a very few have manifested a correct understanding of it. This lack of a clear definition is, curiously enough, very much due to the simplicity of the theory; it has occasioned a vagueness in its formulation which has led to innumerable misinterpretations of its content. Indeed, the poet's words: 'the simple thing is the difficult thing', seem to be more than a rhetoric phrase.

The chief purpose of the present study is to fill this gap in the literature of the history of economic doctrines. The basic line of thought developed in the analysis of the fundamental content of the quantity theory of money is very much due to repeated discussions with my main teacher, Professor Gustaf Åkerman. I wish to express my great gratitude for his willingness always to discuss the problems involved and for his great interest and encouragement shown me throughout my years as a student of economics and without which this work would never have been completed.

To Professor Ivar Sundbom, who originally suggested the undertaking of this study and from whose sober judgements I profited at the early stages of this book, I acknowledge my great debt. Professors Edward C. Simmons and Joseph J. Spengler have both read the manuscript. I am deeply indebted for their constructive criticism, which led to a number of improvements. Also, I should like to express my thanks to Professors Calvin B. Hoover and Erik Lindahl for their interest and encouragement shown to me.

My thanks are also due to the American Scandinavian Foundation and Statens Samhällsvetenskapliga Forskningsråd (The Swedish Social Science Research Council) which enabled me to study at American universities, primarily Duke University, for two years. I wish to acknowledge the interest shown me at all times and the suggestions made by the teachers at these universities.

Finally, I want to thank Mrs. Dorothy Bradsher, who not only scrutinized the linguistic side of the manuscript, but also drew my attention to points of obscure thought.

Gothenburg, October 1951.

HUGO HEGELAND

THE QUANTITY THEORY OF MONEY

INTRODUCTION

Throughout its history, the quantity theory of money (which will always be referred to as the quantity theory) has been stated in so many different ways that there has been little agreement concerning it. The distinctions between some heterogeneous 'quantity theories' have been completely neglected, while even those theories which are approximately alike involve so many formulations and interpretations that some authors, in dealing with the subject, do not attempt to provide definitions.

The very name of the theory is the cause of some confusion; and as it seems impossible to say who originated the name, his original meaning cannot be exactly determined. The greatest complication, however, is due to a confusion of arithmetic relations with causal relations.

The simplest way of enunciating the original quantity 'theory' is as follows: *ceteris paribus*, average prices are always in proportion to the quantity of money. So formulated, it contains only the proposition of proportionality between the quantity of money and the value of the money-unit. This formulation is obviously a truism; but its purpose was to illustrate a specific peculiarity of money, distinguishing it from all other things. This peculiarity consists in the nonexistence of any value of money as such (disregarding the value of its metallic content), so that a great or small quantity of money is of no consequence for the total wealth of a nation. This proposition, which was originally stated by Locke, was directed towards the monetary doctrines of mercantilism, according to which the quantity of money constituted one of the main sources of the total wealth of a nation. Its basic content is that money is primarily a medium of exchange, which, in point of principle, does not add to the amount of riches of a given economy. Locke's proposition, therefore, is *not a theory of the effects of changes in the quantity of money*; it contains merely an *illustration* of the relative insignificance of the amount of money (within certain practical limits), thereby emphasizing *the function of money as a medium of exchange.* If Locke's proposition is to be called a *theory*, it must be labelled as a theory of the nonexistence of any value as such of the medium of exchange.

Generally, however, the quantity theory is formulated in the following way: if other things remain the same, changes in the quantity of money *cause* proportionate price changes. This second version of the quantity theory, also containing a proposition of causality, has been the foundation of a theory for the explanation of actual variations in the price level, for the prognostication of price developments, and, what seems to be the most surprising fact, even for the explanation of individual prices. In this formulation, however, the purpose of Locke's original formulation is lost, which mainly accounts for the inadequacy of this version.

Locke's basic idea — that the function of money is fundamentally that of being a medium of exchange — naturally provides the foundation for a theory of the effects of changes in the quantity of money. According to this third version of the quantity theory, changes in the quantity of money *means* changes in the quantity of money used as a medium of exchange. Since the role of money as a store of value is left out of the picture, changes in the quantity of money will not affect the rate of circulation of money. It is only a question of changes in the amount of the medium of exchange used at the various transactions. This is the basic content of the quantity theory, which is derived from Locke's original proposition of the fundamental role of money, namely of being essentially a medium of exchange. This is also the basic interpretation of the quantity theory as it was apprehended by one of its best known defenders, Irving Fisher. This version of the quantity theory, which we maintain to be the most correct one, deals primarily with the problem of changes in the quantity of money and their effects upon the rate of circulation of money. The effect upon prices is a *secondary* question. If total supply remains constant when the quantity of money changes, prices will vary in proportion to these changes *because* the rate of circulation of money will not be affected. This is a *special* case of the proposition of the relation of changes in the quantity of money to its rate of circulation, *i.e.*, of *the* quantity theory, and should be looked upon as merely a demonstration of the irrelevance *per se* of the amount of money in circulation. Since classical economics dealt with situations of full utilization of total resources only, changes in the quantity of money (used as a medium of exchange and when dealing with long run effects) evidently appeared as a problem of the relation of these changes to average prices only. Peculiarly enough, this special case of the quantity theory of money has been interpreted as the essence of the quantity theory. This has been possible only because of a lack of knowledge of the historical development of the quantity theory.

The purpose of the first part, which also is the main part, of the present study is to scrutinize the development of the various versions of the quantity theory, thereby maintaining that the third version, which is built upon the first version, is the only one that can be properly characterized as *the quantity theory* of money, whereas the second version is partly due to a misinterpretation of the first version and partly based upon a fallacious reasoning in combination with other ideas developed earlier. The main task has not been to find who first stated the quantity theory, but *how* and *why* it was originally enunciated, how it was misinterpreted and confused with other ideas, and how its dominant influence impeded the progress of a realistic monetary theory.

Obviously, it is both impossible and unnecessary to deal with every writer on the quantity theory; but a selection will always be more or less arbitrary. The norms for selecting the economists discussed are mainly based upon the following principles: the author has been frequently mentioned in connection with the early formulation of the quantity theory, *e.g.*, Julius Paulus; he has strongly affected its interpretation, either because of being an outstanding economist, as Ricardo, or because of being very well known in other fields, as Montesquieu; he is a typical representative of the general interpretation of the theory in a certain country, *e.g.*, Helfferich, or merely of a certain interpretation, *e.g.*, Wicksell; he is a pronounced adherent, *e.g.*, F. A. Walker, or critic., *e.g.*, J. L. Laughlin, of the quantity theory; he has tried to verify the theory statistically, *e.g.*, Fisher; or he has formulated a monetary theory based on a different approach, *e.g.*, Pigou. Indeed, the interpretation of the quantity theory shows almost as many variations as the number of its interpreters.

Since the quantity theory deals with the function of money as a medium of exchange only, whereas its function as a store of value is particularly emphasized by Keynes, the second part of the present study is devoted to an attempt to synthesize these two views in a general analysis of the effects of changes in the quantity of money. Both views exemplify two distinct ways of looking at the role of money in a monetary economy and they both go the extreme. By splitting up the total quantity of money into active and passive cash balances, so that the two basic functions of money can be discussed with reference to distinctly separated quantities of money, the merits and weaknesses of the two approaches can be easily demonstrated. The main purpose of the second part is to study the effects of changes in the quantity of money with respect to the basic idea of the quantity theory, namely with respect to its effects on the rate of circulation of money, within the framework of the attempted synthesis mentioned above.

PART I

CHAPTER I

THE ALLEGED FORERUNNERS OF THE QUANTITY THEORY

1. The attempts to trace the origin of the 'simple' form of the quantity theory as far back as possible in the history of economic doctrines have at present halted at the writings of Confucius and his disciples.[1] The validity of any such attempts depends, of course, upon the meaning of the 'simple' form of the quantity theory, and upon the interpretations of these old writings. The 'simple' or 'primitive' form is generally understood as containing only a statement that changes in the quantity of money cause price changes in the same direction, without any affirmation about proportionality. The purpose of such a statement would primarily be to show that the value of money is not something fixed and intrinsic, but is a flexible relation between the quantity of money and commodities.

There is no evidence of Confucius having indicated, even indirectly, this simple relation. He stated only a few principles about money: it is a medium of exchange necessary for the economic life; it is a commodity and hence a part of wealth, and it consists of three kinds, namely, gold, silver, and copper.[2]

In the writings of Confucius' disciples, there are statements that imply the application of the general law of demand and supply to the value of money. Ma-twan-lin declared that is was »the duty of a good ruler of the empire to exercise control over the relative value of commodities and the *quality* of the money. Are commodities heavy the money is light. The fact that money is light results from the quantity of goods. Is it much a law must be passed to suppress it, and in this way to make that it becomes scarce, and consequently heavy; if it then gets too heavy again, a law must be passed to diffuse it, by which it is made light again. Surely, this is the fundamental principle by which

[1] See Chen Huan-Chang: *The Economic Principles of Confucius and His School,* New York, 1911, p. 439.

[2] *Ibid.*, pp. 435—436.

the value of the money is maintained.»[3] The causal relation is first reversed to that of the quantity theory as the lower value of money is the *result* of the diminished quantity of goods. To restore the old value of the monetary unit, the quantity of money has to be lessened, and so the causal relation is again changed. Consequently, there is no question of an exclusive causation. The value of money is thought to be determined by the relation of the amount of goods to the quantity of money, which, however, by many economists is said to be the essence of the quantity theory. But this is not the case, for it fails to include the specific point that the quantity theory brings out. Ma-twan-lin's theory is based upon the opinion that average prices shall not differ from the 'usual' purchasing power of money in *either* direction. To achieve this goal, the ruler had only to act according to the law of demand and supply.

Another disciple of Confucius, Chia Yi, holds exactly the same view: »The government accumulates copper for the control of the value of money. When the value is low, it lessens the quantity by some policy; and when it is high, it distributes the money by some policy. Hence, the price of commodities must be equalized.»[4] The goal of »equalizing» prices must refer to some given price level which is considered desirable, and has nothing to do with any proportionate price-changes. There is no statement whatsoever either of how much the quantity of money, or prices, will change.

It may be worth mentioning that the observations both refer to a period when the government alone had the power to issue coins, and consequently to determine the stamp value of the coin. This might have given the government a great power over the currency, as hardly any other means of payment existed, had it not been counterbalanced by the great amount of counterfeits that very often appeared. The main task for the government was to keep the purchasing power of money equal to its stamp value, which, in the minds of the people, probably represented a certain amount of goods. It is very interesting, indeed, that the modern policy of keeping the price level stable was considered to be the duty of the government even in those days!

Yeh-Tzu-ch'i, apparently influenced by the Confucians, wrote in 1378 A.D. that the best policy for controlling paper money was redemp-

---

[3] W. Vissering: *On Chinese Currency, Coin and Paper Money*, Leiden, 1877, p. 110. The expressions light and heavy refer to the old way of weighing the commodities and the metals when comparing their value.

[4] Chen Huan-Chang, *op. cit.*, p. 439.

tion, attained by having a reserve fund of cash. According to Chen Huan-Chang, the policy should also be »in harmony with the quantity-theory, namely, the paper should not be issued beyond a certain limit even though there is the reserve of cash. But how can we know the exact amount according to which so much paper should be issued? It is judged by the price of all commodities.»[5] But the quantity theory does not contain any judgement about what price level *should* be maintained. In fact, the amount of money issued is of *no* importance, since prices, *ceteris paribus,* will always be in proportion to the quantity of money in circulation.

2. In the long list of writers who have been pointed out as the originators of the quantity theory, Xenophon is the oldest except for the Chinese. He, who is best known as one of the famous disciples of Socrates, has a passage in his pamphlet on revenues which is sometimes referred to as containing a »crude» quantity theory.[6] When discussing how to increase the supply of silver, which would mean an increase in wealth, he points out the different effects of an increase in the production of silver from those of an increase in the production of other commodities, *e.g.*, gold, bronze, wine, *etc.*: »With an increase in the number of bronze-workers articles of bronze may become so cheap that the bronze-worker has to retire from the field. And so again with iron-founders. Or again, in a plethoric condition of the corn and wine market these fruits of the soil will be so depreciated in value that the particular husbandries cease to be remunerative .... But the converse is the case in the working of silver; there the larger the quantity of ore discovered and the greater the amount of silver extracted, the greater the number of persons ready to engage in the operation. One more illustration: take the case of movable property. No one when he has got sufficient furniture for his house dreams of making further purchases on this head, but of silver no one ever yet possessed so much that he was forced to cry 'enough'.»[7]

5 *Ibid.*, p. 443.

6 See, *e.g.*, Louis Baudin: *La Monnaie et la Formation des prix,* Première Partie: *Les éléments* (part VI of *Traité d'économie politique,* publ. under the direction of Henri Truchy), Paris, 1947, p. 512, where Xenophon is mentioned as the first representative of »la notion quantitative», *i.e.*, »les mouvements du niveau général des prix sont dus à ceux de la monnaie, mais non exclusivement et sans leur être forcement proportionnels».

7 *The Works of Xenophon,* transl. by H. G. Dakyns, 4 vols., London, 1892, vol. II, p. 335.

There is a certain resemblance in this statement to the quantity theory, which might explain the attempts to name Xenophon the first quantity theorist. His view that whatever amount of silver, *i.e.*, money, there is, it will be accepted, is also implied in the quantity theory, although the argumentation is quite different. Xenophon's argument is that nobody will ever get too much money — an idea which we will meet later on in the writings of Locke — because silver is the commonly accepted medium of exchange. But according to the quantity theory, there will never be too much money in circulation, because prices will always be in proportion to the amount of money. Both views illustrate a specific pecularity in money; but Xenophon illustrates it from the standpoint of an individual, while the quantity theory illustrates it by using total categories. The difference can also be expressed by saying that Xenophon considers the individual demand for money to be infinite, and on this basis falsely infers that the value of money does not decrease when its supply increases, while the »crude» quantity theory assumes the total demand for the value of the circulation in terms of goods to be given, thereby making the »demand» for the medium of exchange completely elastic.

The crucial point is that silver will not depreciate in value when it becomes superabundant, which means that the general law of demand and supply has no bearing on the value of the commonly accepted medium of exchange. This unique position of silver is accentuated by the fact that gold, in spite of being a precious metal, will decrease in value when its supply is increased. Evidently, Xenophon's statement is diametrically opposed to the quantity theory, and one might instead be inclined to denote him as the first anti-quantity theorist, as is done by Paul Lambert.[8] Yet, even this is hardly correct, since the essence of the quantity theory is not that the value of money will be influenced by changes in the quantity; moreover, the quantity theory was not formulated until the end of the seventeenth century.

3. The Roman lawyer Julius Paulus is sometimes quoted as the first pronouncer of the quantity theory.[9] This is primarily due to the following remark in *Corpus juris civilis*:

---

[8] *La Théorie quantitative de la Monnaie,* Paris, 1938, p. 10.

[9] See, *e.g.,* A. W. Marget: *The Theory of Prices,* 2 vols., New York, 1938—42, vol. I, p. 9; E. F. Heckscher: *Mercantilism,* 2 vols., transl. by M. Shapiro, London, 1935, vol. II, p. 225; E. Kemmerer: *Money and Prices,* New York, 1907, p. 2; and K. Wicksell: *Interest and Prices,* transl. by R. F. Kahn, London, 1936, p. 38.

»The origin of selling and buying lies in the trade of bargain, because in bygone days money did not exist as now and one thing was not called commodity and the other one price .... But since it might not always and not so easily happen so fortunately, that while you had what I wanted, I in return owned what you wanted to possess, a material was chosen, the value of which, being generally recognized and lasting, would remedy the difficulties at the bargaining by the equality of the quantities.[10] And this material, coined by the state, is connecting the right to use and to own not so much on account of its substance (content) as on account of its quantity (number of coins), and so both are not longer called commodities, but one of them price.»[11]

There seems to be a miscomprehension of this quotation and no general agreement on the interpretation has been reached. *Publica ac perpetua aestimatio*, which means the generally acknowledged and lasting value of money, can, of course, be apprehended in different ways. But that Paulus should have meant that the value of money will always remain constant, regardless of the quantity, seems very unlikely, although it is impossible to say definitely what he did mean. Such an interpretation, which is a distortion of the passage, would mean the opposite of what the quantity theory states. It is more likely that Paulus was thinking only of money as always having a value of exchange. Whether this should remain constant or not is not indicated.

More questionable is the word *quantitate* in the phrase *usum dominiumque .... quantitate.* R. Gonnard has found two possible interpretations. According to the first, it is a question of a numerical sum alluding to the value of money as being based upon its function as a legal medium of exchange. This interpretation, which Gonnard holds to be the best one, makes Paulus appear as a nominalist. The other interpretation, which is considered to be more doubtful, is exactly

[10] That is, the equality or the correspondence of the sum of money to the value of the commodity at both transactions, thus first at the selling, and then at the new bargain with this sum of money.

[11] »Origo emendi vendendique a permutationibus coepit; olim enim non ita erat numus, neque aliud merx, aliud pretium vocabatur .... Sed quia non semper nec facile concurrebat, ut, quum tu haberes, quod ego desiderarem, invicem haberem, quod tu accipere velles, electa materia est, cuius publica ac perpetua aestimatio difficultatibus permutationum aequalitate quantitatis subveniret; eaque materia forma publica percussa usum dominiumque *non tam ex substantia praebet, quam ex quantitate*, nec ultra merx utrumque, sed alterum pretium vocatur.» *Corpus juris civilis, L: 1. Dig. XVIII, 1* (about 200 A.D.), Impressio nona, Lipsiae (Leipzig), 1861; italics added.

the opposite, namely, that *quantitate* alludes to the number of units of weight in the total amount of coins.[12]

It is obvious that Gonnard is giving a considerably more comprehensive and suggestive meaning to Paulus' thoughts than Paulus himself ever intended, even if he could possibly be classified as a nominalist when he set down that (the right to use) money was mediated *non tam ex substantia praebet quam ex quantitate.* For this must refer, as A. E. Monroe has indicated,[13] to the legal position of money in purchase contracts. In these contracts a certain amount of money usually was settled upon, not any constant amount of value, and this amount was not changed when the price level went up or down. The word *quantitate* undoubtedly alludes to this numerical sum as distinguished from what the sum represents in value, *i.e.*, then as now, the contracts had as little consideration for the changes of the value of money. Gonnard seems to overlook this and regards it as a question of the determination of the value of money.

What appears as particularly peculiar is that the phrase *non tam ex substantia praebet quam ex quantitate* often is taken as proof of Paulus being the first to state the quantity theory in its most primitive form. Paulus does not speak of any value of money. Instead, he says that »the money coined by the state is connecting the right to use or own not so much on account of its substance as on account of its quantity». He discusses money as an object of legal claims and is not considering an economic-theoretical point of view, which is rather natural since he was a lawyer.[14]

What Paulus means, and, in fact, also says, is that the mediation of the right to use and to own by the instrumentality of money in the first place is expressed by the quantity of money and not by the substance of money, *i.e.*, not by a certain amount of weight, as was originally done.

From what has been said above, it should have become clear that to Julius Paulus cannot be ascribed the 'merit' of having first pro-

[12] R. Gonnard: *Histoire des doctrines monétaires,* 2 vols., Paris 1935—36, vol. I, pp. 54—57.

[13] A. E. Monroe: *Monetary Theory before Adam Smith* (Harvard Economic Studies, vol. XXV), Cambridge, Mass., 1923, pp. 10—11.

[14] The only author found who holds about the same opinion is A. E. Monroe: »The passage from Paulus .... has also been interpreted as implying a fiat theory of the value of money ... Such a reading is misleading, however, it seems to me, for it loses sight of the fact that these writers [the Roman lawyers] were developing a juristic rather than an economic theory of money. They were concerned with the 'paying power' rather than the 'purchasing power' of money» (*ibid.*, p. 11).

nounced the primitive form of the quantity theory. Why that ever has happened can probably only be explained by the attempts of some economic writers to date the origin of the theory as far back as possible in order to claim to have made a discovery.

Nor can one discover any vestiges of a quantity theory or even a discussion of the influence of changes in the supply of money on its value in the writings of the canonists.[15] The Scholastics, however, provided a more advanced discussion of economic problems, and made several statements about the influence of the quantity of money. Henry of Ghent said that the value of money varied just like that of all other things, *i.e.*, in conformity with time, place and quantity.[16] He especially emphasized the supply available. This, however, is not a statement of the quantity theory, the kernel of which is not that the value of money is influenced by its quantity.

Another author who has been mentioned in this connection is Nicole Oresme,[17] one of the great spirits of the fourteenth century, but it has not been possible to find any observations by him which could be interpreted as indicating any primitive form of the quantity theory. Mostly he speaks of the peril of coining below the standard, of some technical details about the alloying, and of the relation of the value of gold to silver.[18] His great follower, Gabriel Biel, who wrote the most important book on money of the fifteenth century, has no passage on the relation between the quantity of money and its value.[19] The book is primarily a discussion, with repeated references to Oresme's writings, of some moral views on falsifying money and under what circumstances the coined value of money might be altered.

---

[15] See W. Endemann: *Studien in der Romanischkanonistischen Wirtschafts- und Rechtslehre*, Berlin, 1883.

[16] E. Schreiber: *Die volkswirtschaftlichen Anschauungen der Scholastik seit Thomas v. Aquin*, Jena, 1923, pp. 132—133. See also A. E. Monroe, who points out that Antonine of Florence indirectly noted the influence of supply »in his remark that, when gold is hoarded, it becomes scarce, and more goods will be given for the same money» (*op. cit.*, p. 26).

[17] See J. Dmochowski: »Nicolas Copernic économiste» (*R: E. p.*, 1925, p. 107) where Oresme's influence on Copernicus is pointed out.

[18] See *Traictie de la première invention des monnaies de Nicole Oresme* publ. by M. L. Wolowski, Paris, 1864. J. Y. Le Branchu, in »La théorie quantitative de la monnaie au XVIe siècle» (*R. E. p.*, 1934, p. 1245), and P. Lambert (*op. cit.*, p. 11) share this view.

[19] *Treatise on the Power and Utility of Moneys*, London, 1930.

4. Nicolas Copernicus, the famous astronomer, has also been designated as the originator of the fundamental content of the quantity theory.[20] This is mainly because of a statement in his *Monete cudende ratio* (1526), in which he declares:

»Money loses its value above all when it is increased too much, for example, when too great a quantity of silver has been transformed into money, so that men will strive to attain bullion rather than the denominator. Money will lose all its 'dignity' when it cannot any longer buy as much silver as it contains, and when it will be profitable to melt it down. The only remedy, then, is not to coin money any more until it has restored its equilibrium and regained a higher value than bullion.»[21]

This quotation says simply that an increased quantity of money will lower the value of it, which could hardly be any novelty. Copernicus' view is rather peculiar, because it says that the value of money can *sink below* the value of the quantity of metal contained. Then the confidence (the »dignity») in the coin as a legal tender will completely disappear and one can use only the uncoined metal as a means of payment, making it profitable to melt the coins and to pay with bullion.[22] So if the metal in question does not appear as coins, its value will increase! It seems inconceivable that the confidence in the coin could be so shaken, but it is possible that Copernicus had such an experience. He was well aware of all the properties of money and was requested to carry out several monteary reforms, *e.g.*, the Prussian Monetary Reform in 1519.[23]

---

[20] See, *e.g.*, P. Lambert, *op. cit.*, p. 11. According to Lambert, Copernicus is the first one to express the fundamental relation of the quantity theory. Of the same opinion are J. Dmochowski, *op. cit.*, pp. 114—115, and Paul Harsin: *Les doctrines monétaires et financières en France du XVIe siècle,* Paris, 1928, p. 10.

[21] *Traité de la monnaie de Copernic,* publ. by M. L. Wolowski, Paris, 1864, p. 53. *Cf.* p. 33, where one reads: »La monnaie doit être rare pour avoir une valeur élevée.» See also J. Y. Le Branchu: *Ecrits notables sur la monnaie,* 2 vols., Paris, 1934, part I, p. 7.

[22] Dmochowski's assertion that Copernicus only said that the prestige (dignitas) and not the value of the money was lost when the quantity was increased, must be due to some misinterpretation (*op. cit.*, p. 115). Copernicus clearly says that money will lose its value when it is increased too much, and when, as a result, one prefers ingots instead of coin, it will *also* lose all of its »dignity»!

[23] See H. Schmauch: »Nikolas Copernicus und die preussiche Münzreform» (in *Personal- und Vorlesungs-Verzeichnis.* 3. Trimester 1940, Staatl. Akademie zu Braunsberg). Nothing is said here as to the causal relation mentioned above. In the Saxon controversy of the new monetary reforms, about 1530, the same causal relation is mentioned (see W. Lotz: *Die drei Flugschriften über den Münzstreit der sächsischen Alber-*

The idea that Copernicus expressed himself carelessly and probably meant that the currency was coined below the standard is not compatible with the statement that it is profitable to melt the coin. His view implies that the value of the currency is completely dependent upon its quantity, exactly as if it had been an irredeemable paper currency. Of course one can characterize such an opinion as *a* quantity theory of the value of money and to that extent Dmochowski is right in saying that Copernicus was the first to enunciate such a principle.[24] But he cannot be characterized as the founder of *the* quantity theory, since he never mentions that specific peculiarity of money which both Locke and Hume so energetically emphasized.

5. Because of his well-known observation of the causal relation between changes in the quantity of money and prices, Jean Bodin was often mentioned, especially before Copernicus' book became known, as the founder of the fundamental content of the quantity theory.[25] It was during the discussion of the considerable increase in

tiner und Ernestiner um 1530, Leipzig, 1893, pp. 58—60 and 62). That discussion was probably influenced by Copernicus' writings. Although this causal relation was known, there was, according to Monroe, no connection between this idea and the theory of prices (Monroe, *op. cit.*, p. 55). *Cf.* Heckscher, however, who mentions that the relationship of little money — low prices, and plenty of money — high prices, was clearly understood as early as the Saxon coinage controversy (*op. cit.*, vol. II, p. 225).

[24] Dmochowski, *op. cit.*, p. 115.

[25] See M. Palyi's article »Die Quantitätstheorie» (in *Handwörterbuch der Staatswissenschaften,* 4 ed., vol. 6, pp. 1147—1152) where he alleges that Bodin's observation is »the starting point of the quantity theory of money»; M. J. Bonn: *Spaniens Niedergang während der Preisrevolution des 16. Jahrhunderts,* Stuttgart, 1896, pp. 12—13; H. Denis: *Les récentes théories monétaires en France,* Paris, 1938, p. XI; A. Dubois: *Précis de l'Histoire des Doctrines Economiques,* Paris, 1903, pp. 185—186, where he calls Bodin the first great quantity theorist; and P. Harsin: »Bodin et la théorie monétaire au XVIe siècle», *Revue belge de Philologie et d'Histoire,* 1928, pp. 1301—1304.

A. Pose declares that one generally has to go back to Bodin to find the origin of the quantity theory, although it was first fully expressed by Locke (»Esquisse de l'évolution de la théorie quantitative», *R. H. e.*, 1926, p. 154). H. Hauser is much too precipitate when he claims that Bodin is the originator of *all* those ideas which led up to the quantity theory by Locke (*Réponse au paradoxe de M. Malestroit,* publ. by H. Hauser with an introduction and under the title: *La vie chère au XVIe siècle, la response de Jean Bodin à M. de Malestroit,* 1568; Paris 1932, p. LXXV). E. J. Hamilton holds about the same opinion (see »American Treasure», *Journal of Economic and Business History,* 1928, p. 33, note 6), but in his great investigation of prices in Spain 1501—1650, he found this causal relation indicated by earlier authors, *e.g.,* Francisco Lopéz de Gómara. He does not think that Gómara had any importance in the spread of the idea in Spain, but that this was accomplished by Bodin's well-known

prices on the continent, particularly in France, that Bodin made his well-known remark that the chief and almost sole cause of the increase was the great imports of precious metals.[26] Other, although, less important, causes, which he mentioned in a later edition of his famous reply to Monsieur de Malestroit's paradoxes, were devaluations, monopolies, the shortage of food, and the extravagances of kings and noblemen.[27] Of these causes, which were more generally known, Malestroit claimed devaluations to be the most important.

Peculiar as it may seem at first, Bodin's often mentioned statement was of no significance in the formulation of the quantity theory. He laid down the main reason for the actual price increase in France during the sixteenth century. Besides, his statement suggests that he by no means considered himself to be the first to establish the causal relation as such, for he refers to the same relation experienced during the reign of the Roman emperors Paulus Æmilius and Julius Caesar.[28] What he did do was to make this idea widely known.[29] The main reason for his remark being so commonly and immediately accepted was its obvious support by facts, as there had been a substantial influx of

---

pamphlet. Nor does he believe that the final word about the origin of the quantity theory can be said before we know more of the history of banking and of the influence of credit on prices at that time; see E. J. Hamilton: *American Treasure and the Price Revolution in Spain 1501—1560* (Harvard Economis Studies, vol. XLII), Cambridge, Mass., 1934, pp. 4 and 292—294.

A more adequate statement of Bodin's relation to the quantity theory is given by A. E. Monroe and A. W. Marget. Monroe mentions that although Bodin was the first to give the influence of the quantity of money on its value its proper place, he by no means said that it was something different in kind or degree from the effect on values in general. But it was Bodin's great emphasis on this statement that was responsible for the development, later in the century, of the monetary theory, wherein only the supply of, and not the demand for, money was discussed (Monroe, *op. cit.*, p. 58).

Marget speaks of »a type of reasoning which goes back at least as far as the time of Jean Bodin», namely, »a formulation with respect to the forces determining 'prices' in which the *quantity of money* was given an unmistakable place» (Marget, *op. cit.*, vol. I, p. 9).

[26] *Réponse au paradoxe de M. de Malestroit,* p. 9.

[27] These causes were not mentioned in the first edition of his reply. See Le Branchu: *Ecrits notables sur la monnaie,* part I, p. 83, which contains the second edition (1578) of Bodin's *Réponse à M. de Malestroit.*

[28] *Cf.* Heckscher (*op. cit.,* vol. II, p. 225) who emphasizes that the idea of prices being determined by the demand for goods on the part of the holders of money is so simple that it occurred at a very early date.

[29] In his introduction to Bodin's *Réponse,* Hauser writes that Bodin became an authority who was constantly quoted by Englishmen (*op. cit.*, p. LXVIII).

precious metals. The deplorable result was, however, that gradually all price increases — and, later, nearly all changes in prices — were said to be caused by changes in the quantity of money, and so the idea of an *exclusive* causal relationship appeared. This idea was then erroneously ascribed to the quantity theory and even to Bodin!

The importance of Bodin's statement is, as Marget points out, that it laid the foundation for the opinion that variations in the quantity of money have a decisive effect on the value of money, *i.e.*, the price level.[30] Obviously, he simply applied the law of demand and supply when explaining the changes in the value of money. This law was then confused with the content of the quantity theory, and thus all the statements about Bodin being the founder of the quantity theory have arisen. Bodin never hinted at the essence of the quantity theory, but he did influence its *formulation,* so that the kernel of the theory was misunderstood.

Bodin's view was taken over by Antoyne de Montchrétien in 1615, but with a very interesting addition, namely, that prices by no means had increased always *in proportion* to he additional quantity of money.[31] Bodin never claimed that, but the remark shows a reflection of eventual proportionate price changes. Whether or not Montchrétien was influenced by the idea behind the quantity theory is impossible to say, but it is very likely that the idea had been in the air long before it was clearly written down by Locke (see Molina, p. 21).

6. The economic writer who most frequently is characterized as »Father of the Quantity Theory» is Bernardo Davanzati.[32] Born

[30] H. Hauser has tried to show that Bodin also maintained a certain proportionality between prices and the quantity of money, but his reference does not give any support to this thought. (»Un précurseur: Jean Bodin, Angevin», *Annales d'Histoire économique et sociale,* 1931, p. 384. Lambert also considers Hauser's opinion untenable (Lambert, *op. cit.,* p. 15). There is no suggestion of any proportionate price changes in Bodin's famous *Réponse à M. de Malestroit.*

[31] Antoyne de Montchrétien: Traicté de l'Œconomie Politique, 1615 (ed. by Funck-Brentano, Paris, 1889), p. 257; also see J. W. Angell: *The Theory of International Prices* (Harvard Economic Studies, vol. XXVIII), Cambridge, Mass., 1926, p. 207.

[32] See, *e.g.*, Gino Arias: »Les précurseurs de l'economie monétaire en Italie, Davanzati et Montanari», *R. E. p.*, 1922, p. 737; J. Y. Le Branchu: »La théorie quantitative de la monnaie», *R. E. p.*, 1934, pp. 1255—1256, although he is more reserved in his statement; Lambert, *op. cit.*, p. 17; and K. Wicksell: *Lectures on Political Eco-*

in Florence, he later became head of the Mint House at Naples. In 1588 he published *Lezione delle Monete*, in which the following passage is generally interpreted as the origin of the quantity theory: »All these earthly things are, by the consent of nations, worth all the gold (and in this I include silver and copper) that is wrought: therefore all men covet all the gold to buy all the things, to satisfy all their wants, to be happy. The parts follow the whole: therefore, however much of the happiness of a kingdom, of a city or of a man depends on a thing, that much is it worth of all its gold or labor.»[33]

The characteristic of this statement is the equalization of the value of the total quantity of money with the value of the total quantity of goods. The idea that the total quantity of money represents a certain value lays one foundation for the derivation of the quantity theory. It follows, logically, that the more units of money there are, *ceteris paribus,* the less their value will be; the relation being characterized by an inverse proportionality. But it does not follow that *if* the quantity of money is increased, while other things remain the same, the *effect* will be that prices will be raised proportionately, since the first statement does not contain a proposition of a causal relationship of that kind under actual conditions.[34]

Davanzati himself did not draw this conclusion, but said that the *parts follow the whole,* characterizing this as »the rule and mathematical proportion which applies to the relation between the goods and gold (money)». Thus, if the value of one commodity constitutes a given part, say one thousandth, of the total value of the commodities (expressed in terms of »labor» or »utility»), then it constitutes also one thousandth of the total quantity of gold. Davanzati equalized the

nomy, transl. by E. Classen, 2 vols., London, 1935, vol. II, p. 144. Angell agrees with Gino Arias that Davanzati was the first to develop a theory of the value of money, and that Bodin, on the other hand, never gave any precise definition, either of the value of money, or of value in general (Angell, *op. cit.*, p. 206, note 3).

33 »tutte queste [le cose terrene] per accordo delle genti (I) vaglion tutto l'oro (e con esso intendo l'ariento e 'l rame) che si travaglia: braman adunque tutti gli uomini tutto l'oro per comperar tutte le cose, per appagar tutte lor voglie e bisogni, per esser felici. Le parti seguon la natura del tutto: però quanta parte di tutta la felicità d'un regno, d'una città, d'un uomo alcuna cosa opera e cagiona, tanta parte vale di tutto 'l suo oro o lavoro.» *Lezione delle Monete* (Scrittori Classici Italiani di Economia Politica, vol. 2), Milano, 1804, p. 32.

34 Commenting on Davanzati's statement, Monroe writes that the implication of it would be that »changes in the supply of the money metals would cause proportionate changes in their value» (Monroe, *op. cit.,* p. 60). This is not the correct way of phrasing the implication, however, as it includes a new proposition of causation.

value of the total quantity of gold both to the total amount of labor invested in all commodities, and to their total amount of utility.[35]

Davanzati's conclusion also came to be interpreted as a theory of individual prices, that is, that the prices of goods were determined by a purely quantitative comparison between the group of commodities in question, the total amount of commodities, and the quantity of gold.[36] If the group of commodities constituted one hundredth of the total amount of goods, then its total price became one hundreth of the quantity of money, and so the price of a single commodity was supposed also to be determined. As Davanzati himself points out, such a comparison requires a constant over-all view of the commodities in order to determine the mathematical proportion of goods to the quantity of money.[37] In this way, he became the founder of a quantitative theory of money which explained individual prices in terms of a purely quantitative comparison between money and goods. It was never explained how the unit of measure, which made the comparison possible, and which, in fact, would have determined relative prices, was determined. The ideas of Davanzati became confused with those of Locke and, especially, with those of Hume, who both formulated the original quantity theory. And so the quantity theory was sometimes criticised as an explanation of individual prices.[38]

There is one instance in which Davanzati speaks of proportionate price changes, though it has nothing to do with the quantity theory. He mentions that after Rome was defeated by Hannibal, the currency was coined more and more below the standard, so that finally it contained only one twelfth of the original content, and the result should have been that prices increased from 1 to 12.[39] When dealing with the effects of the increase of gold and silver from the American countries, he declares that when all that gold turns to the markets in Europe, it will lose its value and become a 'drug'. Accordingly, the value of gold is determined by its scarcity, and so far Davanzati is consistent with

---

[35] *Cf.* F. Hoffman: *Kritische Dogmengeschichte der Geldwerttheorien,* Leipzig, 1907, pp. 16—17, where Davanzati's inconsistency when dealing with the value of all commodities and with one commodity is stressed. The value of a commodity depended upon its utility, scarceness, and to some degree, on the amount of labor invested. *Cf.* also Arias, *op. cit.*, p. 741.

[36] See, *e.g.*, Montesquieu's interpretation, p. 32.

[37] Davanzati, *op. cit.*, p. 33.

[38] See, *e.g.*, Laughlin, p. 78.

[39] Davanzati, *op. cit.*, p. 44.

his theory of value for a single commodity, but not with his idea that the total value of gold equals the value of all commodities.[40]

It seems most probable that Davanzati did not have any influence on the formulation of the quantity theory as it was stated by Locke and Hume.[41] His comparison and false equalization of the quantity of money to the total amount of goods did not aim at a demonstration of the specific property of money indicated by the quantity theory, but at an explanation of the exchange *value* of money. This explanation has sometimes been understood as the essence of the quantity theory and elucidates the opinion that Davanzati founded the quantity theory. Unfortunately, it rests upon a misunderstanding, primarily due to a confusion of its derivation with its content, and of the purpose of the quantity theory. Besides, it is theoretically impossible to determine the value of money in the way proposed by Davanzati, since the quantitative comparison has to be based on a common standard of measure, which implies that the relation of value is already settled.[42] The quantity theory avoids this, simply by assuming that the quantity of money represents (or constitutes) a given value. Davanzati's way of reasoning, however, lends itself very easily to the illustration of the quantity theory, although he never turned this possibility into fact.[43] This was done after the quantity theory was enunciated by Locke.

7. In the middle of the nineteen-thirties, Bernhard W. Dempsey, an American who apparently had a close knowledge of the Spanish

---

[40] Davanzati, *ibid.*, p. 35. Monroe intimates that Davanzati's conclusion does not follow from his principle that »all goods are worth all the gold, silver, and copper, but rather from a consideration of the influence of demand upon the value of the metals». (Monroe, *op. cit.*, p. 60). As Le Branchu points out, one must not interpret this statement too strictly. He believes that Davanzati wanted only to emphasize that too great an increase of gold will have the effect that gold cannot be considered as a precious metal any longer, and that one will have to look for another rare metal. Furthermore, it should be remembered that Davanzati's *Lezione delle Monete* was written only as a lecture to the Academy of Florence (Le Branchu: »La théorie quantitative», *R. E. p.*, 1934, pp. 1254—1255).

[41] He who first adopted Davanzati's opinion outside Italy is said to be Johann Becher in his *Politischer Discurs*, 1656 (see Monroe, *op. cit.*, p. 110).

[42] See, *e.g.*, Wicksell who emphasizes that »there is nothing in the act of exchange as such which can determine the value of money or concrete commodity prices» (*Lectures*, vol. II, p. 22).

[43] Le Branchu holds very much the same opinion (»La théorie quantitative», *R. E. p.*, 1934, p. 1256).

literature of the sixteenth and seventeenth centuries, introduced a new name into the discussion about the founder of the quantity theory. He referred to a book by Luis Molina, a Spaniard, *De Jure et Justitia*, published in 1593, in which one is confronted with the following remark: »The value of money will increase by as much as the supply in a given place is less and, other things being equal, much more can be bought for the same amount of money.»[44] If the translation is correct, the statement undoubtedly contains Hume's conclusion from the proposition of the quantity theory, even though Molina does not use the word 'proportionate'. But Molina's statement, apparently, is not based upon the quantity theory, which is partly indicated by the quotation itself. He emphasizes the *change* in the value of money more than the *proportionality*, as he explicatively adds that the smaller quantity of money will buy more commodities than the corresponding quantity when there is more money (and the same amount of goods). It is still more evident in his assertion that the value of money changes just like that of other things, that is, according to its abundance or scarcity and its demand. These are the causes of its value being lower in one place than in another, and of its differing in the same place at different times.[45] His argumentation is probably directed partly to those who still thought that the value of money was something intrinsic and constant.

It would not be correct to characterize Molina as the founder of the quantity theory. He does not give a satisfactory explanation of *why* the value of money »will increase by as much as the supply in a given place is less», which explains why he did not realize the implications of his statement. Nor does he have any importance in the formulation of the quantity theory as expounded by Locke and Hume. His intention is to explain why the value of money changes, not to indicate any specific property of it. On the contrary, he thought it followed the same laws as all other things. It cannot be denied, however, that he seems to be the first to pronounce a statement — probably casually — which contains roughly the conclusion drawn from the proposition of the quantity theory. There is the possibility, of course, that some ardent investigator of the old monetary literature will find another statement of the same kind that is still older, but is also very likely that it will have the same insignificance for those first formulations of the

44 Quoted from B. W. Dempsey: »The Historical Emergence of Quantity Theory», *Q. J. E.*, 1935, p. 180, who has translated from an edition printed in Amsterdam, 1615.

45 *Ibid.*, 180—181.

quantity theory which aimed at the indication of a specific property of the means of exchange.

There has been some discussion as to whether Molina was influenced by Jean Bodin. Dempsey has not found any reason for making such an assumption, in spite of Molina's remark that the influence of the great import of precious metals on prices was known earlier by his fellow-countrymen. One of them, Fransisco Lopéz de Gómara, had already declared in 1558 that the great flow of precious metals was the real cause of the price increase, and E. Hamilton cannot find any particular reason for honoring Molina.[46] Contrary to Dempsey, he thinks that Molina knew, either directly or indirectly, of Bodin's work, which he believes to have been written several years before 1558. However it might be, it is quite evident that this discussion centers around the question of when the causal relation between changes in the quantity of money and price changes was first indicated, and not around the fundamental content of the quantity theory.

8. Not until a century later did Davanzati get a follower who built upon his idea that the quantitative proportion between goods and money determined the exchange value of money. The man was Geminiano Montanari, professor of mathematics and astronomy at the universities of Bologna and Padua. His discussion is more refined and he does not equalize the value of all goods to the total amount of precious metals, although he refers to Davanzati's statement when making his observation: »all the commodities in commerce between men, taken together, are worth as much as the gold, silver, and copper, coined and in circulation».[47]

This statement is the first comparison between the quantity of money in circulation and the total amount of goods to be exchanged, and differs decisively from Davanzati's all-including comparison. The idea indirectly forms the background of the equation of exchange and has

[46] See Hamilton's rejoinder to Dempsey's article in the same number of the *Q. J. E.*, (1935), pp. 185—192, and *American Treasure and the Price Revolution*, pp. 292—293. *Cf.* also Le Branchu: »La théorie quantitative», *R. E. p.*, 1934, p. 1294, who believes that Gómara's work (Annales) was published in 1557, and therefore puts him before Bodin.

[47] »tutte le comodità degli uomini che sono fra loro in commercio, comprese insieme, tanto vagliono quanto l'oro, l'argento ed il rame coniato che pure fra loro corre in commercio»; *Della Moneta* (Scrittori Classici Italiani di Economia Politica, vol. 3), p. 45. The book was first published in 1683. *Cf.* also p. 89.

probably influenced those economists who formulated similar equations long before Fisher. All these equations have the same purpose as Montanari's comparison, namely to determine the value of money.

According to Monroe, the proposition quoted above »may fairly be said to be the first clearcut statement of the quantity theory».[48] Such a conclusion, however, is based upon a different interpretation of *the* quantity theory. It assumes the quantity theory to be primarily a theory of the value of money, which can be expressed in terms of a quantitative comparison. No doubt such an explanation can very properly be called *a* quantity theory of money, as was pointed out under Davanzati, but it is not *the* quantity theory of money which was formulated by Locke and Hume. The purpose of the latter theory was *not* to determine the value of money, but to emphasize a specific peculiarity of the medium of exchange.

Montanari never alleged any proportionate price changes, only that if the volume of the commodities in the market remains the same, an increased amount of money must result in higher prices. The value of money depends upon the value of the commodities, which in turn derive their value primarily from the wants and desires of the consumers, and secondarily from their utility. He distinguishes clearly between the price level and the relative prices of goods. The former is determined by the amount of goods in relation to wants at a given quantity of money, while the latter depends upon the utility and scarcity of the goods.[49] That derivation of individual prices attempted by use of Davanzati's formulation of a mathematical rule, cannot be found in the writings of Montanari. Nevertheless, it gradually won support.

It is quite clear that Montanari had no influence on the foundation of the quantity theory, although it is possible that his work was of some importance in its later development, which ultimately resulted in the confusion of his quantitative theory of the value of money with *the* quantity theory. In spite of his, in many respects rather advanced, observations on money and coinage, his work was probably not read by English economists until very much later.

9. It is not surprising that the notion of a causal relationship between the value of money and its quantity is very old, but it may seem somewhat strange that it took such a long time before it was commonly recognized.

[48] Monroe, *op. cit.*, p. 109.

[49] Montanari, *op. cit.*, pp. 58—59.

The relation was probably known first by the Chinese, since they had developed a currency system before any other country and therefore had more experience with money. They displayed the idea of regulating the value of money by changing its quantity. The same causal relationship was also recognized by the Romans, although much later, and, as in the case of the Chinese, from experience. But the thought that precious metals had an intrinsic and invariable value must have been very strong. Only in those countries, where there had been more significant changes in the supply of money, was the causation apprehended by some economic writers. The dominant opinion explained price movements in virtue of the conditions on the commodity side, presuming that the value of precious metals, when being used as a common means of exchange, was fixed. This view was also supported by the circumstance that there had been very few significant changes in the price level before the sixteenth century.

Bodin's famous reply to Malestroit, in which he made the great imports of precious metals the main cause of the great price increase, attracted enormous attention. It seemed as if nobody ever thought of that explanation, in spite of the causal relation as such being mentioned earlier by some of the Scholastics and by Copernicus. This lack of realization, however, became more than compensated for after Bodin's observation was commonly accepted. It became the foundation of a monetary doctrine which aimed at explaining the variations, mainly the increases, in the price level as being caused primarily by increases in the quantity of money. Then it was but a short step to assert an exclusive causation. This doctrine, more or less rigorously stated, seized a remarkably strong hold on the economists, and dominated the discussion of the movements of the price level during an extended period. Even in the beginning of the twentieth century, it still had rather many adherents. Peculiarly enough, this doctrine, which has been labelled as a theory of the value of money, has frequently been confused with the quantity theory. It is obvious, however, that this doctrine is only an explanation of actual variations in the price level according to the law of demand and supply, and does not explain the value of money. Such an explanation was proposed by Davanzati and further developed by Montanari. It comprised a theory which asserted that the value of the quantity of money in circulation was equal to the value of all commodities in trade. Hence the value of the money-unit is inversely proportionate to the quantity of money, though neither Davanzati, nor Montanari drew this conclusion.

What the quantity theory has in common with Davanzati's and Montanari's propositions is not the property of being a theory of the value of money, but the presumption that the total quantity of money represents a certain value in terms of goods. Regardless of *how* this value is determined, it follows that there must be a very simple arithmetic relation between the value of one money-unit and the quantity of money. This relation, which contains the proposition of the quantity theory, was often formulated as follows: changes in the quantity of money, *ceteris paribus,* cause proportionate changes in the price level, (even when the purpose was to indicate the proportionality only). When erroneously stated in this way, the theory contains two propositions: one of proportionality and one of causality. Tracing the origin of the content of these propositions, the proposition of causality has been ascribed to Bodin, who in fact only explained an actual increase in the price level, while Davanzati is named as the founder of the other proposition, because it is inherent in his monetary theory. The misunderstanding of the purpose and the erroneous formulation of the quantity theory made it possible to trace its origin much farther back in history than when it was actually enunciated, and connected its foundation with two names, frequently mentioned, which did not have any influence on its first formulation.

Even if a benevolent interpretation of Molina's statement would reveal the idea of the quantity theory, there are obvious reasons for not denoting him as the founder of the theory. The specific peculiarity of the medium of exchange, which the quantity theory illustrates, is not emphasized by any of the authors discussed in this chapter and it is very likely that nobody stated it before Locke.

CHAPTER II

THE FOUNDERS OF THE QUANTITY THEORY AND ITS FIRST CRITICS

1. John Locke never dealt with the functions and characteristics of money as a coherent subject. His observations were incidental to his discussion of the consequences of lowering the rate of interest (from 6 to 4 per cent) and of raising the exchange value of money (by changing its denomination) in his contemporary England. Because of his wellknown confusion of money with capital, his ideas are often very inconsistent and contradictory, which partly explains why he is designated as the founder of the quantity theory by references to completely different statements. Another reason is the different interpretations of the quantity theory itself.

Locke gives the most clear-cut statement of the quantity theory when he advances the example of an island separate from the commerce of the rest of the world and with a given quantity of money which cannot be increased. In such a country »any quantity of that money would serve to drive any proportion of trade, whether more or less; there being counters enough to reckon by, and the value of the pledges being still sufficient, as constantly increasing with the plenty of the commodity».[1] The fundamental content of the quantity theory is mentioned in the first of part of the statement: the quantity of money as such has no importance (within certain limits). The latter part of the statement is interesting, however, because it assumes a causal relationship opposed to what is included in the common presentation of the quantity theory. It is a good illustration of the view that the problem of causation has nothing to do with the main proposition of the quantity theory and is an entirely different question.

---

[1] *The Consequences of the Lowering of Interest,* in *The Works of John Locke,* London and New York (1883?), p. 590. This statement is also quoted by E. Roll: *A History of Economic Thought,* London, 1938, p. 117, and by Heckscher, *op. cit.*, vol, II, pp. 23 and 225—226, as an example of the quantity theory.

The case of an isolated economy is very rare, and when countries trade with each other, the quantity of money in circulation is not insignificant according to mercantile views. Being a good mercantilist, Locke most strongly favors an export surplus in order to receive gold and silver, but as distinguished from most mercantilists, he also says: »Riches do not consist in having more gold and silver, but in having more in proportion than the rest of the world, or than our neigbours, whereby we are enabled to procure to ourselves a greater plenty of the conveniences of life, than comes within the reach of neigbouring kingdoms and states.«[2] As an example, he mentions that nobody would get richer if the quantity of gold and silver were doubled in all countries, emphasizing exactly what is indicated by the quantity theory: money, serving as a medium of exchange, has no value in itself. Consequently, a variation in its quantity does not mean any change in the total wealth of the world. Thus, money is put into a unique position, as compared to other things.

Practically, there are certain limits to the quantity of money in a society. In the case of an isolated economy, there must be enough to give everybody some money (when bartering is excluded), but in the course of trading with other countries, the proportion of money to trade should be great enough to make the exchange value of silver at least the same as in other countries. This idea is based upon Locke's mercantile opinions, which obviously have no relevance in an isolated economy. He also points out that the proportion needed does not depend »barely on the quantity of money, but on the quickness of its circulation».[3]

Those who consider the following explanation to be the main content of the quantity theory, refer to Locke as responsible for the first complete statement: »For the exchange value of money in general, is the quantity of all the money in the world, in proportion to all the

---

[2] *Op. cit.*, p. 565.

[3] *Ibid.*, p. 573. The velocity of money is said to have been recognized first by William Petty, who wrote in the middle of the seventeenth century (see M. W. Holtrop: *De omloopssnellheid van het geld,* Amsterdam, 1928, pp. 1—3). Thanks to his advanced knowledge of statistics, Petty realized that the value of the quantity of money was considerably less than that of the total quantity of goods. Locke was also fully aware of this fact, so Hoffman's assertion that Locke overlooked the velocity of money seems rather peculiar (Hoffman, *op. cit.*, p. 35), as well as A. Pose's statement that Locke equalized the total quantity of money to that of goods (»Esquisse de l'évolution de la théorie quantitative», *R. H. e.,* 1926, p. 155). He believes Locke's assertion — that every change in the quantity of money will change the value of money, when the amount of goods remains constant — implies such an interpretation. Actually, Locke also considered the velocity of money.

trade: but the exchange value of money in any country, is the present quantity of the current money in that country, in proportion to the present trade.»[4] Such an explanation, however, is not specific. Also Locke emphasizes that the exchange value of money is determined in exactly the same way as that of all other things, namely by the relation between demand and supply. »But, because the desire of money is constantly almost every where the same, its vent varies very little, but as its greater scarcity enhances its price, and increases the scramble: there being nothing else that does easily supply the want of it: the lessening of its quantity, therefore, always increases its price, and makes an equal portion of it exchange for a greater of any other thing.»[5] Identifying the desire for money as capital and as a medium of exchange, Locke falsely infers that because people will constantly say »yes» to the receipt of money, there is a constant, that is, unaltered, demand for money.[6] He is also mistaken when he claims that an increase in the price of money, that is, the rate of interest, because of the lessening of its quantity, will make »an equal portion of it exchange for a greater of any other thing». There is no necessity for a given quantity of money to be worth more in respect to its exchange value when the rate of interest increases, a fact even stressed by Locke himself.[7] What Locke apparently has in mind is that a change in the quantity of money will affect both the rate of interest and the exchange value of money. In this respect,

---

[4] *Op cit.*, p. 591. This or similar statements are quoted by economists who interpret the quantity theory as a theory of the exchange value of money. See *e.g.*, Angell, *op. cit.*, p. 18, and Monroe, *op. cit.*, p. 111. Because of his confusion of money with capital, Locke gave exactly the same explanation of the determination of the price of money, *i.e.*, the rate of interest: »The natural value of money, as it is apt to yield a yearly income by interest, depends on the whole quantity of the then passing money of the kingdom, in proportion to the whole trade of the kingdom» (Locke, *op. cit.*, p. 589). *Cf.* the comments by Heckscher, *op. cit.*, vol. II, p. 203, and Keynes: *The General Theory of Employment, Interest and Money,* London, 1936, pp. 343—344.

[5] *Op. cit.*, pp. 584—585.

[6] Marget suggests that Locke's idea of a constant demand for money might be based on the fact that »the demand for (or 'vent' of) money is such that money is less likely to lose its value entirely than are most other commodities»; and that »the probability of sudden and short-period changes in the demand' for money (or its 'vent') is much less than the probability of such changes in the supply of money (or its 'quantity')» (*op. cit.*, vol. II, p. 17, note 39). The explanation seems to be much simpler and based on Locke's false conclusion: people will always want money; hence the demand for money will never decrease. The possibility of an increased demand is never realized, because Locke confuses a constant demand, meaning a permanent demand, with an unchanged demand.

[7] Locke, *op. cit.*, pp. 578—579.

he is consistent, since both are said to be determined in the same way. But his proposition that the demand for money is »constant», and therefore changes in the value of money must depend upon variations in its quantity, implicitly presumes that the amount of trade is constant also! Totally viewed, if trade declines, the demand for money, both as »capital» and as a means of exchange, will decline. Locke overlooks this because his argumentation of a »constant» demand for money is based on an individual's preferences in spite of the fact that he is dealing with total categories. His conclusion, therefore, — irrespective of the confusion of the concept of the demand for money — is consistent with his idea that the exchange value of money is determined by the proportion of money to the amount of goods or trade, since his proposition of a »constant» demand for money implies that the amount of trade remains unchanged. Then, obviously, it is a truism to say that changes in the value of money must depend exclusively on variations in the supply of money. There is no mention in this connection of any proportional changes in the value of money, implying a demonstration of the specific property of money indicated by the quantity theory. Locke says only that »the lessening of its quantity . . . makes an equal portion of it exchange for a greater of any other thing». This is merely a truism. Truly, the formulation of *the* quantity theory is also a truism, but the essence of it is the implications of this truism, and there are no such implications from Locke's truism.[8]

Locke is everything but consistent. Sometimes he alleges that a decrease in the (absolute or relative) quantity of money will stop trade to a corresponding degree, without any alternative; and sometimes that it will do this, or decrease prices proportionately, or increase barter.[9] All these inconsistencies are mainly due to his identification of money with capital and are very improper as examples of an application of the quantity theory. He gives, however, one real example which is in conformity with the content of the quantity theory, namely that »there being ten times as much silver now in the world, (the discovery of the West-Indies having made the plenty) as there was then [in Henry VII's time] it is nine-tenths less worth now, than it was at that time», presuming that the supply and demand conditions of the commodities had not changed.[10]

---

[8] Locke's truism is quoted as a statement of the quantity theory by Laughlin (*op. cit.*, p. 228). *Cf.* Monroe's comments, *op. cit.*, p. 113.

[9] *Op. cit.*, pp. 591 and 679.

[10] *Ibid.*, p. 589.

The emphasis is put upon the proportionality while there is no proposition of a direct causal relationship between money and prices. The statement amounts to exactly the same as saying that if we have $10M$ in the equation of exchange ($MV = PT$), then we must also have $10P$ when V and T remain constant.

When the quantity theory is traced back to Davanzati, it is sometimes understood as an explanation of the (intrinsic) *value* of money. Locke did not take over this idea, and he never makes any attempt to explain the intrinsic value of money by equalizing the value of all commodities to the quantity of gold and silver. His explanation is that mankind has »consented to put an imaginary value upon gold and silver, by reason of their durableness, scarcity, and not being very liable to counterfeit».[11] Once again, however, the great philosopher makes a logical »somersault» as he continues that gold and silver (as money) have »no other value, but as pledges to procure what one wants, or desires; and they procure what we want, or desire, only by their quantity, it is evident that the intrinsick value of silver, and gold, used in commerce, is nothing but their quantity».[12] Their intrinsic value must be that imaginary value mankind is said to have imputed to them, and it is not identical with their quantity, even though their quantity influences this decision. It is also evident that their power to satisfy wants is not related to what constitutes their intrinsic value. Locke's view could be characterized as *a* quantity theory of the intrinsic value of money, as he makes the value of money completely dependent upon its quantity.

In spite of Locke's different and rather confusing »quantity theories», it is clear that he did enunciate a complete statement of *the* quantity theory and did realize its implications, which is shown by his emphasis upon the proportionality between the quantity of money and its value and not upon any direct causal relation. It is also very likely, though of minor significance, that he was the first enunciator of the quantity theory.

It has sometimes been asserted that the quantity theory was stated by English economists before Locke. Some of the names mentioned are John Hales (1581), Gerhard Malynes (1601), Henry Robinson (1641), William Potter (1650), Thomas Mun (1664), and James Hodges (1697). Of these writers, Thomas Mun has probably been named most frequently, but he points out only

[11] *Ibid.*, p. 572.

[12] *Ibid.*, p. 572; see also p. 652.

the old idea of a causal relation: »plenty of money in a Kingdom doth make the native commodities dearer».[13] The observations made by the other writers do not go beyond an awareness of this causation, except for William Potter, who has a very interesting remark:

»If then, in opposition to what is thus undertaken to be proved, it should be objected, that an increase of money would occasion an increase in the price of commodities, proportionable to such increase of money, (that is, if the money were twice as much, commodity would be twice as dear) consequently (going never the further in commodity by the increase thereof) would not occasion any increase in the sale of commodity: therefore not any increase of trade; and yet (by causing the price of commodities to rise) incur an inconvenience contrary to what is before affirmed.»[14]

This quotation may be the first in which proportionate price changes are mentioned. And yet, the idea seems not to be new to Potter, since he can very well imagine it being used as a criticism of his view that an increased quantity of money will cause an increase of trade. He manifests the same confusion as Hume of the necessarily proportionate relation between the quantity of money and prices at a given point of time (*ceteris paribus*) with the *effects* of an increased quantity of money, although his personal belief is that the amount of sales will increase, thereby inhibiting the proportionate price increase. There is no attempt to illustrate any specific position of money by this argumentation. The purpose is to point out the effects of an actual increase in the quantity of money, not to formulate the fundamental idea of the quantity theory.

2. Although Montesquieu did not attain any great importance as an economist, which is understandable, he did, unfortunately, influence the interpretation of the quantity theory. Because of his own peculiar definition of prices, he contributed to a misunderstanding of the quantity

---

13 Thomas Mun: *England's Treasure by Foreign Trade,* in McCulloch's ed. of *English Tracts on Commerce,* London, 1856, p. 104; *cf.* also pp. 138 and 149—151. See the comments on the writers mentioned above by Angell, *op. cit.*, p. 16; Heckscher, *op. cit.*, vol. II, pp. 238—243; Monroe, *op. cit.*, p. 182; and J. Viner: *Studies in the Theory of International Trade,* New York, 1937, pp. 41—45. Viner maintains that several of these early authors presented »some simple version of the quantity theory», and objects to Angell's and Monroe's denial of this view.

The dates within brackets above indicate when the books, in which the quantity theory is supposed to have been stated, were published. For further information, please see the bibliography.

14 *The Key of Wealth,* 1650, p. 13.

theory as a theory of individual prices. His price theory rests fundamentally upon the notion of money as »a sign which represents the value of *all* merchandizes», from which he infers the reversed proposition that »as money is the sign and representative of a thing, every thing is a sign and representative of money».[15]

It does not necessarily follow from these propositions that the exchange value of all commodities is equal to the total quantity of money, but Montesquieu is so strongly influenced by Davanzati and Montanari that such an interpretation is very likely to be what he had in mind. And it is unmistakable that this idea formed the background of his theory of prices. His answer to the question: »How are prices fixed?» admits of no doubt:

»If we compare the mass of gold and silver in the whole world, with the quantity of merchandizes therein contained, it is certain that every commodity or merchandize in particular, may be compared to a certain portion of the entire mass of gold and silver. As the total of the one is to the total of the other, so part of the one will be to part of the other. Let us suppose, that there is only one commodity or merchandize in the world, or only one to be purchased, and that this is divisible like money: a part of this merchandize will answer to a part of the mass of gold and silver; the half of the total of the one, to the half of the total of the other; the tenth, the hundreth, the thousandth part of the one, to the tenth, the hundreth, the thousandth part of the other. But as that which constitutes property amongst mankind is not all at once in trade; and as the metals of money, which are the sign of property, are not all in trade at the same time; the price is fixed in the compound ratio of the total of things with the total of signs, and that of the total of things in trade with the total of signs in trade also: and as the things which are not in trade to-day may be in trade to-morrow, and the signs not now in trade may enter trade at the same time, the establishment of the price of things fundamentally depends on the proportion of the total things to the total of signs.»[16]

---

[15] *The Spirit of Laws,* transl. by Thomas Nugent, 2 vols., London, 1823, vol. II, book XXII, chap II (italics added). These chapters on money were written twenty years before the book was first published (in 1748), according to Joseph Davidsohn: »Bidrag til Liberalismens Historie. Kvantitetsteorin omkring 1. Halvdel af 18. Aarh.», *N. T.*, 1928, p. 206. Davidsohn has a very exaggerated opinion of Montesquieu's economic thoughts. He characterizes him as a great economist, whose fundamental economic doctrines rest upon the quantity theory, which is said to be the starting point for his whole theoretical system.

[16] *Op. cit.*, book XXII, chap. VII.

This price theory is a direct derivation of Davanzati's and Montanari's equalization of all the money (in circulation) to the total amount of goods (in 'commerce') and of the 'mathematical rule' that the parts follow the whole. Certainly, it can be very properly named a quantity theory of prices. It was to this explanation of relative prices that the early cost-of-production theorists mainly objected. Criticising it, they frequently overlooked the weakest point of the whole theory, namely that such a comparison does not tell anything about relative prices, and emphasized instead, among other things, the omission of the velocity of circulation of money. The 'theory' states merely that if the quantity of goods is ten times greater than the quantity of money, then one hundreth of the quantity of goods is ten times greater than one hundreth of the quantity of money. Such a comparison, as has been pointed out, presumes a given unit of measure, which, in fact, would determine the relative prices. Montesquieu, as well as his predecessors, overlooked this completely.

It is not surprising that the quantity theory of money was confused with this 'quantity theory of prices' in the eighteenth century, but it is very surprising that it still could be criticised from this viewpoint in the beginning of the twentieth century (see Laughlin's criticism, p. 78). The confusion originates in the circumstance that both the quantity theory of money and this 'quantitative theory of prices' are based on a comparison of the total quantity of money with a certain quantity of goods. Montesquieu, however, was fully aware of the two different conclusions and never confused them.

Montesquieu's explanation of the great increase in the actual price level is a typical demonstration of the proposition of the quantity theory: »If since the discovery of the Indies, gold and silver have increased in Europe in the proportion of 1 to 20, the price of provisions and merchandizes must have been enhanced in proportion of 1 to 20. But, if, on the other hand, the number of merchandizes has increased as 1 to 2, it necessarily follows, that the price of these merchandizes and provisions, having been raised in proportion of 1 to 20, and fallen in proportion of 1 to 2, it necessarily follows, I say, that the proportion is only as 1 to 10.»[17] This explanation almost invites illustration of the reasoning algebraically, and there is much to Marget's point that

[17] *Ibid.*, book XXII, chap. VIII.

[18] *Op. cit.*, vol. II, p. 94, note 51. A. de Foville illustrates Montesquieu's exposition by the formula $\frac{P}{p} = \frac{M}{m} \cdot \frac{c}{C} \cdot k$ where P and p indicate the price levels to be

Montesquieu's exposition of the quantity theory shows how the equation of exchange was built up historically.[18]

It is far from the author's intention to minimize Montesquieu's views on the causal relationship between money and prices, but the method of demonstrating the proportionate changes in the price level by using figures, can have only one purpose: to emphasize the proportionality. It is not done, however, in order to emphasize a specific proportionality of money, but merely because it necessarily follows from the equalization of the quantity of money to the value of the amount of goods. It is significant, however, that in spite of his clear exemplification of the quantity theory, he did not pronounce its usual formulation.

3. The most elucidating account of the essence of the original quantity theory is furnished by David Hume. He rejects Locke's description of money as the wheel of trade and characterizes it as »the oil which renders the motion of the wheels more smooth and easy». The emphasis is always put upon the subservient role of money, forming no part of wealth. It has merely »a fictitious value arising from the agreement and convention of men», while manufactures and commodities are the only valuable things in commerce. Hence it follows that the quantity of money as such has no importance. His illustration of this idea is stated even more clearly than Locke's: »If we consider any one kingdom, it is evident, that the greater or less plenty of money is of no consequence since the prices of commodities are always proportioned to the plenty of money.»[19] Here is the fundamental content of the quantity theory, and it is quite evident that the question of causation does not belong to it. In that respect, the statement is very significant as compared to the formulation of the quantity theory which later became commonly accepted, namely that an increase in the quantity of money,

---

compared, M and m the quantity of money, and C and c the amounts of goods. The constant k is included because Foville does not think that Montesquieu equalized the quantity of money to the value of the commodities. Taking the velocity of money also into account, the equation reads: $\frac{P}{p} = \frac{M}{m} \cdot \frac{c}{C} \cdot \frac{V}{v}$ (*La Monnaie,* Paris, 1907, pp. 142 and 145). Obviously it is but one step to the equation of exchange, and it is very possible that Montesquieu's clear exposition of the quantity theory influenced the first attempts, which were made in the end of the eighteenth and in the beginning of the nineteenth century, to formulate equations expressing the relation between the quantity of money, the amount of goods, and the price level (see p. 86).

[19] *Essays and Treatises.* A New Edition, 2 vols., London, 1825, vol. I, pp. 279 and 294.

ceteris paribus, causes proportionate price increases. The real issue is not what will happen *if* the quantity of money is increased, but that the actual quantity of money has no significance, since prices are always in proportion to the amount of money. Very few have realized this distinction, but Hume is one of them. He points out the difference between the statement that a greater or smaller circulation is of no importance and what the effect will be of an actual change in the quantity of money. He admits that »since the discovery of the mines in America, industry has increased in all the nations of Europe», which might seem contradictory, and also did to many critics of the quantity theory, »if we consider only the influence which a greater abundance of coin has in the kingdom itself, by heightening the price of commodities».[20] His way out of this seeming dilemma became famous, but also much criticised, especially by James Mill, who could not possibly reconcile it with the quantity theory. Hume declared that the price increase does not follow immediately, but that there is an interval between the increase in money and prices which is advantageous to the owners of the new money and allows them to increase their demand for labor and commodities. The effect is an increased trade and the final price rise will be in proportion to the increase in money *and* trade.[21] Thus he showed that an *actual* change in the quantity of money will *not* cause proportionate price changes and referred to the well-known fact that prices had increased only three or, at most, four times since the discovery of the West Indies, while coin had increased much more.[22] It is rather surprising, therefore, that the quantity theory became interpreted mainly as a proposition of what would happen if the quantity of money were changed under hypothetical conditions.

The difference between the result of an actual change in the quantity of money and a presumed, instantaneous change is alluded to in Hume's famous example in which he supposes everybody in England, by miracle,

---

[20] *Ibid.*, p. 283.

[21] J. Viner mentions that the same idea was already put forward by James Hodges (1697), who strove for an increased amount of circulation (in England), because this would lead to a greater increase in sales than in prices (*op. cit.*, p. 44). The same opinion was held by François Forbonnais (1767), a Dutchman, who stressed how the gradual price increase would stimulate production, by means of which the price increase would also be partly counterbalanced; and in agreement with Hume, he said that it was the temporary price increase that was favorable to a country, not the higher price level (according to Angell, *op. cit.*, pp. 208 and 217). See also Potter's statement, p. 31).

[22] *Op. cit.*, pp. 289—290.

to get five pounds slipped into his pocket one night. The example is not at all a good one, since there is no reason to expect a proportionate price increase.[23] But the point Hume wants to make is that nobody will get richer if the quantity of money is proportionately increased: »We fancy, because an individual would be much richer, were his stock of money doubled, that the same good effect would follow were the money of every one increased.»[24] This principle, which is brought out by the quantity theory, is undeniable, but Hume's way of demonstrating it was wrong. He confuses the self-evident maxim that the sum of the prices of the goods sold must always correspond to the amount of money paid,[25] with the propostion that *if* the quantity of money is increased, even by miracle, *ceteris paribus*, the *result will be* a proportionate price increase. This distinction has not even been realized by the critics of the quantity theory, who instead claim that other things will *not* remain constant. Hume's formulation unintentionally brought a proposition of causation into the content of the quantity theory, which led astray the understanding of the real content and purpose of the theory.

Contrary to Locke, Hume maintained that low prices were advantageous to a nation because they increased its possibility to export, thereby increasing trade and production. He was also consistent with the maxim that prices are determined by the relation of money to goods. Hence differences in the price levels between trading countries were automatically adjusted by exports or imports of precious metals or commodities.

When the quantity theory is understood as a theory of the determination of the exchange value of money, or even as a theory of individual prices, Hume is quoted as a supporter of these ideas. He considered

---

[23] *Ibid.*, p. 297; see, *e.g.*, Wicksell's criticism of this example (*Lectures*, vol. II, pp. 160—161).

[24] *Ibid.*, p. 315.

[25] Hoffman writes Hume's quantity theory as $(G - H + K) : (G_1 - H_1 + K_1) = (P - W) : (P_1 - W_1)$, where G means the total amount of money, H that part which is not exchanged, K the amount of credit, P the amount of goods and W that part of P which is bartered. The index refers to the period of comparison. Hoffman characterizes the equation as a naive quantity theory of money, probably because the velocity of money is omitted *(op. cit.*, p. 42). Regardless of the confusion of the equation as such with the quantity theory, Hume never said that there was any proportionality between the quantity of money and the amount of goods in a country as compared to different periods. But the equation can illustrate his theory of international prices, if the index refers to another country instead.

it a maxim, almost self-evident, that it is »the proportion between the circulating money, and the commodities in the market, which determines the prices. Goods that are consumed at home, or exchanged with other goods in the neighbourhood, never come to market, they affect not in the least the current specie.»[26] There is no doubt that 'prices' refer to individual prices, which may account for the misinterpretation of the quotation as an acceptance of Montesquieu's quantitative theory of prices. It is rather obvious, however, that Hume speaks of prices not as expressing the relative values of the commodities, but as expressing the exchange value of money. And the self-evident maxim is that the exchange value of money is determined by the law of demand and supply. Hence it follows that those parts not entering into the demand or the supply side of money have no influence whatsoever on the determination of the exchange value of money. The application of the general law of demand and supply to money is not to be confused with *the* quantity theory. The purpose of the proposition of the quantity theory, that prices are always in proportion to the amount of money, is not to bring out *how* prices are determined, but, using a phrase of Hume's, that the »absolute quantity of the precious metals is a matter of great indifference».[27]

---

26 *Op. cit.*, p. 289.

27 *Ibid.*, p. 292. A. Hansen interprets Hume's exposition of the quantity theory somewhat differently: »The pure version of the quantity theory was forcefully stated as early as 1752 by Hume.... The Hume version, refined and elaborated, determined economic thinking throughout most of the nineteenth century. The price level was thought to be a function of the quantity of money.» (*Monetary Theory and Fiscal Policy*, New York, 1949, p. 48). Though we unreservedly agree to Hume's influence, we cannot share the interpretation. This can best be illustrated by quoting Hansen's summary of the main ideas in Hume's writings: »Here are the root ideas that permeated monetary thinking in much of the nineteenth century. Thrift and productivity determine the rate of interest; the money supply determines the level of prices. The demand for money is interest-inelastic. International gold and silver are distributed in proportion to the level of industry and commerce in each country and thereby the price levels of different countries are kept in line» (*ibid.*, p. 218).

But Hume never meant that the price level was determined only by the quantity of money, which seems to be Hansen's opinion of the quantity theory. Hume said that it was »the proportion *between* the circulating money *and* the commodities in the market, which determines the prices». Consequently, the price level is not determined by the quantity of money more than by the quantity of goods in circulation. Here actually lies the misinterpretation and also the distortion of Humes' ideas which fostered the notion, already partly provided by Bodin, that the price level was *solely* a function of the quantity of money.

4. In 1757, Joseph Harris anonymously published *An Essay upon Money and Coins*, which contains a very typical exposition of the derivation and proposition of the quantity theory. His views are based on a coalescence of the thoughts of Davanzati, Locke and Hume. From Davanzati, he took over the idea of setting off the total quantity of money against the total amount of goods, and that the 'parts follow the whole'; from Locke, the view that the quantity of money could never exceed the whole demand; and from Hume, that only those goods exchanged by money are to be compared to the amount of money in circulation.

The combination of these ideas gives an excellent illustration of the background and content of the quantity theory and the part of the proposition of causation. Thus Harris asserts that »the value of a given quantity or sum of money, in any country, will be less or more, according as the sum total, or the whole quantity of money in currency, is greater or less, in proportion to the whole of the commodities of that country, exchangeable for money: Or, *the value of a given sum of money will be always, pretty exactly, in a reciprocal proportion to the sum total, or the whole quantity in circulation*; that is, the more money there is in currency, the less will be the value of a given sum in proportion to other things; and *vice versa*. Hence again, it naturally follows, that, *if*, in any country, *the whole quantity of money in circulation, be either increased, or diminished; the value of a given sum will be accordingly lessened or increased; and that in proportion, as the said sum becomes thereby, a lesser or greater part, of the whole stock in currency.*»[28]

Only the first sentence in italics contains the basic proposition of the quantity theory, but Harris seems not to be aware of the purpose of the statement. He emphasizes the logical correctness of the proposition as a result of the equalization of the quantity of money to the amount of goods in circulation. Then he makes that logical mistake which has included a proposition of causation to the formulation of the quantity theory, namely that *if* the quantity of money is increased or decreased, *ceteris paribus*, the value of money will be proportionately lessened or increased.[29] But it is evident that *it does not follow from this arithmetic*

[28] *An Essay upon Money and Coins* (in *Old and Scare Tracts on Money*, London, 1933, pp. 391—392); Harris' italics.

[29] Harris does not use the phrase *ceteris paribus*. The first to adopt this expression is said to be Bishop Berkeley, who asked in his *Querist*: »Whether, *ceteris paribus*, it be not true that the prices of things increase as the quantity of money increaseth, and are diminished as that is diminished?» (*The Works of George Berkeley*, ed. by A. C. Fraser, 4 vols., Oxford, 1901, vol. IV, *The Querist*, No. 465, p. 464).

proportion that changes in the quantity of money will cause proportionate price changes. It is exactly the same logical mistake which has been made so frequently by many economists when they illustrate the quantity theory by using the equation of exchange or some similar quantity equation. The only thing the equation of exchange demonstrates is some arithmetic relations between the symbols included. Nothing can be said as to causal relationships between the different elements. Harris' proposition has to *presume* that there is a direct causal relationship between changes in the quantity of money and in the price level. Then it follows from his first proposition in italics that the price changes will be in exact proportion, *ceteris paribus*, to the increased or decreased quantity of money. Thus his second statement in italics contains two propositions: 1) prices will be directly influenced by the change in the quantity of money, and 2) price changes will be exactly proportionate to that change. The assumptions, upon which these two propositions are based, are 1) a direct causal relationship between changes in the quantity of money and in prices, and 2) that other things remain equal. Evidently the value of Harris' second statement is no greater than that of the first, and both are mere truisms. But they both illustrate a specific property of money which constitutes the justification of their formulation, although Harris only wanted to demonstrate a necessarily arithmetic relation and probably never thought of the implied presumption of causation. That problem is completely different and is not directly related to the proposition of proportionality. Unfortunately, Harris' second statement became the commonly accepted formulation of the quantity theory, even when the purpose was to emphasize the proportionality only; and so the quantity theory was criticised both as a proposition of proportionality and of causality. Later, when the statement of proportionality was considered a truism, the question of causation became the main point of criticism.

5. The essence of the quantity theory was overlooked by its first critics, who objected to immaterial issues. The misinterpretation is due partly to the ambiguous formulation by the founders themselves, because of the confusion of the proposition of proportionality with an unintentional proposition of causality, and partly to the inability of the critics to see the real purpose of the 'theory'. Thus Richard Cantillon, although he did not deny that absolute prices were determined partly by the quantity of money in circulation and that changes in the quantity of money will influence the price level, criticises Hume's view

that an increased quantity of money will lead to *proportionate* price increases. Despite Hume's distinction between an actual change in the quantity of money and an imaginary change, Cantillon enumerates all those factors which work against an exactly proportionate price increase. It is simply impossible, he says, to estimate how much prices will rise, because one does not know beforehand which ways or channels the additional money will take, or how much it will influence different commodities. The primary effect will always be an increase in consumption, but the resulting dearness will not be equally distributed among the prices of all the commodities, since demand will increase differently for different commodities, and often turn in new directions.[30]

Cantillon objected also to the assumption of a constant velocity of money, accentuating the influences of an increased quantity of money. He asserted that changes in the velocity of money have the same effect on prices as changes in the amount of circulation.[31] This view was accepted by adherents of the quantity theory, who extended the theory to include the proposition that changes in the velocity of money, *ceteris paribus*, will cause proportionate price variations also. The essence is still the proposition of proportionality.

Cantillon is always characterized as a quantity theorist when the theory is confused with the idea of a causal relationship between changes in the quantity of money and in prices. He maintained that prices are determined by the quantity of money, that is, high prices mean plenty of money, low prices scarcity of money, when other things remain equal.[32] One implication of the quantity theory is, of course, that one of the price-influencing factors is the quantity of money. The best illustration of that view is unquestionably given by the equation of exchange, the correctness of which nobody will deny nowadays. Can-

---

[30] *Essai sur la nature du commerce en général,* 1755, pp. 235 and 329. The book was published anonymously, but is ascribed to Cantillon. According to Lambert, the book was written about 1733 (one year before Cantillon's death), but was first published in 1755 *(op. cit.*, p. 26).

[31] *Op. cit.*, p. 213. A. Pose maintains that even if Cantillon was not the first to draw attention to the velocity of money, he was, at least, the first to underline its great importance (*De la Théorie monétaire à la Théorie économique,* Paris, 1930, p. 157).

[32] »Lorsqu'on afferme des terres à haut prix c'est une marque l'argent abonde dans l'Etat; mais lorsq'on est obligé de les affermer bien plus bas, cela fait voir, tout autres choses étant égales, que l'argent est rare.»

»Suivant les principes que nous avons établis, les quantités d'argent qui circulent dans le troc, fixent & déterminent les prix de toutes choses dans un Etat, eu egard à la vîtesse ou lenteur de la circulation» (*op. cit.*, pp. 247—248 and 381—382).

tillon's observations actually contain two of those truisms which follow from the acceptance of that equation; namely, the relation betwen M and P, and V and P, respectively, when the values of the other symbols remain constant. But he does not mention any proportionality, although it is very possible that he would not have denied such a statement if there were no implication of causation. His criticism of the statement of an over-all proportionate price increase apparently prevented him from the conclusion which is so easily found.

There is one instance where Cantillon evidently would agree to proportionate price changes. The example is interesting in so far as it is used by Fisher in order to illustrate the content of the quantity theory (see p. 88). If, namely, the numerical value of the coin is increased, then prices will increase (presumably in the same proportion), when the actual content of precious metal is the basis of the price determination.[33] Cantillon wants to bring out that to the state as a whole and in its relation to foreign countries, it is a matter of indifference what denomination the coin has as long as the *quantity* of money is not changed. Individuals are said to gain or lose according to their economic engagements. This statement, however, overlooks the proportionate changes in incomes. The mistake is due to his consideration of the problem of causation, which, in fact, is of no importance for the illustration of the idea. A change in the quantity of money, though, will change the situation of the country in conformity with is mercantile views.

It is rather obvious that this example is not related to the basic content of the quantity theory. It is an illustration of the truism that prices will always be in proportion to the standard of value. The *denomination* of coins, therefore, is irrelevant, both in relation to individuals, to the state, and to other countries. The essence of the quantity theory, that the *quantity* of money is irrelevant, is overlooked even by Fisher when he tries to illustrate it by employing the same example as Cantillon used to demonstrate the first-mentioned proposition.

There is no direct denial of the essence of the quantity theory in Cantillon's work, nor is there any clear statement of it. The main reason is probably his very realistic approach to economics, which made him ask *how* a change in the quantity of money takes place and what the effect would be. This realistic view made him overlook the purely hypothetical assumption of a change in the quantity of money in the formulation of the quantity theory, and made him an ardent critic of the

---

33 *Ibid.*, p. 208.

asserted proportionate price changes. The thorough analysis, on the other hand, which he undertook in order to disprove this proposition, by tracing all the different channels in an economy through which money passes, and the results of changes in wages and prices when the production of precious metals increases, constitutes one of the main reasons for the high esteem of Cantillon's work and for the characterization of it as the »Cradle of Political Economy».

6. Another early and more important critic of the quantity theory is James Steuart. He is interesting because he criticises both the 'quantitative theory of prices', as it was first outlined by Montesquieu, and the proposition of the quantity theory as it was stated by Locke and Hume. He interprets the quantity theory as primarily an explanation of individual prices in terms of the amount of money paid for the different commodities. Such a price theory seems to him very inconsistent: »Were there a determinate proportion between certain quantities of gold and silver, and certain quantities of things vendible, I do not see how prices could vary while the proportion of quantity to quantity between metals and things remained the same.»[34]

This 'quantitative theory of prices' is decidedly rejected, and Steuart emphatically declares that individual prices are not determined by the quantity of money but by the conditions of demand and supply, which he summarizes as 1) the abundance of the things to be valued, 2) the demand for them, 3) the competition between the demanders, and 4) the extent of the faculties of the demanders. He makes an attempt, however, to reconcile the two theories, by saying that the price of every commodity is proportionate to the quantity of money 'destined' for that commodity, since this amount of money is the measure of demand. But it does not mean that prices are regulated in this way. They can only be settled by an agreement between the buyer and seller at the final transaction, not by the quantity of money as such.[35]

Steuart's criticism of Hume's statement that changes in the quantity of money will cause proportionate price changes is different from Cantillon's objections. He flatly denies that changes in the

[34] *An Inquiry into the Principles of Political Economy,* 5 vols., 1796 (first published in 1767), vol. III, p. 6; *cf.* also vol. II, p. 187. In his discussion of the quantity theory, Laughlin takes into consideration only Steuart's criticism of this 'quantitative theory of prices', which is an indication of Laughlin's own similar interpretation of the quantity theory (Laughlin, *op. cit.*, pp. 235—236).

[35] *Op. cit.*, vol. II, p. 187.

quantity of money itself will have *any* effects on prices whatsoever, if it does not lead to changes in demand. It is not even possible to increase the circulation when the demand has not increased. If the amount of money increases, but not the demand for commodities, the result will be merely that the new coins are locked up or converted into plate.[36]

This criticism has merits in that Hume was wrong when he concluded that changes in the quantity of money will *cause* proportionate price changes, but it manifests, even as Cantillon's criticism, a misunderstanding of the purpose of Locke's and Hume's statement. Steuart's opinion is that the prevailing quantity of money in circulation is just the proper amount to serve the desires and wants of the inhabitants in a given economy; therefore, it is simply impossible to increase the circulation, whereas a decrease will hurt the industrious and retard the circulation, or even stop the industry, if no symbolic money is invented.[37] Even if it were feasible to raise the circulating amount of money »in ever so great a proportion, commodities will still rise and fall according to the principles of demand and competition».[38] The argument, which does not invalidate Hume's proposition, is an illustration of Steuart's interpretation of the quantity theory as a theory of individual prices.

Steuart makes an honest effort to follow Hume's reasoning, however: »Suppose», he says, »the specie of Europe to continue increasing in quantity every year, until it amounts to ten times the present quantity, would prices rise in proportion?» If the industry is increased proportionally, there will be no increase in prices. If, on the other hand, »the scale of demand could be supposed to preponderate, so as to draw all the wealth into circulation without having the effect of augmenting the supply (which I take to be impossible) their prices would rise ten times the present standard, at least in many articles.»[39]

Though this conclusion coincides with Hume's proposition, it is evidently based on a fundamentally different principle, namely that individual prices, *ceteris paribus*, will change in proportion to changes in the demand. The barrier which kept Steuart from realizing the essence of the quantity theory was not only the inability to distinguish individual prices from absolute prices; basically, it was his confusion of

[36] *Ibid.*, vol. II, pp. 180—181.

[37] *Ibid.*, vol. II, pp. 189—190 and 197.

[38] *Ibid.*, vol. II, p. 181.

[39] *Ibid.*, vol. II, pp. 197—198.

money with wealth, which indeed was the fallacy that Locke's and Hume's proposition was meant to illustrate.

7. The quantity theory as stated by Locke unmistakeably contains only *one* proposition: prices are always, *ceteris paribus*, in proportion to the quantity of money. Hence it follows that the quantity of money as such has no importance. The purpose of this conclusion is to emphasize the specific peculiarity of the means of exchange as constituting no part of wealth in itself. This idea was more than sorely needed in the heyday of mercantilism. Is was then taken over by Hume who, unfortunately, committed himself to a logical fallacy when he tried to demonstrate Locke's proposition. His false conclusion was that a *change* in the quantity of money will *cause* proportionate price changes. The emphasis, however, is still put on the proposition of proportionality, since the purpose is to prove that prices will always be in proportion to the quantity of money in circulation. But this formulation of Locke's idea brings a proposition of causality into the statement, which has a completely different implication than the original idea. It means that there is a direct causal relationship between changes in the quantity of money and in prices, so that an *actual* increase (or decrease) in the quantity of money, if other things remain equal, will raise (or lower) prices proportionately. Hume does not seem to realize this implication, but evidently thought that he was only illustrating the proposition of proportionality. As his formulation of the quantity theory became the accepted one, Locke's original purpose was overlooked, and the theory was — very rightly according to its formulation — understood as containing *two* propositions. Interestingly enough, the first two more important critics attacked one proposition each. Thus Cantillon criticised the idea of proportionate price changes, while Steuart denied a direct causation between changes in the quantity of money and in prices. And they both missed the purpose of the quantity theory.

Not only was the essence of the quantity theory misunderstood by the critics from the very beginning of its enunciation, but it was often confused with other ideas, some of which were undoubtedly a part of its background. The explanation for this confusion is simple. The name of the doctrine as »the quantity theory of money» was not yet used. Instead, it was at first referred to as the doctrine of Locke: that prices are always in proportion to the amount of money in circulation; and later, as the doctrine of Hume: that changes in the quantity of money will cause proportionate price changes. The latter, finally, became the commonly accepted version of the quantity theory. One reason for its acceptance is principally that the idea of a causal relationship was so commonly accepted. This idea goes back to Bodin's famous explanation of the price increase in the sixteenth century and was taken for granted, which may explain Hume's conviction that changes in the quantity of money *cause* proportionate price variations.

Locke's doctrine rests on several assumptions which have frequently been confused with the essential idea itself, partly because these assumptions were also stated by Locke and Hume, although as distinct propositions. They said that (absolute) prices are determined by the proportion of money to the amount of goods to be exchanged, which evidently was the foundation of the illustration of the quantity doctrine. The content of this proposition is very simple as it implies merely that plenty of money, *ceteris paribus*, means high prices and scarcity of money low prices. Obviously, it amounts only to the application of the general law of demand and supply, presuming that the exchange value of money is determined in exactly the same way as that of all other things. This presumption was considered as an axiom, and so was the idea that the supply of money is equal to the total amount of money (in circulation), and the demand for it equal to the total supply of commodities (to be exchanged for money). Hume's statement, therefore, as illustrating the application of the law of demand and supply, refers to prices as expressing the exchange value of money. Peculiarly enough, some economists interpreted it as alluding to individual prices expressing relative values, and so the statement was confused with Montequieu's 'quantitative theory of prices', where relative prices were elaborately explained as the result of a quantitative comparison between the total quantity of money and commodities. The confusion is basically due to the derivation of both ideas from this quantitative comparison.

The designation of Locke's and Hume's doctrine of proportionality between prices and money as the quantity theory of money, is certainly not adequate. It is no theory of money, only a proposition indicating a specific peculiarity of money. Nor was it named a quantity theory of money, either by Locke or by Hume. But their successors made it a theory of money by interpreting it at first as a statement of what would happen if the circulating amount of money were changed under actual conditions, and later, as an *explanation* of actual variations in the price level. This last idea was primarily based on Bodin's famous explanation. And so an endless discussion began about *if* it were possible to change the amount of money in circulation, and *what* would be the effects. The beginning was made by Cantillon and Steuart, but it is difficult to determine any end to this discussion, which to such a great extent seemed to be so meaningless because of the lack of clear definitions and distinctions. The participants in these controversies were mostly talking over each other's head.

CHAPTER III

THE QUANTITY THEORY DURING THE CLASSICAL PERIOD

1. Adam Smith's theory of value is partly directed against Montesquieu's 'quantitative theory of prices' and partly against Steuart's demand and supply theory. He firmly objects to the explanation of relative prices as being determined by the amount of money given in exchange for goods. Money is only the nominal price of the commodities, while their real price is determined by the amount of labor necessary for their production.[1] The value of money is determined in exactly the same way, not by any quantitative comparison of the total amount of goods to the total quantity of money, and depends upon the quantity of pure silver or gold contained, not upon its stamp or denomination. If the currency is coined below the standard, prices will rise until they correspond to the same amount of precious metals which was given at the lower prices, that is, the price increase will be in proportion to the devaluation.[2] This example, which is the only instance of Adam Smith's mentioning proportionate price changes, is the same as used by Fisher in order to illustrate the quantity theory (see p. 89). Adam Smith, however, only demonstrates his theory of value, which, in his opinion, is a disproof of the quantity theory. Fisher's argument for the resulting proportionate price changes is that since a constant amount of goods (or transactions) will be turned over by a nominally increased quantity of money, the result is mathematically necessary, while Adam Smith maintains that since the quantity of money still constitutes the same amount of labor, it has to be exchanged for the same amount of labor.[3]

---

[1] *The Wealth of Nations* (ed. by G. Bell & Sons), 1901, p. 33; also see *Lectures on Justice, Police, Revenue and Arms,* delivered in the University of Glasgow by Adam Smith. Reported by a student in 1763 and edited with an introduction and notes by Edwin Cannan, Oxford, 1896, pp. 173—182.

[2] *The Wealth of Nations,* p. 47.

[3] Fisher asserts that the quantity theory was accepted by Adam Smith, but we have not been able to find any explicit statement supporting this view (*The Purchasing Power of Money,* New York, 1911, p. 14, note 1).

In conformity with his theory of value, Adam Smith claims that only a certain quantity of coins, constituting a given amount of labor, can circulate a given quantity of goods.[4] Therefore, he criticises the assumption in the commonly accepted formulation of the quantity theory of a (sudden) change in the circulating amount of money. It is simply impossible, *ceteris paribus,* to increase the amount of money in a free currency system. If the circulation of a country consists of coins, then the issuing of notes or news coins will drive out an exactly corresponding amount of coins abroad, as long as the additional quantity is not needed for the circulation.[5] The quantity of money in circulation is an exclusively *passive* factor — the fundamental view of the Banking School — and it is determined by the demands of circulation and by its cost of production. Every increase or decrease in the amount of circulation depends on a change in either of these factors. Thus, the cause of the great increase in prices in the middle of the sixteenth century was due to the lower costs of mining the precious metals: »The discovery of the abundant mines of America reduced, in the sixteenth century, the value of gold and silver in Europe to about a third of what it had been before. As it cost less labour to bring those metals from the mine to the market, so when they were brought thither they could purchase or command less labour.»[6] The causal relation is obviously the opposite of Bodin's famous observation and of the proposition of causation in the incorrect, but accepted, formulation of the quantity theory. This is also the basis for Adam Smith's disavowal of the quantity theory. He could only think of a decrease in the value of money, *i.e.*, of coins, being occasioned by cheaper costs of production, which would result in an increased amount of money. But he forgot to mention what providence made the quantity of the precious metals, that could be mined at the lower costs of production, correspond exactly to the demands of circulation at the new price relation!

Adam Smith also criticises the quantity theory when discussing its application to paper money: »The increase of paper money, it has been said, by augmenting the quantity, and consequently diminishing the value of the whole currency, necessarily augments the money price of commodities. But as the quantity of gold and silver, which is taken

---

[4] Adam Smith never discusses any changes in the velocity of money. The only observation he makes is that because small coins have a greater velocity of circulation than notes, they turn over just as great sums of value (*The Wealth of Nations,* p. 302).

[5] *Ibid.*, p. 294.

[6] *Ibid.*, pp. 32—33.

from the currency, is always equal to the quantity of paper which is added to it, paper money does not necessarily increase the quantity of the whole currency.»[7] This representation of the theory is incorrect, since the very fundamental basis of its formulation is the presumption that the value of the whole currency is constant; therefore, a greater quantity of money, *ceteris paribus*, necessarily means higher prices, not the diminishing of the value of the whole currency. The theory assumes an increased quantity of money, but Adam Smith tries to disprove its proposition by presuming the quantity of money to remain constant, while only the composition of this quantity will be changed from coins to paper money! But if »the quantity of gold and silver, which is taken from the currency, is always equal to the quantity of paper which is added to it», then there can be only one conclusion: paper money does *not* increase the quantity of the whole currency. The conclusion that »paper money does not necessarily increase the quantity of the whole currency» is evidently incorrect. Further, to disprove the quantity theory, he mentions that food was cheaper in Scotland in 1759 than ever before during the same century, in spite of there being considerably more notes circulating that year than earlier!

In the case of an inconvertible paper currency, the value of money is determined by the security and the date of its future redemption, while the quantity of money has no direct influence on its value.[8] Also in this case, Adam Smith denies the proposition of the quantity theory as he cannot see any justification for the assumption of a change in the quantity of money, if other things remain equal.

Fundamentally, Adam Smith agrees with the essence of the quantity theory: the main function of money is to circulate consumable goods: »In the same manner as [the worth of] a piece of ground does not lie in the number of highways that run through it, so the riches of a country does not consist in the quantity of money employed to circulate commerce, but in the great abundance of the necessaries of life.»[9] But

[7] *Ibid.*, p. 329.

[8] *Ibid.*, p. 330.

[9] *Lectures*, p. 191; also see pp. 192 and 199—200. Interestingly enough, and also inconsistently enough, Adam Smith praised Hume's explanation of international price movements, which was based upon the latter's famous idea that the quantity of money must always bear a certain proportion to the quantity of commodities in every country. Adam Smith describes Hume's reasoning as »exceedingly ingenious» (*Lectures*, p. 197). With respect to Locke, however, Adam Smith misinterprets his ideas as he speaks

his approach is entirely different: the quantity of money which circulates in a country is determined by the value of the consumable goods to be turned over annually.[10] Therefore, the quantity of money plays only a passive role, and it is simply impossible to increase the circulation. The inclusion of a proposition of causation in the formulation of the quantity theory was, for Adam Smith, an anomaly which he could not reconcile with his own opinion, although basically, the two views coincided.

2. Jean Baptiste Say, the greatest classical economist outside England, accepted the quantity theory, but objected to the way of demonstrating it by equalizing the total amount of money to the total amount of commodities. To him money was a commodity, not different from other commodities, except by dint of having an indirect utility, and obeyed the same laws of value.[11] Thus he affirmed that since a doubling of the harvest of wine in a certain year would decrease the price of wine by half, one could suppose that a doubling of the quantity of money in circulation would double prices! And this relation does not indicate that the total value of money is equal to that of all commodities any more than it indicates that the total value of all wine is equal to that of all other commodities. This peculiar phenomen derives its existence from the relation of the commodities to each other, and not from their relation to other commodities.[12] Consequently, Say assumes an elasticity of demand for all commodities equal to unity; and since he holds that money obeys the same laws that govern commodities, changes in the quantity of money must cause proportionate price changes. This way of deriving the common version of the quantity theory is evidently diametrically opposed to the usual way. Instead of illustrating a specific peculiarity of the means of exchange, it makes this peculiarity a property of all commodities, and *hence*, also of money! Accordingly, there would be no reason for speaking about the quantity theory of *money*, but of the quantity theory of exchange values applicable to all commodities and money.[13]

---

of Locke's notions as being »founded on the idea that public opulence consists in money» (*ibid.*, p. 198; *cf.* the remarks of the editor of the *Lectures*, pp. 198—199, note 3).

10 *The Wealth of Nations*, p. 345.

11 *Traité d'économie politique*, publ. by Horace Say, 6 ed., Paris, 1841 (first published in 1803), p. 257.

12 *Ibid.*, p. 279.

13 Say not only criticised the idea of comparing the total value of goods to the total quantity of money, but also the proposition that the prices of commodities were

The quantity theory is also derived in the usual way. If the circulation in France amounts to two billion francs and is suddenly increased to four billion, while no change has taken place in the total amount or supply of commodities, then one will be offering double as much money as before for the same amount of commodities. But the four billion francs will not be worth more than the previous two billion francs; consequently, the value of one franc will be halved.[14] Though Say is well aware of the extremeness of the assumptions made, he asserts that a less considerable and a more gradual increase (or decrease) in the quantity of money will lead to a proportionate change in the value of the monetary unit.

The difference in the views of Adam Smith and Say, in respect to the quantity theory, rests upon their different theories of value. Say did not accept the cost of production theory, but agreed to Steuart's theory of value, although he emphasized more utility as a decisive factor. An increased quantity of coins, according to Adam Smith, meant an increase of value, and could not cause proportionate changes in the value of the coins. Hence one could not increase the circulation if there were no increase of the demand for money at the same time. The whole line of reasoning, therefore, in the quantity theory became irrelevant. But Say shared Adam Smith's opinion that the value of the circulation could not be increased, because it was determined by the amount of transactions. The *value* of the circulation was a passive factor, but not the *number* of coins or paper money. Consequently, the quantity of money could very well be increased; but since the total value of the circulation could not be increased, the effect must be, *ceteris paribus*, a proportionate decrease in the value of the monetary unit. To this way of reasoning, Say could not find any theoretical objection, though he realized its highly hypothetical character.

Say never maintained that the effect of actual increases in the quantity of money would necessarily raise prices in the same proportion. Instead, he criticised Locke for not having considered that the supply of the

---

determined by this comparison, especially as it was stated by Montesquieu. Do a seller and a buyer know all that is offered and demanded of the commodities, he asked. And if they should know, would it affect that special commodity they are interested in (*ibid.*, p. 280).

[14] *Ibid.*, p. 248. *Cf.*, p. 256. Say may, at first glance, seem to make the same mistake he criticises, but actually he never equalizes the value of the total amount of commodities to the total circulation. His demonstration is based upon the assumption that the quantity of money in circulation represents a *given* value.

precious metals might be augmented without any corresponding decrease of their value. Thus, the reason the value of the precious metals did not sink to a tenth when their supply was increased tenfold (since the discovery of America), was because the demands of trade, the arts, and luxuries, which were simultaneously increasing, raised the desirability of the precious metals considerably.[15]

From one point of view, Say's position is unique, as he did not look upon the quantity theory as based upon a specific peculiarity of the means of exchange, but held its applicability to all things, *including* money. He tacitly *presumed* the elasticity of demand for every commodity to be unity, and hence, also for money, whereas the quantity theory actually is based upon this arithmetic relation being true only in respect to money. Even though it is conceivable that there are some commodities with an elasticity of demand equal to unity (within certain limits), Say's view, which seems to be mixed up with his famous idea that supply creates its own demand, is obviously untenable. He has probably confused the fact that the '*average* elasticity' of demand for all commodities must be unity, with a given money supply, with the elasticity of demand for individual articles. For it is self-evident that a doubling of the total volume of goods, when the quantity of money and its velocity remain the same, requires a halving of the price level.

Although Say himself never stated it directly, it is obvious that his famous law of markets, or of the indestructibility of purchasing power, implies the acceptance of the quantity theory. The statement can also be turned around, thus saying that the acceptance of the quantity theory also means the acceptance of Say's law of markets. For in both cases, the fundamental point is that money is only a medium of exchange, used in order to facilitate the circulation of goods. In other words, money is only a veil of the real circulation of goods for goods. Basically, Say's idea, that real purchasing power is only created by the production of goods and that the introduction of money cannot destroy this purchasing power, is sound if we look at it from a social point of view. From this viewpoint, money has fundamentally only one special function, namely of being the generally accepted medium of exchange, since we cannot speak of money as a store of wealth when we are dealing with total categories in a closed economy. The purely *formal* character of money is then obvious. Say's law is, therefore, also opposed to the mercantilist idea which regarded money as such as constituting wealth.

[15] *Ibid.*, pp. 339—340.

But both Say and all the other quantity theorists forgot that *individual* cash holders do not look upon their money from a social point of view. To them money has also a second important function, although based upon its first function, namely of being a store of value. Therefore, changes in the quantity of money will not mean corresponding changes in purchases, *i.e.*, the velocity of money will not remain constant; nor will production create its own demand if the income receivers choose to increase their cash holdings (in real terms). Consequently, Say's law and the quantity theory are applicable only to an economic system in which money has the sole function of being a medium of exchange, implying that cash holdings are reduced to a minimum for meeting daily expenses. Under competitive conditions, such a system will become manifest in an equilibrium situation of full employment and perfect foresight.

3. The quantity theory is generally understood as a theory of the value of money, according to which the value of money is regulated (or determined) by its quantity. One of the best examples of the incorrect deduction of this view is provided by James Mill. Using the same way of illustration as Montesquieu did in order to prove his 'quantitative theory of prices', Mill concludes that the value of money is regulated entirely by its quantity:

»If we suppose that all the goods of the country are on one side, all the money on the other, and that they are exchanged at once against one another, it is obvious that one-tenth, or one-hundreth, or any other part of the goods, will exchange against one-tenth, or any part of the whole money; and that this tenth, &c. will be a great quantity or small, exactly in proportion as the whole quantity of the money in the country is great or small. If this were the state of the facts, therefore, it is evident that the value of money would depend wholly upon the quantity of it.»[16]

The reservation refers to the velocity of money, implying that there is no instantaneous exchange of all goods, because the total quantity of money is smaller than that of the commodities. Although the conclusion is not that individual prices, as expressing relative values, are determined by the quantity of money, it is rather understandable that this seeming inference was drawn by other economists, especially the critics of the quantity theory, who interpreted the statement as a repetition of Montesquieu's 'quantitative theory of prices'.

[16] *Elements of Political Economy*, London, 1821, p. 95.

The exemplifications which are given in the quotation are obviously merely a series of truisms based upon certain presumptions. The conclusion, however, that the value of money depends wholly upon its quantity, is founded on a logical fallacy, making the conclusion completely unrelated to the presumptions. This is very important, because the common idea of the quantity theory as a theory of the value of money is frequently based upon the same kind of argumentation. The fallacy lies in Mill's confusion of the total amount of money with the value of a money-unit as a means of exchange. At first he compares the total amount of money to the total amount of goods, supposing them to be exchanged instantaneously. In doing so it is evident that there cannot be any kind of an exchange relation between the two 'goods'. They are simply exchanged against each other, without any kind of a standard of measure or a means of exchange. It is rather meaningless to say that one-tenth, or one-hundredth, of the goods is exchanged against one-tenth, or one-hundredth, of the money, since such a comparison can only be made with respect to the group of money itself, not to another group; that is, one-tenth of a given amount of money will be half of one-tenth of another group of money, being double as large as the given amount. This is all that these truisms say. The value of one money-unit can have no other import than to constitute a certain part of the total value of the money group, however it is defined. It cannot mean the value of money as a medium of exchange in the hands of the consumers; it is simply the value of one unit of a homogeneous group, which is instantaneously exchanged for a given amount of commodities. The concept of money as a medium of exchange has then lost all its bearing; accordingly, it is logically incorrect to conclude, on the assumptions advanced, that the value of money, as a means of exchange, depends upon its quantity.

Even if this logical error is not made, it is rather obvious how barren this 'quantity approach' is as a contribution to the explanation of the causes determining the value of money in the hands of the consumers. The content of it is that the quantity of money determines its value. It is very questionable whether such a statement has any meaning. It merely says: Suppose two money-units are paid for a certain commodity, instead of one at an earlier date. Thus the value of the money-unit has decreased by half. Conclusion: the quantity of money determines the value of money! This is a simple illustration of the false conclusion made by all those who claim that the quantity of money regulates its value. They have confused an arithmetic truism with a causal relation. And there are innumerable economists who have said that the value of irredeemable paper money is *determined* (or regulated) by its quantity! Significantly enough, this confusion is fundamentally based upon a confusion of Locke's original proposition of proportionality with a proposition of causality. Of course, James Mill belongs to this group. But he did ask: What determines the quantity of money? The answer was that the amount of coins depends upon the cost of production of bullion, which really means that the value of coin is determined by its cost of production also. Paper money, on the other hand, is regulated entirely by its quantity, which is determined by the government or the Central Bank.

James Mill's confusion of the proposition of proportionality as implying a statement of causality is best illustrated in the following quotation: »In whatever degree, therefore, the quantity of money is increased or diminished, other things remaining the same, in that same proportion, the value of the whole, and of every part, is reciprocally diminished or increased. This, it is evident, is a proposition universally true. Whenever the value of money has either risen or fallen, (the quantity of goods against which it is exchanged and the rapidity of circulation remaining the same,) the change must be owing to a corresponding diminution or increase of the quantity; and can be owing to nothing else. If the quantity of goods diminish, while the quantity of money remains the same, it is the same thing as if the quantity of money had been increased; and if the quantity of goods be increased, while the quantity of money remains unaltered, it is the same thing as if the quantity of money had been diminished. Similar changes are produced by any alteration in the rapidity of circulation.»[17]

The proposition, universally true, is evidently that of proportionality, which is so clearly illustrated by the equation of exchange, $MV = PT$. Mill's statement amounts merely to a demonstration of the truism that if the value of one symbol is changed, while that of two other symbols is constant, the remaining symbol has to change also. It is typical that the fourth possibility is left out, since the price level is thought of as a passive factor. Besides, he does not maintain any exclusive causal relationship, as he lays the emphasis upon the proportionate relation.

The demonstration above provides a good illustration of how the *indications* of a change in the exchange value of money were confused with the *causes* of the change. The interpretation of the quantity theory

---

[17] *Ibid.*, pp. 97—98.

since the end of the eighteenth century is based upon this conclusion, which appears to be self-evident because of the necessary proportionality in the changes.

In the paragraph quoted, Mill makes the same mistake as Adam Smith when declaring that the value of the *whole* quantity of money will vary inversely to variations in its quantity. If so, price changes would be more than in proportion to the variations in the amount of money, which is incongruous with the assumptions made.

James Mill is so fully convinced of the truth of his universal law of proportionate price changes that he denies every increase in money giving rise to anything but proportionate price changes, not observing the different assumptions made by other writers. Therefore, he criticises Hume's very advanced opinion that an increase in money may stimulate production because of the new demand and the rising prices. As much as prices increase, just as much the value of money decreases! (As if two different definitions of the same thing could be used as an argument.) Consequently, the entrepreneurs will receive a constant amount of value when selling their commodities, so there will be no incentive to producing more, nor will it happen! If it is objected that commodities of the same kind not yet being sold would still have their prices unchanged, he agrees, but adds that the price increase will soon be spread by the additional quantity of money, constituting a fresh demand for those other articles, though not by any other money. Unsold goods have the same influence on prices as if they were never brought to the market, that is, no influence at all.[18] This opinion, which at first may sound a little peculiar, is later to be found held by even such a well-known authority as Francis A. Walker (see p. 76). The idea, which is rather unfortunately formulated, is probably best illustrated by referring to the equation of exchange. What they both have in mind is that those commodities not entering into the transactions, T, will not influence the value of T, and hence not P. But the statement was sometimes understood as meaning that the quantity of money determined individual prices.

4. The foundation of David Ricardo's formulation of the quantity theory is the idea that the circulating amount of money represents a certain value which cannot be increased when 'other things' remain constant. The size of this amount of value depends upon the

---

[18] *Ibid.*, p. 125.

velocity of money, the extent of credit and the banking system.[19] Any increase in the quantity of money in circulation above the proportion required will lead to a corresponding export of coins. Only in the case of a paper currency will it be possible permanently to increase the total circulation. Adopting Hume's fallacious way of reasoning, Ricardo emphatically affirms that the result of an increased quantity of money will be a proportionate price increase: »If the Bank were restricted from paying their notes in specie, and all the coins had been exported, any excess of their notes would depreciate the value of the circulating medium in proportion to the excess. If 20 millions had been the circulation of England before the restriction, and 4 millions were added to it, the 24 millions would be of no more value than the 20 were before, provided commodities had remained the same, and there had been no corresponding exportation of coins; and if the Bank were successively to increase it to 50 or 100 millions, the increased quantity would be all absorbed in the circulation of England, but would be, in all cases, depreciated to the value of the 20 millions.»[20] While Hume compared the total quantity of money to the total quantity of goods, Ricardo compares the total value of the circulation to a certain amount of paper money. In both cases, the total value of the circulation is given; hence, it necessarily follows that the value of the currency unit will be in an inverse proportion to the number of units. But it does *not* follow from this proportionate relation that an *actual* increase in the number of units, *ceteris paribus,* will *cause* proportionate price changes. This is a logical fallacy which not only Ricardo repeats, but also all those who have taken Hume's formulation of the quantity theory for granted. The necessarily proportionate relation is demonstrated by the different figures employed, but the causal relation cannot be proved in that way; it is a proposition which remains to be proved.

Although Ricardo employs the same kind of argumentation as

---

[19] *The High Price of Bullion* (in *The Works of David Ricardo,* ed. by J. R. McCulloch, London, 1846, pp. 284—285). Hoffman affirms that according to Ricardo's thinking, the quantity of money equals the supply of goods, because he overlooked the velocity of money (*op. cit.*, pp. 110—111). This interpretation is definitely incorrect since there are several instances where Ricardo points out how small the circulating quantity of money is in relation to the total amount of transactions, *e.g.*: »In England, so many means of economizing the use of circulating medium have been adopted, that its value, compared with the value of the commodities which it circulates, is probably (during a period of confidence) reduced to as small a proportion as is practicable» (*op. cit,*. p. 284).

[20] *Ibid.*, p.285.

Hume, his purpose is different. This is indicated by the different foundation of their similar assumptions of a circulation representing a given value. According to Ricardo, money has a value, not because of its being a means of exchange representing the value of the commodities, but because of its cost of production (and to a certain degree, because of the scarcity of the precious metals). Hence an increase in the quantity of money would mean an increase in the quantity of labor, and thus in value, and no proportionate price changes would be expected. Sharing Adam Smith's view that under given conditions only a certain amount of circulation can be employed, he cannot, without qualifications, accept Hume's proposition of the result of an increase in the total amount of money. Ricardo attempts to show that an increased quantity of paper money will raise prices proportionately because it does not mean an increase in the total value of the circulation, as it would if the amount of coins were increased.[21] The purpose of this statement is *not* to indicate a specific property of money, but to point out what will actually happen *if*, *ceteris paribus*, the quantity of irredeemable paper money is increased above the amount of coins it substitutes, thereby supposedly providing a strong theoretical argument for his opinion that the contemporary high price of bullion was due to the increase in the quantity of paper money.

The similarity between Hume's and Ricardo's statements, both of which contain the proposition of the quantity theory, veiled the different purposes of their formulations. While the emphasis in Hume's statement is on the proportionality in order to illustrate a specific peculiarity of money, Ricardo's emphasis is on the causality between changes in money and prices. As Ricardo became the great authority during the nineteenth century, his formulation and interpretation of the quantity theory was commonly accepted, which meant a decided shift of the original content and purpose of the quantity theory. Not only was the emphasis put upon the causal relationship, but the purely hypothetical formulation of the quantity theory was used as a strong support for the idea of explaining changes in the price level as being caused by changes in the quantity of money. A quantity theorist was then understood, not as a person who accepted the formulation of the theory as such, since it was considered to be logically undeniable, but as a person who tried

[21] Wagemann offers an interpretation which seems to miss the very specific way of Ricardo's derivation of the quantity theory: »So gelangt er [Ricardo] von dem Satz vom Angebot und Nachfrage zur Quantitätstheorie hinüber« (*Allgemeine Geldlehre,* Berlin, 1923, p. 128).

to explain changes in the price level in terms of changes in the circulating quantity of money. Thus Ricardo is generally considered to be a quantity theorist because he explained the great price increase in England in the early part of the nineteenth century to be caused mainly by the increase in the amount of currency.

There has been much discussion as to whether Ricardo's expounding of the quantity theory referred only to inconvertible paper money, or if it also applied to a circulation of coins. The quantity theory is then primarily understood as an explanation of changes in the value of money. Since Ricardo explained the relative values of commodities (including the precious metals) in terms of their cost of production, it has been asserted that the quantity theory was to be applied only to irredeemable paper money.[22] It is evident, however, that the quantity theory is *no explanation* of changes in the value of money. In Ricardo's statement quoted above (see p. 57) it is merely demonstrated that the value of money is inversely proportionate to its quantity. This explains neither the causes of changes in the value of money, nor what constitutes the value of money. In the case of coins, these answers were supposedly provided by his cost of production theory, which obviously could not be applied to paper money. And so it was concluded that Ricardo's quantity theory was supposed to furnish the answers in the latter case. It can easily be proved, however, that he did apply the same propositions to a metal currency.

Ricardo differentiated between the 'intrinsic' value of money, *i.e.*, coins, which was determined by the costs of production, and the 'market' value of money, which tended to coincide with its intrinsic value, but might differ temporarily because of changes in demand and supply. Therefore the value of coin determined the number of coins that could be employed at a given demand, while the quantity of paper money determined the value of the irredeemable currency-unit.[23] Thus the causal relation of the value of coin to its quantity is opposite to the proposition of causality. Hence, the quantity theory, in Ricardo's formulation, cannot be applied to a free circulation of coins. In illustrating the effects of temporary changes in the quantity of coins, however, Ricardo employs the same arguments. He declares that the discovery of a gold mine, resulting in an increase of circulating coins, will have exactly the

[22] Adolf Wagner, especially, favors this opinion very strongly. See *Die Geld- und Credittheorien der Peel'schen Bankacte,* Wien, 1862, p. 47.

[23] Ricardo, *op. cit.*, pp. 83, 114 and 213—214.

same effect on prices as an increased issue of bills, namely a proportionate price increase.[24] There is no discussion whatsoever of why prices will rise in proportion to the increased quantity of coins. The explanation must be his idea that the circulation represented a certain value, which could not be changed by an increase in its quantity as long as the demand for that value was constant. Consequently, Ricardo did apply his quantity theory both to a free currency system and a restricted paper currency; but in doing so he overlooked the fact that he originally formulated the quantity theory for a paper currency only.

5. The quantity theory became more and more to be understood as a theory for explaining price changes in terms of variations in the amount of circulation, especially after Ricardo's writings in the discussion of the causes of the great price increase after the Bank of England had been released from its duty of redemption. The first severe attack on this explanation was advanced by Thomas Tooke, who therefore is commonly characterized as a pronounced anti-quantity theorist. He asserted that the causal relation between money and prices was just the opposite to what the 'quantity theorists' held, basing his view on the results of his and Newmarch's investigation of the price development in England since 1797: »The whole tenour of the facts and reasonings adduced has been to establish the conclusion that the great alterations of prices originated, and mainly proceeded, from alterations in circumstances distinctly affecting the commodities, and not in the quantity of money, in relation to its functions.»[25]

Apparently Tooke also comprehended the quantity theory as a theory of the determination of individual prices, based upon the misunderstanding of Hume's statement that prices are determined by the quantity of money in circulation.[26] Ricardo's explanation of the causes of the price changes was therefore understood also as an explanation of individual price changes. Tooke's great attack was on the question of causality,

---

[24] *Reply to Mr. Bosanquet's Practical Observations on the Report of the Bullion Committee* (*op. cit.*, pp. 341—342).

[25] *A History of Prices,* 6 vols., London, 1838—57, vol. II, p. 350; also see vol. V, p. 344, and vol. VI, pp. 232—233, where the same conclusion is stated. W. Stanley Jevons came to the opposite result when he investigated the relation of the quantity of money to the price level during the same period, finding that »an expansion of the currency occurs one or two years previous to a rise of prices» (*Investigations in Currency and Finance,* London, 1884, p. 107).

[26] See especially Tooke's criticism of this idea in *An Inquiry into the Currency Principle,* London, 1844, pp. 74—75.

and as the commonly accepted idea of the quantity theory put the emphasis on the causal relationship, the discussion centered mainly around this question. It is very curious, indeed, that the acceptance or refutation of this proposition, which originally did not belong to the quantity theory, now became the dividing line between adherents and critics of the quantity theory. Furthermore, Tooke objected to the view, held by some so-called 'extreme quantity theorists', that *every* increase or decrease in the gold stocks of a country (caused by an increased or decreased import or export of the metal) would lead to corresponding changes in the circulating amount of money, and hence in prices. Here he certainly was right when he proved that there could be significant transfers of gold between different countries without prices being affected.[27] His criticism gives a slight notion of the inconceivably strong influence of the idea of a permanent causal relationship between changes in the amount of precious metals and prices. This view, going back to Bodin's famous explanation, had such a strong hold that it was very difficult for Tooke to convince his opponents in spite of elaborate and pointing statistics.

Tooke recognized the possibility of increasing the circulation of irredeemable paper money, causing higher prices,[28] but his main thesis is that the quantity of money is ordinarily, and always when the coinage is free, a *passive* factor, adapting itself to changes in prices. Only that part of the circulation constituting the different revenues influences the aggregate of money prices.[29] His discussion of the role of the quantity of money in determining prices was mainly based upon a misunderstanding of the essence of the quantity theory. Tooke's criticism is not directed towards the basic content of this theory, but towards the explanation of a certain price development in England and towards the idea of an exclusive causal relationship between changes in money and prices.

6. Ricardo's and Tooke's different views on the causes of the general price increase in England after 1797 gave rise to two schools, which dominated the monetary discussion in that country during the first

---

27 *An Inquiry*, pp. 121—122.

28 *Ibid.*, pp. 69—70.

29 *Ibid.*, p. 123; see also p. 71 and *History of Prices*, vol. III, p. 276. A. Hansen brings out, in an interesting discussion, the main differences between the quantity theory and the income approach, in which he correctly places Tooke as the originator of the income approach in the determination of the variations in the price level (*op. cit.*, pp. 87—88 and 117—118).

half of the nineteenth century. One of them, the Currency School,[30] whose foremost exponents were Lord Overstone, Mr. G. W. Norman and Colonel Torrens, was founded on the thinking in Ricardo's pamphlet *The High Price of Bullion*, in which the price increase was said to be the result of a too great issue of paper notes, made possible by releasing the bank from its obligation of redemption. Only if the Bank of England were imposed not to issue more notes than what corresponded to its gold stocks, would the notes preserve their denoted gold value and vary as the costs of production of gold.[31] Furthermore, the export and import of gold should be regulated through the issue of the bank, while the price of gold was indicated by the rates of exchange.[32]

The other opinion was represented by the Banking School, led by Thomas Tooke, who had on his side, among others, John Fullarton, James Wilson and Bonamy Price. They considered the causes of the price increase to be wholly explained by circumstances pertaining to the commodity side, and the increased circulation to be a result of those changes. The banks could not increase the amount of circulating money at will, as was maintained by the Currency School, because that amount was determined by the demands of transactions, which finally depended upon the price level. A too great issue of notes, therefore, soon resulted in a return of the notes to the banks, so there was no reason to base the issue of notes on the price of gold. Furthermore, the total currency did not consist of specie

---

[30] According to Tooke, Mr. Norman was the first to use the names of the Banking and Currency Schools. He characterized the idea that the circulation adapts itself to changes in the quantity of gold as the Currency principle, and the opposite view, namely that the circulation adapts itself to prices, as the Banking principle (*History of Prices*, vol. IV, p. 166). Viner mentions that William Ward (a member of the currency school group) in 1832 spoke of »the principle of the currency» as a characterization of the main doctrine of this school, and Samuel Jones Lloyd, *i.e.*, Lord Overstone, (in testimony before the Committee on Banks of Issue in 1840) referred to the same doctrine as the »currency principle», and to that of the other group as the »banking principle». After 1840 these groups were usually referred to as the »currency school» and the »banking school» (*op. cit.*, p. 220, note 1).

[31] As Viner points out, this would be true »only if the velocity of circulation of bank notes and of specie would under like circumstance be identical» (*ibid.*, p. 221).

[32] Adolf Wagner holds that one of the great mistakes of the Currency School was the identification of the total amount of precious metals in a country with the circulating amount of money (*op. cit.*, p. 222). He also maintains that another mistake was the application of Ricardo's quantity theory to redeemable notes (*ibid.*, pp. 36—37), but as has been shown above, this was done by Ricardo himself.

and bank notes only, but also of bank deposits and bills of exchange, which influenced prices just the same as did the former.

This controversy has, by some economists, been said to deal primarily with the question of causality between money and prices, which has been identified with a controversy on the correctness of the quantity theory,[33] while others have asserted that it was primarily a debate on the possibilities of banks increasing the quantity of money at will.[34] The main issue in this discussion of the regulation of the English banking system was undoubtedly the question of the possibility of increasing the circulation at will.[35] The answer depends very much, although not exclusively, on the acceptance or the refutation of the idea of a causal relation between money and prices. Regardless of this answer, however, the issue is obviously not on the correctness of the original quantity theory. But even if the later version of the quantity theory were accepted, *i.e.*, that changes in the amount of circulation, *ceteris paribus*, will cause proportionate price changes, the controversy is not on the fundamental content of this formulation either, which still is the proposition of proportionality. For this formulation has to *assume* the possibility of a causal relation between changes in money and prices. Then the question is to what degree is this assumption justified, if emphasis is laid on the proposition of causation. The Currency School could certainly not refer to this version of the quantity theory as a *support* of its opinion, though it was erroneously done. What they did was merely to maintain an actual causal relation which coincided with an unexplained assumption in the distorted formulation of the quantity theory. In that respect, it was the Currency School which supported the proposition of causality, not the reversed relation, if it could be proved.

7. The cost of production theory in its relation to the quantity theory, interpreted as an explanation of the value of money, is given a considerably more penetrating analysis by William Nassau Senior than by anyone else of his contemporaries. In criticising James Mill's statement that changes in the quantity or velocity of money would permanently influence the real (intrinsic) value of money, he considers why this should be true of the value of coins more than it is of the

[33] See, *e.g.*, Laughlin, *op. cit.*, pp. 256—257.

[34] See, *e.g.*, F. Walker, *Money,* New York, 1883, pp. 420—421.

[35] This view is supported by Viner's summary of the general position of the two schools (*op. cit.*, pp. 220—224). Viner's discussion of »English Currency Controversies, 1825—1865» is the most penetrating and clarifying available.

value of any other commodity (omitting fluctuations in the short run).[36] The value is not determined by the quantity of circulating coins or by the velocity of circulation, nor by the amount of transactions or the use of barter or credit. There is only one cause determining the value of money: the cost of its production, which depends upon the cost of producing coins under the least favorable circumstances.[37] Money has a special position, however, in so far as it is the cost of producing it which determines the demand for it, not the demand which determines how much money will be produced.[38] It is the same view as that held by Adam Smith, namely that with a given velocity of money and a given amount of transactions to be carried out, the quantity of money is determined by its costs of production, which is determined by the price level. Thus the quantity of money is a *passive* factor in respect to its value, and can never *cause* any changes in its value; nor can the velocity of circulation. An increase or decrease in the velocity of money will not, except for short periods, affect the value of money; only the quantity of money in circulation (if there were no changes in the cost of production at the same time).

According to the cost of production theory, the quantity of money in circulation depends upon the value of money, while the 'quantity theorists' said the opposite, *i.e.*, that the value of money depends upon its quantity. James Mill's conclusion that the value of money is determined by its quantity was certainly incorrect in view of its assumptions, but Senior's criticism is based on a misunderstanding of the assumption of a change in the amount of money, which demonstrates the 'universal law' of proportionality. This is very easily explained by the dubiousness of the formulations themselves of the quantity theory. While the so-called quantity theorists simply *assumed* the quantity of money to be changed, and inquired as to the effect of that change under certain given conditions, Senior asked *why* the quantity of money had changed, looking for the cause. The *cause* could only be a change in the value of money, which was treated as an effect by the quantity theorists; consequently, the two ways of reasoning were incompatible.

Senior's theory of the value of coins being determined by the cost of producing the precious metals is said to be applicable only to countries which have any gold and/or silver production. For other countries, the

---

[36] *Three Lectures on the Value of Money* (1829), reprinted as No. 4 in *Series of Reprints of Scarce Tracts in Economic and Political Science,* London, 1931, pp. 8—9.

[37] *Ibid.*, pp. 30 and 33.

[38] *Ibid.*, p. 36; also see p. 55.

value of the coined metal is determined by the cost of producing that quantity of goods which is given in exchange for the amount of precious metals. If prices in such a country are low, the reason is not because the circulation is small, as maintained by the 'quantity theorists', but is because of the great costs of producing the commodities exchanged.

This explanation is probably not so striking as it may at first appear. Thinking of how small a part the foreign trade constituted of the total trade of the interior countries on the European continent (to which the explanation referred), and of that part which was exchanged for gold and/or silver, it seems doubtful whether the cost of producing the goods exchanged really determined the price level. Were the imports of gold and silver relatively small in comparison to the total amount of precious metals in the country, it seems still more questionable.

Denying the possibility of increasing a currency of coins without a change in the cost of producing bullion, Senior agrees with the 'quantity theorists' that an increased amount of paper money will raise prices, since no problem of the cost of production is involved. He even thinks that prices will go up more than in proportion to the additional amount of currency, as a result of »the spirit of speculation» which is created by an excess of money.[39]

In his account of the Mississippi bubble, Senior uses the propositions in the distorted formulation of the quantity theory as a support of the explanation of what happened: »It appears to us obvious, that when the currency of the country [France] was suddenly tripled, all prices must have experienced at least an equal rise.»[40] The price rise might be more if the »spirit of speculation» is influenced, which just means an increased velocity of money. Evidently he is the object, like nearly all 'quantity theorists', of the same confusion of the proposition of proportionality with that of causality.

Senior, when scrutinizing the quantity theory, resembles Ricardo, but is more consistent. His acceptance of the theory as an explanation of changes in the value of paper money is based upon the same way of argumentation. Thus he mentions that if the circulation of Great Britain contains 45 million sterling and were replaced by an issue of notes with the nominal value of 90 million sterling, the effect would

---

[39] *Three Lectures on the Cost of Obtaining Money* (No. 5 in *Series of Reprints*), p. 38.

[40] *Ibid.*, p. 74.

be that wages, salaries, and profits doubled.[41] This purely arithmetic example forms, as did Ricardo's examples, the foundation of a fallacious causal proposition.

8. John Stuart Mill, who presented a restatement of much of classical doctrines, also tried to forge the different monetary theories into one unified theory. This sometimes made him appear quite contradictory, and the critics were not long in pointing it out. His inconsistencies, however, are very much reduced if they are read in their proper connections. There is no difficulty in showing, by the help of detached quotations, how Mill at first lays down the quantity theory as the most fundamental proposition in monetary theory, but later says that it would be childish to think that the value of money is determined by its quantity. This would not imply any contradiction if the quantity theory is interpreted in the original sense given it by Locke; but even when understood as a theory of the value of money, it is still in conformity with the essence of Mill's monetary theory.

Money is looked upon as a commodity, the market (or exchange) value of which is determined by its demand and supply, while its natural (or intrinsic) value is determined by its cost of production. The supply of money is the quantity which people are willing to circulate, whereas the demand for money, which holds a special position, is the amount of commodities offered for it in the market. The latter differs from the demand for other things by being limited only »by the means of the purchaser», so »there is always a demand for as much money as can be got», whereas the demand for other things is limited.[42] This is the same idea as Locke's (see p. 28). It constitutes one of the bases of their formulations of the quantity theory, implicitly in the case of Locke, but explicitly as stated by Mill, where it supposedly justifies the assumption of a doubled, tripled, *etc.*, quantity of money being practically feasible.

Of course, Mill had the right to define the demand for and the supply of money as he preferred, but he overlooked that these deceptive definitions do not have the same import as the general definitions of these concepts. This is the source of the great confusion of the application of these terms to money. Thus the demand for money, in Mill's definition above, can have no other meaning than another

---

41 *Ibid.*, pp. 52—53.

42 *Principles of Political Economy* (ed. by W. J. Ashley), London, 1923, p. 490; also see p. 493.

definition of the total monetary value of goods being exchanged for money. It is not related to the usual concept of the demand for something (*i.e.*, in the sense of schedules). It is impossible to use this definition when analyzing the exchange value of money, because it is not a question of a demand for just another commodity. The same criticism applies to the concept of the supply of money.[43] It is merely another way of defining the total quantity of money given for a certain amount of goods and has nothing to do with the concept of supply in relation to individual goods. The 'supply of money' only indicates the total quantity of goods demanded and taken at a certain price level, which is also indicated by the 'demand for money'. The application of these terms to the total quantity of money in circulation is an example of how fallacious it is to use concepts only applicable to micro-economics when dealing with total categories.

Mill asserts that an increased quantity of money, *ceteris paribus*, will always raise prices, because it is equal to an increased demand, and because the additional quantity of money will be accepted everywhere.[44] This argument is fundamentally different from Locke's and Hume's propositions which aimed at demonstrating the proportionality between the quantity of money and prices. Mill puts the emphasis on the change in demand. The increase in demand is actually an upward shift in the demand schedule, since the supply of goods is presumed to be constant. If there were to be an exactly proportionate rise in all prices, the structure of demand would have to be constant. Considering this as only theoretically possible, Mill criticises Hume's famous example in which all people are assumed to wake up one morning with an extra guinea in their pockets. The result would not be a proportionate price increase on all goods, but only an average increase. If, for example, the quantity of money were increased by one-fourth, *ceteris paribus*, some prices would rise more than others, but »the average rise would be one-fourth. This is a necessary consequence of the fact that a fourth more money would have been given for only the same quantity of goods.»[45]

Both Mill's and Hume's statement are merely truisms as they obviously coincide with the same argument that a greater quantity of money is given for a constant amount of goods. But Mill accentuates

[43] Wicksell, particularly, stresses how meaningless these concepts become when applied to money (*Lectures*, vol. II, pp. 20—21).

[44] *Op. cit.*, pp. 490—491.

[45] *Ibid.*, p. 493.

that an increase in the quantity of money means an increase in demand. The primary thing is not the change in the quantity of money as such, but in demand, although this fact is veiled by his peculiar definitions of the demand and supply of money.

The supply of money is said to be determined by the quantity of money multiplied by its velocity of circulation, to which Mill gave a rather peculiar interpretation: »The phrase, rapidity of circulation, requires some comment. It must not be understood to mean the number of purchases made by each piece of money in a given time. Time is not the thing to be considered. The state of society may be such that each piece of money hardly performs more than one purchase in a year: but if this arises from the small number of transactions — from the small amount of business done, the want of activity in traffic, or because what traffic there is, mostly takes place by barter — it constitutes no reason why prices should be lower, or the value of money higher. The essential point is, not how often the same money changes hands in a given time, but how often it changes hands in order to perform a given amount of traffic. We must compare the number of purchases made by the money in a given time, not with the time itself, but with the goods sold in that same time.»[46]

The assertion not to take time into consideration is to obscure the whole concept of the velocity of money, making it dependent on the value of money and depriving it of any independent significance.[47] The greater the value of money is, the less the velocity of money will be, according to Mill's argument. The velocity of money is then a passive factor, without any influence on the value of money. If it increases, *ceteris paribus*, it merely means that the amount of goods will be exchanged faster, while the value of money remains constant. This peculiar opinion is probably best explained by Mill's artificial views on the demand and supply of money. He assumed the total demand for goods, at a given moment, to be formed by the quantity of money in circulation multiplied by the velocity of money. Seemingly, the velocity of money then appears not to depend upon time, but on the amount of money and goods, and can be obtained easily by a simple division of the total value of goods by the quantity of money. Obviously, however, the turnover requires a certain time, and the average velocity of circulation will be equal to the number of times which the quantity

[46] *Ibid.*, p. 495.

[47] See Wicksell's criticism of James and Stuart Mill's concepts of the velocity of circulation (*Lectures*, vol. II, p. 60).

of money is turned over during a certain period in order to perform a given amount of transactions. If the value of goods is four times that of the quantity of money at a certain point of time, that does not mean that the velocity of money is four during the given period of time because the quantity of money has to circulate four times in order to perform the transaction of the whole amount of goods. The decisive thing is how long a time it takes to turn over a given amount of goods, which in this case is four times greater than the value of the currency. If it should take one year, and the year is the period considered, the velocity of money would be 4, but it would be 48 if it took only one month. Mill's intention was probably to emphasize that the decisive element in the velocity of money is »not how often the same money changes hands in a given time, but how often it changes in order to perform a given amount of traffic». But then his assertion that »time is not the thing to be considered» is incorrect, as he does, in fact, take time into consideration. The defects in his way of arguing caused only confusion as to the meaning of the concept of the velocity of money.

In conformity with his father, Mill did not maintain any exclusive causal relationship as to the cause of variations in the value of money. A change in the amount of goods would produce the same effect on prices as a change in the quantity of money.[48] The argumentation is exactly the same as if it were based on the equation of exchange; that is, the amount of money paid for the goods exchanged must equal their total monetary value. Mill is fully aware of the far-reaching abstractions necessary for the propositions mentioned, but he seems not to realize that they can have no other meaning than to illustrate purely arithmetic relations. He evaluates the quantity theory according to its ability to throw light on the causes of actual changes in the value of money when pointing out its limitations: »That an increase of the quantity of money raises prices, and a diminution lowers them, is the most elementary proposition in the theory of currency, and without it we should have no key to any of the others. In any state of things, however, except the simple and primitive one which we have supposed, the proposition is only true other things being the same.»[49] As the banking system becomes more developed and credit begins to play an important role in the exchange of commodities, the connection between

[48] *Ibid.*, p. 493.

[49] *Ibid.*, p. 495. The proposition in the first part of the quotation is stressed also by R. G. Hawtrey in the preface to his book *Currency and Credit*, London, 1919.

changes in the quantity of money and in the price level is said to become looser and looser. The content of the quantity theory, therefore, becomes rather insignificant in forecasting the effects of a change in the quantity of money on the value of money. This is the basic reason for Mill's great surprise over there being »some authorities who, still adhering to the doctrine of the infancy of society and of political economy, that the quantity of money compared with that of commodities, determines general prices, think it important to prove that bank notes and no other forms of credit are money, in order to support the inference that bank notes and no other forms of credit influence prices. It is obvious, however, that prices do not depend on money, but on purchases.»[50]

There is no clear distinction, however, between the concept of *influencing* and *determining* prices in these two quotations. Mill agrees to the proposition that in a society using only coins and/or bank notes, changes in the quantity of money will affect prices, apparently in proportion to the variations in the circulation, since no other means of exchange are used and the amount of commodities are tacitly assumed to be constant. But the value of money, *i.e.*, the price level, is not determined by a comparison of the total quantity of money with that of goods. It is determined by the cost of producing the means of exchange. In a society with a highly developed banking and credit system, the amount of coins and bank notes only forms a small part of the total means of payments. Therefore, a change in the quantity of coins or banknotes will only influence prices if the amount of other means of payment has not changed. In the infancy of society, a change in the quantity of money meant an equal change in the amount of purchases, but it does not any longer, since the amount of purchases no longer equalizes the total quantity of money. This is his fundamental idea. It is not a denial of the quantity theory as Mill understands it, nor any new explanation of the determination of the value of money. The lack of distinction between the words influence and determine may partly be compensated for by the different emphasis put upon the words, depending on the connection in which they are used. Thus Mill's concept of the quantity theory must be that prices are determined or, rather, influenced by the quantity of money inasmuch as changes in the quantity of money influence prices. The theory is not understood as an explanation of what determines the value of money. The permanent value of money, *i.e.*, coins, is determined by the cost of producing the precious metals, though temporarily influenced by variations in the

[50] *Op. cit.*, pp. 538—539.

'supply' of coins. Therefore, Mill did not see any dilemma between the cost of production theory and the quantity theory. On the contrary, the latter is a complement to the first. The »statement that the value of money depends on its quantity combined with the rapidity of circulation.... is simply the law of demand and supply, which is acknowledged to be applicable to all commodities, and which, in the case of money as of most other things, is controlled, but not set aside, by the law of cost of production, since cost of production would have no effect on value if it could have none on supply».[51] Because of the use of the concepts of the demand and supply of money, Mill evidently differs from Adam Smith and Senior on the quantity theory. Irrespective of the suitability of these concepts, however, they indicate Mill's realization of the correctness of the idea behind the equation of exchange, which made him treat the value of money in its relation to the cost of production theory as a special case. And so he declared that changes in the cost of production of the precious metals will only influence the value of money as much as they influence its quantity, whereas the value of other things are immediately influenced. In other words: the value of money, $\frac{1}{P}$, could not be influenced because of a mere change in the cost of production of the precious metals, as long as M, V and T were constant. The influence of anticipations is neglected, as well as the effects of changes in the production of the precious metals upon the velocity of money and upon the production of other commodities. A decrease in the value of money is the same as an increase in prices; but as long as the quantity of money and its velocity of circulation remain unchanged, a certain part of the commodities will not be sold, which makes it impossible to keep up prices, according to Mill. The velocity of money is always treated as a passive factor, more or less given, which excludes any alterations in it as a compensating element.

Mill's approach to the quantity theory, understood as an explanation of temporary changes in the value of the money-metal, is characterized by an attempt to combine it with the cost of production theory. This was possible since the quantity theory was not interpreted as a theory of the value of money (*i.e.*, coins); consequently it was not an alternative to the cost of production theory, which was considered to explain the relative values of all things, including money, and the causes of variations

[51] *Ibid.*, p. 504.

in values. Instead, the quantity theory appeared as a necessary supplement to the cost of production theory when applied to money. In the case of inconvertible paper money, the value of money depended exclusively on the quantity of money.[52] But since the relation between changes in the quantity of (paper) money and the price level had become very loose because of the extended use of other forms of payment and of credit, Mill dismisses the 'quantity theory' as an unsatisfactory explanation of changes in the purchasing power of money in a society with a highly developed monetary and banking system. His emphasis upon 'purchases' as determining prices was a step in the right direction toward solving the problem.

9. The classics' discussion of the quantity theory is very indicative of the ambiguity of its real meaning. Adam Smith, Ricardo, and John Stuart Mill represent three rather different interpretations. Adam Smith views the theory as a theory of the determination of the value of money (*i.e.*, coins); hence, he discards it since his cost of production theory is thought of as having general applicability. For he cannot connive at the assumption of a sudden increase (or decrease) in the quantity of money; instead, he immediately inquires as to the cause of this sudden change. And for him this change must be the effect of a change (absolute or relative) in the cost of production of money. One might perhaps say that Adam Smith thinks in economic terms and relations only; therefore the purely mathematical formulation of the quantity theory appears as an unmeaning statement to him.

Ricardo, on the other hand, conceives of the quantity theory as exposing an undeniable mathematical relation. His exemplification of the theory runs in terms of arithmetics. The neglect of the limited applicability of mathematical relations to economic relations has actually led to a vast source of propositions in economics which are true in themselves but are just without economic significance. Ricardo's formulation of the quantity theory receives economic meaningfulness only if it is looked upon as an illustration of some economic principle. Unfortunately, Ricardo made the great mistake of apprehending his purely hypothetical example as a support of his explanation of the contemporary price increase.

Though John Stuart Mill is strongly influenced by Ricardo's reasoning, he differs from him by emphasizing that the assumption in the quantity theory of a change in the quantity of money implies a

[52] *Ibid.*, p. 543.

corresponding change in demand. Thereby he leaves the field of pure mathematics and deals with relations of economic relevance. But because of the assumption of other things being equal, the content of the quantity theory is reduced to a truism. For if total demand increases by, say ten per cent, *ceteris paribus*, then it is self-evident that the average price increase will amount to the same figure, since it means that the schedule illustrating total demand is shifted upwards by ten per cent. Mill's conclusion was that since other things will not remain equal and the total quantity of money, *i.e.*, coins and notes, constitute only a part of the total means of payment, the quantity theory has no relevance in advanced economies. The theory, accordingly, is looked upon as a *prediction* of what will happen under real conditions, the value of which must be judged according to the correspondence of its assumptions with actual conditions. Indeed, we have not been able to find any writer in this period who interprets the quantity theory in line with Locke's and Hume's basic idea.

There is one remark by Senior which is worth special attention, namely that an increase or decrease in the velocity of money will not, except for short periods, affect the value of money, only the quantity of money in circulation (see p. 64). From a very critical point of view, the statement appears as tautological, containing one definition phrased in two different ways; *i.e.*, changes in the velocity of money is merely another way of defining changes in the quantity of money in circulation. This would be true if Senior defined changes in the distribution of active and passive (idle) cash holdings as changes in the velocity of money. Instead, this definition is inherent in his statement. But it also implies that the rate of turnover of a *given* quantity of money is increased. This is actually the basic reason for the diminished quantity of money in circulation. Only then will it be true that prices will remain constant. Consequently, the statement is reduced to a truism, since the correctness of the proposition that the value of money will not be affected depends wholly upon the tacit assumption that changes in the velocity of money are counterbalanced by inversely proportionate changes in the quantity of money. Senior is merely saying, if we refer to the equation of exchange, that if V changes, then M must undergo the exactly opposite changes because P will not be influenced and T is assumed to be constant. But how does he know that $\frac{1}{P}$, that is, the value of money, will not be influenced? His statement, as long as he has not provided any statistical support for it, can be correct only if he *presumes* that *P* will remain unaffected; that is, the proposition is reduced to a truism.

Senior's proposition is of interest because the only intelligible theory, or rather, hypothesis, that can be formulated on Locke's and Hume's basic idea of money as a pure medium of exchange is that changes in the quantity of money, because of this primary function of money, will not influence the velocity of the circulation of money. This is also Fisher's interpretation of the basic idea of the quantity theory. But if this version of the quantity theory is reformulated so as to include the assumption that other things remain equal, that is, that the velocity of money, *i.a.*, will remain constant, in order to prove the truth of the proposition, then it is reduced to the same truism as that of Senior. If, however, Senior's proposition is formulated in a meaningful way, then it is of interest to contrast his view with the 'developed' quantity theory. Senior thus maintains that changes in the velocity of money will not influence prices, but will cause inverse (and proportionate) changes in the quantity of money in circulation (if the number of transactions remains the same), whereas the developed quantity theory (*i.e.*, the Fisherine and Wicksellian version) reads: changes in the quantity of money will not influence the velocity of money, but cause (proportionate) price changes (if the number of transactions remains the same).

CHAPTER IV

AMERICAN ADHERENTS AND CRITICS OF THE QUANTITY THEORY

1. One of the very well-known American economists in the latter part of the nineteenth century, Francis A. Walker, was the most extreme 'quantity theorist' of his time. He not only defended the quantity theory against all kinds of attacks, but also maintained that the value of money was completely determined by its quantity and that individual prices were determined by the quantity of money in circulation.

The quantity theory is conceived as a special case of the general law of demand and supply. The acceptance of it, therefore, is not an advance of any new theory, but only the application to a specific instance of a principle, which has been proved by induction and has never been challenged.[1] The »quantity theory *in general*» is the principle that value is determined by the relation between demand and supply, while the »quantity theory *of money*» is the principle that the value of money is determined by the relation between the demand for money and the supply of money. Walker well realizes that the issue at stake is not the correctness of this general principle as such, but the assumption that the concepts of demand and supply can be applied also to money: »The only hypothesis in the case of the quantity-theory *of money* is that demand and supply have the same dominion and potency here which they have in all other cases of exchange. It is assumed that a principle admitted to be otherwise of universal application can safely be applied to this particular instance, no reason why it should not be so applied having ever been adduced.»[2]

---

[1] »The Quantity Theory of Money», *Q. J. E.*, 1895, p. 372. See also Walker's article »The Relation of Changes in the Volume of the Currency to Prosperity», *Economic Studies*, American Economic Association, 1896, No. 1, p. 27: »But those who hold the quantity-theory of money are not bound to prove their case. That theory is simply the application, to the special case of money, of the general principle that value is determined in the relation between demand and supply.»

[2] »The Quantity Theory of Money», pp. 374—375. Wesley C. Mitchell, in criticising Walker's view, asserts that the law of demand and supply, applied to the

The specific position of money, as a general means of exchange, makes such a hypothesis inadmissible. It is unnecessary to repeat the criticism of Stuart Mill's definition of the demand for and supply of money, which Walker had entirely appropriated to himself. His argument that prices are merely values expressed in terms of money and therefore can be explained by the relation between the demand for and the supply of money, is untenable. Though changes in the value of money can take place only via variations in prices, the causes of these variations cannot be analyzed in terms of the very dubious concepts provided by Stuart Mill.

Walker went much farther than his great teachers Ricardo and Stuart Mill in stressing the role of the quantity of money. The value of money, he said, is completely determined by the quantity of money — used as a means of exchange — in relation to the demand for money, not by its cost of production. The value of money (coins) is determined only by a direct exchange for commodities. It has no relation whatsoever to the cost of production of the precious metals. There is no possibility of distinguishing between the function of money as a means of exchange and as a measure of value, since it serves as a measure of value only by being used as a means of exchange. And so he draws the same conclusion as Hume and James Mill: That only those goods exchanged for money will influence the price level, *i.e.*, the value of money: »It will be observed that every time a barter transaction is substituted for buying and selling, the demand for money is thereby diminished and its value thereby lowered (the supply remaining the same), while the higher prices of commodities which result from the sales actually effected by the use of money, are carried over, in estimation, to the commodities remaining unsold, or to those whose transfer is accomplished by a direct exchange of goods for goods.«[3] The best thing for a seller to do would be obviously to bring only one of his commodities to the market, keeping the rest of them stored. Then the money price would be »carried over in estimation to the commodities unsold« and he would make an enormous profit by a direct

---

price question, proves that the quantity theory is inadequate because it does not take into consideration all those factors which determine the price level (»The Quantity Theory of the Value of Money«, *J. P. E.*, 1896, p. 145).

[3] *Money*, New York, 1881, pp. 64—65; also see »The Quantity Theory of Money«, p. 373. H. P. Willis could hardly imagine any theory of prices which neglected the influences of the cost of production of commodities as entirely as Walker's explanation (»The History and Present Application of the Quantity Theory«, *J. P. E.*, 1896, p. 438).

exchange of these goods for other goods! This 'price determination' would be possible only if the same relations of demand and supply were present when goods are exchanged for money as when there is a direct barter. Actually, it is a denial of the working of the market mechanism when a general means of exchange is not used, since the exchange relations for all bartering are settled in another market. Such a price theory is void of anything which would make it a sensible theory of prices. The confusion is due particularly to a lack of distinction between absolute and relative prices, and between price theory and pure arithmetics.

The foundation of Walker's price theory is easily illustrated by the equation of exchange, $MV = PT$ (*cf.* Hume, p. 36). The equation can evidently be applied to only one single exchange of a commodity for money. That makes $V = 1$ and $T = 1$, thus $M = P$; that is, the price of a commodity is equal to the amount of money paid for it. The more transactions of different commodities included in the equation, the closer one gets a value of P, which, compared with some earlier data, might be said to indicate the changes in the value of money. The value of P, that Walker is discussing, lies somewhere between the price of one commodity and the average price of all commodities. He is merely saying that every time T is diminished or increased, P will vary, because M and V are supposed to be constant. This is pure arithmetics, which neither gives any clue to what causes the changes in the different elements, nor to what determines their values. Walker's very extreme quantity theory of prices is fundamentally based upon the confusion of this necessarily algebraic identity with causal relations. Once again the quantity theory was made the foundation of a theory of individual prices and of the explanation of actual changes in the price level.

2. J. L. Laughlin has characterized Walker as the 'most ardent supporter of the quantity theory in the United States', and can himself be appropriately described as the most ardent critic of the same doctrine, especially of all its different misformulations and misapplications, which he unfortunately identified with the essence of the theory. The awareness of how difficult it is to discuss the quantity theory because it is not stated in the same way by any two of its adherents,[4] has not made Laughlin as careful in dealing with the subject as might be expected. In spite of being one of the few researchers of the history of the quantity theory, he has been led to interpret the doctrine as a theory of prices,

[4] »The Quantity Theory of Money», *J. P. E.*, 1924, p. 276.

basing his arguments on statements which by no means are related to the essence of the quantity theory.

The fundamentals of the doctrine are said to be that the pricing process can take place only by an actual exchange of commodities for money, and that the price level is determined by a comparison of the number of exchanges to be performed with the amount of money in circulation (taking into regard the velocity of money): »The central error of the quantity theory lies, in my judgement, in the assumed premise that prices are fixed by a comparison between the goods to be exchanged (*i.e.*, the money work) and the media of exchange by which the work is done .... What, for instance, regulates the price of wheat? Why, of course, the amount of the medium of exchange for which it is in fact exchanged.»[5] But this central error belonged only to the 'quantitative theory of prices', which was a doctrine of the determination of individual (or relative) prices. It is very surprising that Laughlin is able to interpret the quantity theory in that same way. It should be altogether unnecessary to recall to mind that the quantity theory deals with average prices (close to a multiple factor). Laughlin, however, is hard to convince and perseveres, despite all kinds of objections, by saying that there is no abstract price level, independent of individual prices; only an average of the single prices of the different articles. True; but such an argument cannot possibly invalidate the fact that the price level is partly related to the quantity of money. Had the criticism referred only to the statement that *average* prices are *fixed* by a comparison of the amount of goods with that of money, it would have been a duly legitimate objection to a very common conclusion drawn from the content of the quantity theory, since there can be *no determination* of the price level in that way. Undoubtedly there had been a tendency to believe the price level to be settled independently of individual prices. So far Laughlin was correct, but he overshot the mark in criticising statements which he erroneously identified with the quantity theory.

Laughlin also confused separate statements of so-called quantity theorists with the quantity theory. He thought the theory to be founded on the presumption that individual prices can be determined *only* by

[5] *The Principles of Money,* New York, 1926, p. 315; also see »The Quantity Theory», p. 273. Laughlin's interpretation is shared particularly by J. S. Nicholson: ». . . the essence of the quantity theory is that money determines prices by being actually used» (*A Treatise on Money and Essays on Monetary Problems,* London, 1901, 5 ed., p. 144).

an actual exchange of money for goods. This is more easily accounted for as several pronounced 'quantity theorists', *e.g.*, Hume and Walker, advanced that proposition in connection with their expounding of the doctrine. They had confused the idea, that only those goods being exchanged for money will influence the number of 'monetary transactions', with the pricing process.

Nothing in Laughlin's criticism is directed against the essence of the quantity theory. He is mainly criticising all those incorrect conclusions which were drawn from the original formulations. He was particularly right in saying that the concepts of demand for and supply of money were misapplied; that changes in the quantity of money did not automatically mean changes in the demand for commodities; and that the use of the concept of a total demand made the demand for particular goods independent of the goods on which the demand was based.[6]

The quantity theory is not conceived as containing an exclusive causal relationship. On the contrary, Laughlin is somewhat ironical over the opinion — ascribed to the quantity theory — that prices cannot decrease with a constant amount of circulation, unless the supply of goods has increased. All statements of this kind, emanating from so-called 'quantity theorists', are always based on the idea of that necessary identity, which was later clearly exposed by the equation of exchange; consequently, they were completely correct, according to their assumptions. Very often, however, these assumptions are not explicitly stated; but even when they are, Laughlin is repeatedly criticising statements of this kind by referring to all those different elements that enter into the determination of individual prices, and thereby also into the determination of the price level.

The quantity theory is basically understood as a theory of prices. A satisfactory theory of prices must take into consideration all those factors which influence the ratio of exchange between money and commodities. The adduced weakness of the 'quantity theory' — to discuss this problem from the monetary side only — and its artificial assumptions which make it impossible to use it as an instrument in the determination of the causes of variations in the price level, is the fundamental reason for Laughlin's rejection of the doctrine.[7]

---

6 *Principles of Money*, p. 325.

7 *Ibid.*, pp. 314, 327, 358 and 362; also see *Money and Prices*, New York, 1924, p. 30. The quantity of paper money has no influence on its value of exchange if it has none on its redemption, which is the decisive factor (*A New Exposition of Money, Credit and Prices*, 2 vols., Chicago, 1931, vol. II, p. 710).

3. F. W. Taussig is a typical representative of the opinion that the quantity theory is merely a special case of the general law of demand and supply: »Double the quantity of money, and, other things being equal, prices will be twice as high as before and the value of money one-half. Halve the quantity of money, and, other things being equal, prices will be one-half what they were before, and the value of money double. That an increase in quantity tends to lower value, is a proposition holding good of all commodities. The special proposition concerning money is that its value tends to vary precisely in proportion to its quantity. This constant relation does not hold good of any other commodity.» Taussig expresses the same thing by saying that the elasticity of the demand for money is unity, which implies that »the position of money is unique».[8] The demand for money is defined, in conformity with Stuart Mill's concept, as the quantity of commodities of all sorts being 'offered' for money. Since the elasticity of this demand is constant and equal to one, prices will always vary in an exact proportion to changes in the quantity of money. The supply of goods will not be influenced; it changes regardless of variations in the circulation. This is the foundation for Taussig's acceptance of the common version of the quantity theory.

At first it may appear that the quotation in the preceding paragraph is perfectly correct in all its simplicity and cannot be denied logically. Similar statements have also been accepted for over a century as self-evident. And yet this formulation of the quantity theory is wholly untenable. Again it includes a causal proposition for which there is no proof. The supposed evidence is the general law of demand and

[8] *Principles of Economics,* 3 ed., 2 vols., New York, 1933, vol. I, pp. 232 and 234.

Taussig's opinion is shared, *i.a.*, by E. Cannan, who finds it »reasonable to assume that we should expect the elasticity of the demand for currency to be equal to unity» (*Modern Currency and the Regulation of Its Value,* London, 1931, p. 70). Cannan, however, is more careful in his statement and warns us against making any precipitous conclusions, for if it were universally true, he says, then »issues of legal tender could go on buying goods and services with new issues indefinitely» (*loc. cit.*). Cannan's point is that the elasticity of the demand for currency is unity only within certain limits. This argument cannot be accepted, however, for either we are dealing with purely arithmetical relations, and then the concept of a unitary elasticity is merely another name for an indisputable arithmetic relation; or we are dealing with actual conditions, which means that nothing can be said about »the elasticity of the demand for currency».

Cannan views the quantity theory as a proposition that the value of money, *ceteris paribus*, depends upon its quantity. He finds it »very astonishing if this were not true, since it is true of every commodity other than money» (*ibid.*, p. 65).

supply, which is behind the uncritical acceptance of the causal proposition as the most self-evident fact in economic theory. Taussig overlooks that the application of the concepts of demand and supply to money as a means of exchange needs very important qualifications, which make the bearing of those concepts entirely different from the ordinary apprehension of them. Correct as it is that »an increase in quantity tends to lower value, is a proposition holding good of all commodities», it is equally incorrect to think that this relation, in respect to money, can be *expressed* and *proved* in the way adduced.

As mentioned above, Taussig's conclusion is based upon the idea that the elasticity of demand for money is constantly unity, which is alleged to make money appear only as a means of exchange. This would, of course, be true *if* Taussig's assumption were correct. He seems to think that his formulation of the quantity theory, which actually is based upon this assumption also, provides the justification for the assumption and for the proposition that the supply of goods will not be influenced by changes in the quantity of money. Therefore, Taussig, like Stuart Mill, criticises Hume for his opinion of the advantageous effect on production of an additional quantity of money, neglecting the fact that the criticism is based on a purely hypothetical proposition, used in a vicious circle. Taussig asserts that the result must be proportionate price changes, since the consumers will not change their habits, *i.e.*, dispositions of money. Then there will be no reason for raising production. Only if the increase of (paper) money takes on so great proportions as to shake the confidence in its value, will the demand for money be influenced and cause a shift in its structure, leading to a different price development.[9] Curiously enough, Taussig uses the same kind of argument against Hume, as Hume used in order to prove the same proposition as Taussig. It illustrates that amazing lack of distinctions which has made these futile discussions continue for centuries. Taussig's argument is that there is no reason why the consumers should change their habits if they all suddenly received twice as much money in their hands. The only thing they can do is to spend the money. If the amount of goods is constant, one single result remains: a doubled price level. This is an exact copy of Hume's argument, and yet they disagreed, simply because Taussig thought only 'in terms of the equation of exchange'. Accordingly, he maintained that the same effects of changes in the quantity of money would follow,

---

[9] *Ibid.*, pp. 237—238 and 246—247.

ceteris paribus, if the rapidity of circulation varied, and the opposite effects if the amounts of goods changed.[10]

As the fundamental content of the original quantity theory is apprehended as a statement of what the effect will be if the quantity of money, constituting the *only* means of exchange in a given society, is changed, the propositions above will only be true under very 'simple conditions'. Taussig makes exactly the same reservation as Stuart Mill: the concept of the quantity of money has a very indefinite meaning under actual conditions, and does not comprise all those different means of exchange which are employed in the performance of transactions. Consequently, there will not be any proportionate relations between changes in the amount of 'real money, *i.e.*, coins and notes, and in the price level. This requires a reformulation of the quantity theory: »Instead of saying that the general range of prices depends (other things being equal) on the quantity of specie, we must say that it depends on the total quantity of money equivalents, or of the available *total purchasing power* in terms of money.»[11] This total purchasing power includes specie, paper money, and the whole credit machinery. The main difficulty is to determine how great an influence the changes in the amount of 'pure' or 'real' money has on the total purchasing power. Even if it should be impossible to distinguish an immediate connection between changes in the quantity of money and in the price level — a proportionate relation is not to be considered — nevertheless, Taussig believes it to be possible to substantiate such a relation in the long run (*cf.* Fisher, p. 92).

This development of the quantity theory, which went astray from Locke's and Hume's original purpose, and which put the emphasis on the proposition of causality in connection with a definite means of exchange, *i.e.*, coins and banknotes, as distinguished from other means of payment, *e.g.*, bills of exchange, checks, *etc.*, is an attempt to preserve a certain part of the original proposition, which is of a formal character only and without any real importance. It is conceded that such an interpretation might seem to be the first that would come to mind, since Locke's intention was to point out that the quantity itself of gold and silver, as means of exchange and disregarding their industrial uses, was of no importance to an isolated economy or to the world as a whole. The statement referred only to the quantity of coins; but the essence was that the quantity of the medium exchange had no significance,

[10] *Ibid.*, p. 238.
[11] *Ibid.*, p. 247.

because prices would always be in proportion to the amount of coins in circulation. As different forms of the medium of exchange developed, the quantity of coins and redeemable notes became a gradually declining part of the total amount of the means of exchange; then the relation between the quantity of coins and notes and the price level could no longer be directly proportionate.

4. One of the first attempts to use an equation as a foundation of a statistical analysis of the relation between variations in the quantity of money and in the price level was made by Edwin W. Kemmerer. The equation used was $M R = N E P$, or $P = \frac{M R}{N E}$. In this formula M represents the quantity of money in circulation, R the number of times M is turned over in a given period, N the amount of commodities exchanged, E the number of times N is exchanged, and P the (average) price of the commodities.[12] $M R$ is said to represent the monetary supply, $N E$ the commodity supply, and $N E P$ the monetary demand.

Kemmerer, in following Stuart Mill and Taussig — to mention only two — makes the same fallacious statements of the demand for and supply of money. $M R$ is not the monetary supply, as compared to what import the concept has in relation to other things; it is merely a misleading definition of the total monetary value of a given amount of economic transactions, expressed in terms of the product of the total quantity of money in circulation and a certain number, defined as its velocity of circulation during the relevant period. It is just as meaningless to signify $N E P$ as the 'monetary demand' since it also merely betokens the total monetary value of a certain amount of commodities (or transactions), expressed as the product of the amount of commodities, times its average number of exchanges, and its average price.

In the case of commodities, we obviously can speak of a total supply or demand. But $N E$ is definitely not the commodity supply. It is

---

[12] *Money and Credit Instruments in Their Relation to General Prices,* New York, 1907, p. 13. Taking into account other means of exchange the equation is written $P_8 = (M R + C R_c) : (N E + N_c E_c)$ or $P_8 = (M_8 R_8) : (N_8 E_8)$, where C represents the total amount of checks employed in the transactions. R_c, N_c, and E_c have the same import as in the basic equation, *mutatis mutandis.* In the last equation $M R + C R_c$ is equal to $M_8 R_8$, and corresponds to the principle amount of means of transactions employed during the period in question. $N_8 E_8$ denotes the amount of goods turned over, expressed by some standard other than the standard of value (pp. 74—75).

the amount of commodities demanded and taken (expressed in some standard of measure other than the standard of value) during a certain period of time! As Kemmerer has defined the symbols in the equation, only those commodities of the total supply during the relevant period, which have been demanded and taken, are included. Evidently, the equation can comprehend whatever amount of commodities desired. Then the question arises: What amount of commodities, or better, transactions, should the equation comprise in order to be of any significance as an implement for economic analysis, particularly with reference to a study of the causes of variations in the purchasing power of money? Unfortunately, there is no answer to that question, because the equation provides no information about causal relationships, regardless of what amount and kind of transactions it contains; the equation determines, in fact, the velocity of money only. It is an old story that the equation is a truism. But all equations are, in some way, truisms, and it is merely a question of our ability to realize the self-evidency of the identities that draws the line of distinction. The greatest value of Kemmerer's, as well as of Fisher's, equation seems to be its fitness for illustrating the original content of the quantity theory.

Kemmerer, however, is fully convinced of the possibility of demonstrating causal relationships between the different symbols in the equation: »In the formula $P = \frac{MR}{NE}$, a variation in N, E, or R is just as effective in causing a change in P as is a variation in M.«[13] Nearly all enunciators of similar equations have committed themselves to the same confusion of necessarily direct or indirect proportionate variations in two numerical values, when the others remain constant, with *causal* relationships. Kemmerer also believes that the factors included in the equation are the sole regulators of the value of money, and are evidence that the quantity theory does not maintain any exclusive causal relationship.

Under given conditions of credit development and amount of business, and when business confidence remains constant, an increased amount of money will increase bank reserves proportionately, and *vice versa*; that is, the amount of checks (C) is said to be a direct function of the quantity of money in circulation (M). With these assumptions, Kemmerer affirms that »the quantity theory, in spite of all the complexities of the modern industrial régime, still holds true as a general principle; and general prices, *other things being equal,* vary

[13] *Ibid.*, p. 31.

proportionately and in the same direction with variations in the money supply».[14] To support this general principle inductively, Kemmerer refers to statistics demonstrating the relation of changes in the quantity of money to variations in the price level in the United States from 1879 to 1904. A proportionate relation is considered to be out of the question, since 'other things' have not been equal. The purpose of the investigation has been to answer the following question: What relation does the amount of money in circulation have to the price level? Kemmerer found — both inductively and deductively, he thought — that a *change* in the quantity of money *caused* variations in the price level in the same direction.[15]

His conclusion is that »the value of money is determined, like the value of other commodities, by the fundamental law of demand and supply, but that *caeteris paribus*, a change in economic prices can only find expression, and therefore only take place, through proportionate changes in the relative monetary supply».[16]

Kemmerer seems to be not quite aware of the fundamental idea behind the quantity theory. When his propositions contain the *ceteris-paribus* premise, then they are reduced to arithmetic truisms, and when this premise is left out, then he is primarily emphasizing the relation between changes in the quantity of money and prices. But the significant relation for demonstrating the correctness of the quantity theory is that between changes in the quantity of money and its velocity of circulation. Therefore, Kemmerer's book, although a pioneer work, did not have the same influence and importance as Fisher's so vigorously debated *The Purchasing Power of Money.*

5. When *The Purchasing Power of Money* was first published (in 1911), it roused considerable attention, because it was, throughout, a defense of the validity of the propositions of the quantity theory under actual conditions in the long run. Since the time of the classics, nobody has striven so energetically to rehabilitate the reputation of the theory as Irving Fisher. The characteristic of Fisher is the attempt to deduce and verify the (reconstructed) quantity theory both deductively

[14] *Ibid.*, p. 87; *cf.* pp. 139—140.

[15] W. M. Persons, in criticising Kemmerer's approach, states that »the statistics presented by Kemmerer do not demonstrate that general prices move in sympathy with relative circulation» (»The Quantity Theory as Tested by Kemmerer,» *Q. J. E.*, 1908, p. 289). Persons also asks if the theory *explains* any facts (p. 274).

[16] *Op cit.*, p. 149; see also his later work, *Money* (New York, 1935, pp. 64—66) in which the same conclusions are restated.

and inductively by help of his well-known equation of exchange, $MV = PT$, where M represents the quantity of money in circulation, *i.e.*, all coins and bank notes held for circulation,[17] V its velocity, P the average price level, and T the total volume of transactions.

Fisher and Kemmerer were far from the first to use an equation as a starting point for a theoretical analysis of the changes in the value of money and their causes. The oldest known formula of this type was proposed by Henry Lloyd in 1771, though it did not include a term for the velocity of money. Lloyd's work was not noticed by his contemporary England, but by some Italian economists, among others Pietro Verri, and later by F. Fuoco; so it is not surprising that the next equation to be found was proposed by an Italian economists, Cagnazzi (in 1813). It reads $Mc = DC$, where M indicates the quantity of money, c its velocity, D the amount of goods, and C the velocity of goods. His fellow countryman Fasiani criticised the equation for not containing any term for prices. Marget, however, maintains that its purpose is to illustrate an equilibrium position, where prices are constant and, therefore, it is merely a formal error.[18] Obviously, Cagnazzi could not avoid the use of prices in some way, when equalizing a given quantity of money to a certain amount of goods. Shortly after, in 1819, Samuel Turner wrote the equation $a = bc$. The symbol b stands for the quantity of precious metals in circulation in a given country, c the number of times b is turned over, and a the value of the commodities transacted in the relevant period. The formula coincides completely with that of Roscher presented in 1854, $u = ms$, where m is the amount of money, s the velocity of money, and u the monetary sum of all transactions in one year. Some time before, in 1840, an equation was published anonymously by Sir John W. Lubbock, namely $\Sigma a_x + E = 1D + mB + nC$. Expressed in better known terms, it says that $\Sigma pq + E = M'V' + M''V'' + MV$. Σpq, MV, and $M'V'$ have about the same meaning as in Fisher's equation, $M''V''$ denotes the amount of bills of exchange used as means of payment times their velocity of circulation, and E indicates roughly the amount of monetary transactions not corresponding to any actual fulfilments.[19] In the following year, 1841, K. H. Rau published an equation mainly in conformity with that of Fisher. When it became known, it was suggested that the equation of exchange be called the Rau-Fisherine equation. This was before the other equations, just mentioned, were discovered. Additional equations of the Fisherine type were proposed in the middle of the nineteenth century by, among others, Bowen (in 1856), who built directly upon Stuart Mill, and by Levasseur (in 1858).

The equation which influenced Fisher's formula most was enunciated by Simon Newcomb (in 1885). With the exception of Kemmerer's equation, it is the only one that has had any direct influence on the Fisherine equation, as is admitted by

---

[17] *The Purchasing Power of Money,* New York, 1911, pp. 11 and 13. Thus cash reserves held by banks (and the monetary authorities) and »hoarded» money are excluded.

[18] See Marget (*op. cit.*, vol. I, p. 10 ff.) from whom most data on the historical development of this kind of equation are taken; also see E. Petersen: *Macro-Dynamic Aspects of the Equation of Exchange* (Skrifter utgitt av Det Norske Videnskapsakademi i Oslo, II. Hist.-Filos. Klasse. No. 6), Oslo, 1938, pp. 15—18.

[19] Viner mentions that Lubbock was the first to use different terms for various means of circulation and their respective velocities of circulation *(op. cit.*, p. 249, note 23).

Fisher himself and further emphasized by his dedication of *The Purchasing Power of Money* to the memory of Simon Newcomb. Newcomb's equation reads $V \times R = K \times P$. V represents the volume of currency, R the average rapidity of circulation, K the total of transfers of wealth and services during the unit of time, measured in dollars of absolute money, and P the ratio of the actual scale of prices to the unit scale.[20] The formula is called the equation of societary circulation, as it demonstrates the identity between the flow of goods exchanged and the flow of money paid for the goods. Newcomb did not employ the equation for the illustration of the quantity theory. Instead, he used about the same type of example as Hume by supposing a beneficent government giving five dollars to every person. The conclusion that »the final results would be that all prices and all current wages would rise in nearly the same proportion»,[21] is built upon an analysis of what would happen under actual conditions. Newcomb, in fact, never mentioned the quantity theory; only the law of value applied to money.

Fisher starts from the equation $MV = \Sigma\, p\, q$, where p is the price of every single commodity and q the corresponding quantity. The sum of all those commodities being sold must be equal to the amount of money paid for them. Thus M indicates the quantity of money in circulation and V its velocity during the relevant period of time. In order to make this identity useable, so that a comparative study of price levels can be carried out, the so-called 'dollar unit' is selected. It is defined as the unit of any commodity which constitutes a dollar's worth. The price of every commodity and service, so expressed, will then be one dollar; accordingly, the average price will also be one dollar. The number of times the 'unit dollar' can be divided into a given amount of goods indicates the quantity of that group. If a certain basic year is selected, P will be equal to unity and the value of P in the comparative year will then directly indicate the shift of the price level. The number of units is represented by T.[22]

By this equation, Fisher sets out to prove that the proposition that, other things being equal, »prices vary proportionately to money», is both theoretically and practically correct. »From the mere fact,

[20] *Principles of Political Economy,* New York, 1886, p. 328; also see p. 338.

[21] *Ibid.*, pp. 343—344.

[22] *Op. cit.*, pp. 26—27; also see pp. 96 and 286. For various comments on the equation of exchange see, *i.a.*, L. V. Chandler: *An Introduction to Monetary Theory,* New York, 1940, ch. II; G. Halm: *Monetary Theory,* Philadelphia, 1942, pp. 21—24; F. von Hayek: *Prices and Production,* New York, 1932, p. 3; Marget, *op. cit.*, vol. I, p. 81 ff; A. W. Marschak: »Die Verkehrsgleichung», *A. f. S.*, 1924, pp. 344—388; and Kjeld Philip: »Betragtninger over Kvantitetsligningen», *N. T.*, 1943, pp. 93—118. Hawtrey's statement, that »Irving Fisher's well known Equation of Exchange was designed to rid the quantity theory of the limitation that all other economic conditions must be given», seems rather strange, since this was never Fisher's real purpose (*Currency and Credit,* 4 ed., London, 1950, p. 34; also see pp. 37 and 41).

therefore, that the money spent for goods must equal the quantities of those goods multiplied by their prices, it follows that the level of prices must rise or fall according to changes in the quantity of money, *unless* there are changes in its velocity of circulation or in the quantities of goods exchanged.»[23] Thus Fisher makes the same logical error as Kemmerer by interpreting the pure arithmetic relations between the symbols of the equation of exchange as also indicating causal relations. For it is incorrect, as a matter of principle, to say that »the price level *must* rise of fall *according to* changes in the quantity of money», referring to the equation of exchange. The proportionate relation is true, not because M *influences* P in any way, but because the identity is a non-functional equation. It illustrates that if $M V = P T$, then $2 M V = 2 P T$, *i.e.*, a doubled M *means* a doubled P, and *vice versa*, when V and T are kept constant. Hence one cannot presume M to double, *ceteris paribus*, asserting that the *result* will be a doubled P. Fisher points out himself, though, that the equation does not reveal which factors are causes and which are effects,[24] but disregards this when the content of the quantity theory is illustrated.

»As a first illustration, let us suppose the government to double the *denominations* of all money; that is, let us suppose that what has been hitherto a half dollar is henceforth called a dollar, and that what has hitherto been a dollar is henceforth called two dollars. Evidently the number of 'dollars' in circulation will then be doubled; and the price level measured in terms of the new 'dollars', will be double what it would otherwise be. Everyone will pay out the *same coins* as though no such law were passed. But he will, in each case, be paying twice as many 'dollars'. For example, if $3 formerly had to be paid for a pair of shoes, the price of this same pair of shoes will now become $6. Thus we see how the *nominal* quantity of money affects price levels.»[25] The statement is theoretically correct as a purely arithmetic example of a self-evident relation; but it is logically incorrect to say that from this »we see how the nominal quantity of money *affects* the price level» (referring implicitly or explicitly to the equation of exchange). The quotation tells us only that *if* the nominal quantity of money *is* twice as much as at some earlier date, *ceteris paribus*, then the price level is also twice as great. There is no evidence of any causal relationship between M and P in this illustration. The only thing demonstrated is

[23] *Ibid.*, pp. 19—20; also see pp. 14 and 29.

[24] See, especially, pp. 149—150 and 298 (*ibid*).

[25] *Ibid.*, pp. 29—30.

the proportionality between changes in the nominal quantity of money and the price level. So far it is merely an arithmetic example of the simplest kind, not even illustrating the quantity theory, since the *number* of coins and/or bills is still the same.[26] The illustration is slightly reminiscent of the formulation of the quantity theory; it indicates that the nominal value of a given quantity of money has no importance (within certain limits), because prices will be in proportion to it. The essence is merely the truism that the *numerical* value of the *standard of measure* is irrelevant, since all things are measured by the same standard.

As a second illustration, Fisher uses a debased currency: »Suppose a government cuts each dollar in two, coining the halves into new 'dollars'; and, recalling all paper notes, replaces them with double the original number.... prices in the debased coinage will again be doubled just as in the first illustration. The subdivision and recoinage is an immaterial circumstance, unless it be carried so far as to make counting difficult and thus to interfere with the *convenience* of money.»[27] This illustration is wholly illusive. There is no *a priori* reason why prices will be doubled, since it cannot be assumed that the individuals will act in the same way after such a remarkable change in the quantity of money. Nobody knows how they will react, and hence, what the effects will be. The illustration needs just so many assumptions as is necessary to reduce it to a self-evident arithmetic example.

In his third illustration, Fisher supposes that »the government *duplicates* each piece of money in existence and presents the duplicate to the possessor of the original. (We must in this case suppose, further, that there is some effectual bar to prevent the melting or exporting of money. Otherwise the quantity of money in circulation will not be doubled: much of the increase will escape.) If the quantity of money is thus doubled, prices will also be doubled just as truly as in the second illustration, in which there were exactly the same denominations.»[28] Nor can this illustration spirit away Fisher's fallacious reasoning. As the assumption within brackets indicates, it is supposedly a statement of what will *actually* happen under certain assumptions. But then

---

[26] The same proposition was earlier stated by William Petty, who asserted that a revaluation of the nominal value of coins, without any change in the bullion content, would only increase prices proportionately [*The Economic Writings of Sir William Petty*, ed. by C. H. Hull, 2 vols. (paged continously), Cambridge, 1899, pp. 87—88].

[27] *Op. cit.*, p. 30.

[28] *Ibid.*, pp. 30—31.

so many unrealistic assumptions are necessary as to reduce again the illustration to a simple arithmetic relation. In fact, the quantity 'theory' can only be theoretically illustrated in a purely arithmetic way. There is no escape from that if the consistency of the reasoning is to be maintained.

In order to give the equation of exchange a greater value as an analytical tool of the causes influencing the value of money, 'credit' is taken into consideration. M' is defined as bank deposits subject to check, and V' as their velocity of circulation. The equation of exchange then reads $MV + M'V' = PT$.[29] That part of the quantity of money which forms the coins and notes, M, is now said to have a less direct influence on the price level. It is maintained, though, that there is a constant relation between M and M', partly because bank reserves are generally kept in a certain proportion to bank deposits, and partly because individuals, firms, and corporations also keep such a proportion of their cash holdings to their check-transactions. Hence the quantity of deposit currency is said to vary directly with changes in the quantity of money;[30] and so Fisher concludes that »it is still true that (1) prices vary directly as the quantity of money, provided the volume of trade and the velocities of circulation remain unchanged; (2) that prices vary directly as the velocities of circulation (if these velocities vary together), provided the quantity of money and the volume of trade remain unchanged; and (3) that prices vary inversely as the volume of trade, provided the quantity of money — and therefore deposits — and their velocities remain unchanged.»[31] But again all these provisos which have to be included in order to justify the conclusions, confine their relevance to obvious arithmetic relations. What Fisher is saying here amounts to the same demonstration of self-evident arithmetic relations as without the inclusion of deposits and their velocity of circulation in the formula. All causal relations are excluded from this demonstration.

---

[29] *Ibid.*, p. 48; also see p. 196.

[30] *Ibid.*, pp. 47 ff. and 150. According to the statistics, however, which Fisher provides himself (p. 304), the relation $\frac{M'}{M}$ increased by more than 50 % from 1896 to 1912. Since this period was characterized by a considerable price increase, Fisher would very likely describe it as a period of transition; hence his statement would not be applicable. But it sustains Wicksell's view that the virtual velocity of money increases during periods of price increases.

[31] *Ibid.*, p. 150.

The main purpose of Fisher's book is »to explain the causes determining the purchasing power of money», thereby proving that changes in the quantity of money will normally affect the price level only.[32] This means that he has to demonstrate that the velocities of money and deposits, and the amount of transactions will not be influenced by variations in the quantity of money. In this respect he is different from most 'adherents' of the quantity theory;[33] and yet, this is the fundamental idea of the quantity theory! In our opinion this is a striking example of how misunderstood the quantity theory really has been, which is also the main reason for the extended discussion of its correctness.

Analysing the subject, Fisher deduces that the velocities of money and of deposits depend upon technical and institutional conditions, and are not related to the quantity of money in circulation or to the price level.[34] Hence he concludes that *changes* in the quantity of money will not affect these velocities in the long run. Thus it is alleged that a doubled quantity of money (by doubling all cash holdings in existence) necessarily must lead to everybody's doubling his expenses and reserves, because everybody »will want to exchange this relatively useless extra money for goods».[35] Such a statement is not sufficient as an evidence of the effect. The assumption of a sudden doubling of all cash holdings is also very unrealistic, which reduces the relevance of the conclusion. But *if* this assumption once were realized, there would be no justification for the proposition that all cash holders will act in the same way. It depends, among other things, upon their reactions and anticipations, and the present economic situation. Fisher tries to escape this dilemma by distinguishing between the effects during periods of transitions, *i.e.*, periods when prices either are rising or falling, and ultimate effects.[36] But this is no way out of the dilemma.

Fisher seems to be correct in his statement that the velocity of money does not depend upon the quantity of money except under very special assumptions. The weakness of his argument is that he has confused the proposition that the quantity of money as such (within

---

[32] *Ibid.*, p. 13; see also the preface.

[33] This is particularly emphasized by A. Aftalion in *Monnaie, Prix et Change,* Paris, 1927, pp. 114—115.

[34] *Op. cit.*, p. 152.

[35] *Ibid.*, p. 154.

[36] *Ibid.*, pp. 55—56 and 155.

[37] *Ibid.*, p. 155; see also p. 156.

certain limits) has no direct relation to the velocity of money with the effect of *changes* in the quantity of money.

Nor will the volume of transactions (T) be affected by a change in the quantity of money, except for periods of transition because the »stream of business depends on natural resources and technical conditions, not on the quantity of money».[37] Here, again, Fisher is undoubtedly correct that the *quantity* of money (within certain limits) does not govern the volume of business; but this does not permit the conclusion that *changes* in the quantity of money are irrelevant, except for periods of transition, for the volume of business.

Fisher by no means holds that no other cause can influence V, V', and T at the same time. Indeed, this is the reason that the variations in the price level will not be in direct proportion to the variations in the quantity of money, though the tendency will always be there;[38] the only absolutely passive element in the equation of exchange is normally the price level.[39] This is not correct, for prices can very well be an active factor among the symbols of the equation of exchange, even under 'normal' conditions.

Fisher also claims that the symbols included in his equation actually determine the price level.[40] He even goes so far as to maintain that »the price level is not determined by individual prices, but that, on the contrary, any individual price presupposes a price level».[41] By this he means that any discussion of what determines individual prices in terms of money is incomplete until the value of money is determined. Thus »there are always just one *too few equations* to determine the unknown quantities involved»;[42] and the missing equation in each case to supplement the equations of demand and supply is just the equation of exchange. This can hardly be correct. First, it is evident that a price level presupposes individual prices, since the price level is merely an average of individual prices, weighted according to certain rules, which always will be more or less arbitrary. The analysis of individual prices in terms of demand and supply has to *assume* a given price level, but this does not mean that the price level is determined first. Secondly, if the system of equations set up either by Walras or Cassel is determinate 'close to a multiplicative factor', this multiplicative factor

---

38 *Ibid.*, pp. 21 and 157—159.

39 *Ibid.*, p. 172.

40 *Ibid.*, p. 150; see also p. 319.

41 *Ibid.*, p. 180.

42 *Ibid.*, p. 174.

is institutionally determined, just as the international prototype of the metre is agreed upon, being a national and international measure of length, and is not determined by any equation.[43] Finally, the equation of exchange does not determine the purchasing power of money, *i.e.*, P. As mentioned above, this P is merely a weighted average of all individual prices. The numerical values of the different symbols in the equation of exchange are, at first hand, a function of the length of the period chosen. When the period is settled, the numerical values are actually determined. How these values are functionally related within each other is another question, not answered by the equation of exchange. Since one equation can provide the numerical value of only one of the symbols involved, the question remains: Which factor is actually determined by the equation of exchange? If we limit the discussion to the formula $M V = P T$, it is quite evident that the only thing actually determined is the value of V. The values of M, P, and T are not determined by any equation; but the determination of V requires knowledge of M and the amount of transactions which are to be included, *i.e.*, $P T$.

[43] Fisher's idea that the equation of exchange provides the missing equation in the Walras system was later taken up by F. Divisia (*Economique rationelle,* Paris, 1928, p. 402 ff.) and further developed by J. Mosak (*General-Equilibrium Theory in International Trade,* Cowles Commission Monograph, No. 7, Bloomington, 1944, p. 36 ff.). Mosak's discussion has been criticised by D. Patinkin (»Relative Prices, Say's Law and the Demand for Money», *Econometrica,* 1948, pp. 135—154) and still more by J. Marschak (»The Rationale of the Demand for Money and of Money Illusion», *Metroeconomica,* 1950, pp. 71—100). Patinkin demonstrates that Mosak's solution is inconsistent, an opinion shared by Marschak, who goes further, however, and proves that also Patinkin's attempt to reach a solution is impossible without imposing certain restrictions on his system. This criticism, however, is answered in Patinkin's article »The Invalidity of Classical Monetary Theory» (*Econometrica,* 1951, pp. 134—151); and in K. Brunner: »Inconsistency and Indeterminacy in Classical Economics» (*ibid.*, pp. 152—173). See also B. Hansen: *A Study in the Theory of Inflation* (The Library of Economics, section 2: New Works, 4, London, 1951, p. 190 ff.) in which it is argued that when Walras' law is not identically valid, it cannot be employed in demonstrating that the number of independent equations is not greater than the number of unknowns in the system.

The simplest objection, it seems, to these various attempts, lies in the circumstance that the very introduction of a *numéraire* in the system — and this is unavoidable as soon as the number of goods is greater than two — implies that absolute prices *are* also determined. For this *numéraire* must then appear as the medium of exchange and every comparison between the medium of exchange and the other goods actually means a comparison in absolute terms. The selection of a *numéraire* does not mean the introduction of a new equation, thereby making the number of equations greater than the number of unknowns (also see note 18, p. 185).

This criticism does not minimize the great significance of Fisher's work, especially of the statistical investigations of the relations between M, M', V and V'. There he did prove that changes in the quantity of money (M), will not influence the velocity of money (V),[44] which is the basic idea of the quantity theory, resting, ultimately, upon »the fundamental peculiarity which money alone of all goods possesses, — the fact that it has no power to satisfy human wants except a power *to purchase* things which do have such a power».[45]

What Fisher overlooked, however, was the circumstance that this power to satisfy human wants by purchases can be effectuated with different time lags; in other words, the importance of the role of money as a store of wealth was left out of the picture. Consequently, one cannot, from a logical point of view, draw the conclusion that, if the volume of transactions remain constant, the price level will vary in direct proportion to changes in the quantity of money,[46] since purchases do not necessarily vary in the same proportion. This is due to the other fundamental property of money, namely, that of being a relatively costless store of potential wealth.

6. The quantity theory experienced a revival in the United States in the end of the nineteenth century. The interpretation of the theory as an exclusive explanation of actual changes in the price level logically turned it into a business cycle theory; consequently, the depression in the seventies was explained as the cause of a decreased quantity of money.[47] The remedy would be to increase the amount of currency, which would raise prices and thereby encourage trade and industry.

Walker's very affirmative propositions of the infallibility of the quantity theory gave rise to a very strong criticism, which induced several

---

[44] See the statistics for the period 1896—1909 in the United States, (*op. cit.*, p. 304). V', however, has changed according to these statistics.

[45] *Ibid.*, p. 32.

[46] See, for example, pp. 157 and 181—183, *ibid.*

[47] See, *e.g.*, E. Benjamin Andrews: »The Bimetallist Committee of Boston and New England», *Q. J. E.*, 1894, p. 322, and F. A. Walker: »The Relation of Changes in the Volume of the Currency to Prosperity», *Economic Studies*, American Economic Association, 1896, No. 1, pp. 33—35. Walker and Andrews are characterized by H. P. Willis as the most rigid interpreters of the quantity theory as »a competent theory of prices» (»The History and Present Application of the Quantity Theory», *J. P. E.*, 1896, p. 439). W. S. Parker defended the opinion that an increased quantity of gold would increase prices, though not proportionately (»An Increase in Gold and the Price-Making Process», *J. P. E.*, 1903, p. 629).

studies of the actual relation between the quantity of money and prices during this period.[48] The weakness of the quantity theory as an explanation of changes in prices was best displayed by Wesley C. Mitchell. He reproved the adherents of the theory for not having clearly stated what kind of money affected prices and how it affected them, and the neglecting of other factors that influence prices.[49]

While Kemmerer's primary purpose was to investigate the relation between the quantity of money and prices, Fisher's intention was to prove a very definite relation. Both his method and his conclusions originated a flow of discussions of the factors that determine the price level. Many subsequent studies, based upon the same methodology, were made in several countries. It was 'proved' — most often by inadequate statistics — that there was no definite relation, either causal or proportionate, between the quantity of money and prices. Fisher's approach was very vigorously criticised by his fellow-countryman B. M. Anderson, whose principal objection was that the equation of exchange could not be used as an instrument for determining the universal laws of money, as it appeared as merely a provincial equation of exchange.[50]

The great importance of Fisher's work lies primarily in its very elaborate statistical analysis and thorough discussion of the factors included in the equation of exchange, especially the determination of the rate of turnover of money (V). It gave rise to new impulses within the field of monetary theory, especially in Great Britain, where it partly inspired the setting up of the so-called Cambridge Quantity Equations. Its influence and dominating position in American monetary theory lasted almost up to the appearance of Keynes' *General Theory*. This book divided the economists in the United States, as well as in other countries, into roughly two groups: (1) those who accepted

---

48 See, *e.g.*, Sarah M. Hardy: »The Quantity of Money and Prices, 1860—1891», *J. P. E.*, 1895, pp. 145—168. She did not find any certain relation between the quantity of money and prices.

Willard Fisher maintained that the majority of transactions were performed by means of checks and drafts, without any use of money; hence, prices depended upon the amount of these other means of exchange, which also determined the quantity of money in circulation (»Money and Credit Paper in the Modern Market», *J. P. E.*, 1895, p. 393).

49 »The Real Issues in the Quantity Theory Controversy», *J. P. E.*, 1904, pp. 407—408.

50 *The Value of Money*, New York, 1917, p. 167. Another critic, Hugo Bilgram, firmly denied the possibility of proving the quantity theory by mathematics (»The Quantity Theory Scrutinized», *J. P. E.*, 1921, p. 761). G. R. Davies, on the other hand, stressed the importance of Kemmerer's study as providing an intelligible explanation of the movements of prices (»The Quantity Theory and Recent Statistical Studies», *J. P. E.*, 1921, p. 221).

— with or without qualifications — the Keynesian monetary approach, and (2) those who still regarded — with or without recognizing any importance in the former approach — the Fisherine approach as being of substantial value for monetary analysis and policy. This division also drew a line of distinction between economists who considered monetary policy ineffective and effective, respectively. Even though all classification of men with various opinions must be rather arbitrary, one might say that the latter group includes names like Milton Friedman, Henry C. Simons, Lloyd W. Mints, and Clark Warburton, whereas the former group seems to be best represented by Alvin Hansen and Paul Samuelson. But this line of distinction is not identical with an acceptance or refutation of the quantity theory. Those days when such a division had any justification are, fortunately, gone. The correctness of the basic idea of the quantity theory should not be a matter of controversy any longer; it should be one of the fundamentals in every textbook of monetary theory.

CHAPTER V

THE QUANTITY THEORY AND THE CAMBRIDGE SCHOOL

Although it was realized early that the quantity theory did not provide any satisfactory explanation of the causes of the variations in the price level, the distorted formulation of the theory was perpetually repeated by most economists as an eternal truth, and this repetition entailed a lingering of the great interest in the quantity of money as such. An attempt to break away from this barren approach was made by the Cambridge School, which laid the emphasis, not on changes in the *quantity* of money in circulation, but on changes in the *value* of the total amount of money that people wanted to keep in the form of cash balances, *i.e.*, coins, banknotes and demand deposits, as being of primary importance in the fluctuations of the price level. Instead of speaking of changes in the quantity of money, the school turned its attention to changes in the amount of individual cash holdings (in real terms) and their effects upon the price level. This approach is more realistic; but the way of illustrating it is based mainly upon the same kind of argumentation as used by the quantity theory, thas is, by help of merely arithmetic truisms, which largely reduced the economic significance of the argument.

1. The foundation of the Cambridge School is mainly the thought of Alfred Marshall. He has, more or less, influenced the best known representatives of this school: Hawtrey, Keynes, Pigou and D. H. Robertson. Theoretically, Marshall has no objection to the quantity theory; but in a restatement of its proposition, he advances a peculiar illustration which serves more as a confusion than as the clarification it is supposed to bring to the content of the theory: »If a railway company adjusted its tickets to the lengths of the corresponding journeys, a long ticket might be more desirable than a short one: but if the lengths of all the tickets were doubled, the

increase of lengths would merely cause a little inconvenience. In a like manner an increase in the volume of a country's currency, other things being equal, will lower proportionately the value of each unit. In fact, if that increase threatens to be repeated, the value of each unit may fall more than in proportion to the increase already made.»[1] This example is not well chosen, for if the length of the tickets were doubled, their value would remain unaffected and still be in proportion to the length of the journey; but if the quantity of money were doubled, *ceteris paribus*, the value of each unit would be halved. One similarity of the examples to which one might agree is that the changes may »cause a little inconvenience», although the illustration is apparently meant to be a little more sophisticated. Marshall's idea may be that the doubling of the length of the tickets will make the value of a given unit of the length of a ticket worth only half of its earlier value, and that a doubling of the quantity of money will be followed by the same decrease of the value of a monetary unit. The comparison is then based on the assumption that the value of the total amount of money and the value of a ticket will remain the same. Such a discussion of the relation between changes in the quantity of money and in the length of the tickets and their respective 'effects' is obviously of merely arithmetic interest and has no economic significance. Beside, a comparison of the value of a railway ticket with the value of money is very dubious and still more so when it is a question of comparing changes in quantity and length.

The conclusion that the velocity of money might be influenced because of repeated increases in the quantity of circulation is evidently inconsistent with the presumption of other things being equal. Having started with a purely theoretical example, Marshall turns — unconsciously or not — to considering also what results one may expect if the quantity of money were doubled several times under actual conditions. Then he realizes that the confidence in the currency might be shaken, which would lead to an increased velocity of money. This inconsistent reasoning is met with in the works of several other economists, for instance of Ricardo and Say, and may indicate that the presumption of other

---

[1] *Money, Credit and Commerce,* London, 1923, p. 38. Marshall does not deal with the quantity theory in his great standard work on the principles of economics. The theory is best discussed in *Money, Credit and Commerce,* though it is also discussed in the report to the *Gold and Silver Commission of 1887 and 1878,* especially questions 9629, 9645—9648 and 9696. See *Official Papers by Alfred Marshall,* ed. by J. M. Keynes, London, 1926.

things being equal is thought of as being least realistic in respect to the velocity of money.[2]

One of the fundamental ideas of the Cambridge School is that the demand for currency is not for a definite quantity of money but for a definite amount of 'value' expressed in real terms of some commodity and represented by the amount of money in circulation. This view was also stated by Adam Smith. Marshall developes it further by explaining that the total value of the circulating quantity of money in a country tends to correspond to »the amount of ready purchasing power, which its members care to hold in hand».[3] With this proposition as a background, he enunciates the original content of the quantity theory, that is, the proposition of proportionality without any proposition of causality. Let us suppose, he says, that »the total value of the currency will be a million quarters of wheat .... If then the currency contains a million units, each will be worth a quarter of wheat; if it contains two millions, each unit will be worth half a quarter.»[4] This is the same way of illustrating the proportionate relation between the quantity of money and the value of one unit that Locke used. Instead of analyzing those causes which determine the amount of purchasing power held in hand by the members of society, Marshall uses this proportionate relation as a basis for a causal proposition, thereby making the same fallacious conclusion as Hume and all his followers made. Thus Marshall declares that »whatever the state of society, there is a certain volume of their resources which people of different classes, taken one with another, care to keep in the form of currency; and, if everything else remains the same, then there is this direct relation between the volume of currency and the level of prices, that, if one is increased by ten per cent., the other also will be increased by ten per cent. Of course, the less the proportion of their resources which people care to keep in

[2] Lambert criticises Marshall's illustration from other viewpoints. He maintains that the *ceteris-paribus* premise implies a neglect of the effects of a change in the quantity of money on the velocity of money, on the amount of transactions, and on hoarding; furthermore, there are no such corresponding factors present in the case of a railway ticket, which makes it impossible to carry out such a comparison satisfactorily (*op. cit.*, pp. 149—150): From a purely logical point of view, however, there is nothing which prevents the comparison from being made if the aim is only to demonstrate a certain proportionate relation, although the comparison is void of any economic relevance.

The reason for the author's dealing with this example in such detail is because this kind of illustration of the quantity theory causes a misunderstanding more often than a clarification of the theory.

[3] *Money, Credit and Commerce,* p. 39.

[4] *Ibid.*, pp. 44—45.

the form of currency, the lower will be the aggregate value of the currency, that is, the higher will prices be with a given volume of currency.»[5]

This statement is best illustrated by Keynes formula $n = p\,k$, in which n represents the volume of currency, p the price of a so-called consumption unit, and k the amount of consumption units that people are willing to keep in cash (see p. 108). Assuming k to remain constant, Marshall asserts that if n is increased by ten per cent, p will also be increased by the same percentage. The concluding remark in the quotation above — that the less proportion of their resources which people will care to keep in the form of currency, the lower will the aggregate value of the currency, k, and the higher will prices, p, when the volume of the currency, n, remains constant — is tantamount to saying that an increase in the velocity of money, *ceteris paribus*, will increase prices proportionately. This is a hint of the change in emphasis, which is represented by the Cambridge School in its stressing the importance of the variations in the velocity of money, regarding the factors affecting the price level. There is no justification, however, for the assumption that the volume of currency will be kept constant when people want to diminish the aggregate value of their currency; hence such a desire need not be related to price changes.

Marshall's appraisal of the quantity theory is somewhat inconsistent. He criticises it for not taking into account those factors wich are supposed to remain constant when the quantity of money is changed, nor of those which govern the velocity of money. This criticism is beside the point, particularly since he underlines that the content of the quantity theory is that »*an increase in the amount of money in a country does not increase the total services which it performs* . . . . . It [the quantity theory] merely means that the purpose of a currency is firstly to facilitate business transactions».[6] The essence of this statement is the same as that of Locke: The amount as such of the means of exchange is of no significance in the total wealth of a given country. Thus Marshall, in his final judgement of the quantity theory, shows a correct understanding of the essence of the theory, in spite of his misapplied criticism and incorrect inference of a causal relationship.

2. An obvious weakness of the equation of exchange as a foundation for analysis, is the general import of its terms. Those elements, the

[5] *Ibid.*, p. 45.
[6] *Ibid.*, p. 49.

changes of which having the greatest importance for the determination of the fluctuations in the value of money, do not appear directly. The perhaps most 'psychological' factor, V, becomes a rather meaningless and abstract average figure with no correspondence to reality. Similarly, a number of different elements are concealed behind the symbol T. In order to demonstrate more explicitly the importance of psychological factors in the analysis of changes in the value of money, Pigou proposed (in 1917) an equation in which the emphasis was laid upon the role of changes in the amount of cash holdings. If R is the total amount of resources, *i.e.*, of wealth, of a community expressed in terms of wheat, k the proportion of these resources that is kept in the form of titles to legal tender (*i.e.*, actual legal tender including token coins, bank notes, and bank balances against which checks can be drawn), M the number of units of legal tender, and P the value per unit of those titles (in terms of wheat), then the equation $P = \frac{kR}{M}$ is obtained.[7] This equation is said to represent also the demand schedule for titles to legal-tender money. If k and R are taken to be constant, P varies inversely to M in an exact proportion; that is, we have the equation of a rectangular hyperbola.

From this 'demand schedule', Pigou derives a demand schedule for legal tender itself. Let c be the proportion of titles to legal tender that a representative individual chooses to keep in actual legal tender. Then $(1—c)$ is the proportion he keeps in bank notes and bank balances. If h is the proportion of actual legal tender that bankers choose to keep (against the notes and balances held by their customers), then the derived equation of the demand for actual legal tender will be $P = \frac{kR}{M} [c + h (1—c)]$,[8] which is commonly known as the »Cambridge Quantity Equation». If k, R, c, and h are constant then P varies in an inverse proportion to M. Obviously the equation is as void of any causal relations as the Fisherine equation.

Pigou's intention is to show that the decisive factor in the variations of the purchasing power of money is changes in the individual cash holdings, not changes in the quantity of money, which is looked upon more as a secondary factor. Accordingly, his view is in opposition to Fisher's, but not in respect to the quantity theory, since it does not say which factors have the greatest importance in the variations of

[7] »*The Value of Money*», *Q. J. E.*, 1917—18, p. 42.

[8] *Ibid.*, p. 43.

the value of money, although it has often been misinterpreted in that way. Demonstrating the connection between his and Fisher's equation, Pigou rewrites the equation of exchange as $\frac{M V}{T} = \pi$, where π is the price per unit of 'commodities' in terms of money. In Pigou's equation P is the price of money in terms of wheat from which it follows that $P = \frac{1}{\pi}$. Hence $\frac{k R}{M} = \frac{T}{M V}$ or $k V = \frac{T}{R}$. »Evidently in given conditions of production and trade $\frac{T}{R}$ may be taken as a constant. It follows that $k V$ also is a constant. So soon as this is perceived, the relation in which the two equations stand to one another is at once apparent. When people decide to keep half as much of their resources as before in the form of titles to legal tender, this *means* that the velocity of circulation is doubled.»[9]

This is the same conclusion as Marshall made (see pp. 99—100). To say that people have decided »to keep half as much of their resources as before in the form of titles to legal tender» is merely an indirect way of saying that the velocity of money has doubled. Hence, it is meaningless to say that *because,* or *as a result,* of an increase (or decrease) in the velocity of money, people keep less (or more) of their resources than before in the form of titles to legal tender, since it is the same thing differently defined.

Pigou prefers his equation to the equation of exchange, because it is »a somewhat more effective engine of analysis. It focusses attention on the proportion of their resources that people choose to keep in the form of titles to legal tender instead of focussing it on 'velocity of circulation'».[10] But since these two concepts, between which Pigou wants to differentiate, indicate the same relation, it cannot be said that his equation 'focusses attention on the proportion of their resources that people choose to keep in the form of titles to legal tender *instead* of focussing it on the velocity of circulation'. The difference between Pigou's and Fisher's equations lies primarily in Pigou's indirect

---

[9] *Ibid.*, p. 53. This arithmetic identity has led to the false conclusion that the two approaches, which these equations exemplify, are fundamentally the same. A. Hansen, *i.a.*, draws attention to this fallacy: »Arithmetically k is ... the reciprocal of V in the equation $M V = P O$. But it does not follow from the mere fact that $V = \frac{1}{k}$, as an arithmetic identity, that therefore the Marshallian *analysis* is in fact the same thing as the Hume-Fisher analysis» [*i.e.*, based upon the quantity theory] (*op. cit.*, p. 49).

[10] *Ibid.*, p. 54.

definition of the velocity of money. Fundamentally, the two equations express the same relationship; and they become almost identical when the total resources in a given economy, R, correspond to the total amount of transactions, T, during the relevant period.

Pigou's equation demonstrates that the total number of the means of exchange, multiplied by a certain unit of value, is equal to the total value of the cash holdings, expressed as a fraction of the total resources of a given society. From the viewpoint of economic theory, however, it is rather meaningless to say that if the value of the total cash balances, $k\,R$, is changed, then P also has to change when M is constant (if the purpose is not to demonstrate the proportionate relation only), since such a statement has only arithmetic relevance. The economic problem is *why* the value of $k\,R$ has changed: and what the effects will be. The equation does not throw much light upon that problem.[11]

The principal aim of Pigou's discussion is to bring out the chief determinants of the variations in the value of money; therefore, he also

[11] Pigou's equation has, like Fisher's, been strongly criticised. One of the most often heard objections is directed against expressing the value of money in terms of wheat, which, as pointed out by Keynes, rather aggravates the problem than solves it (*A Treatise on Money,* 2 vols., London, 1930, vol. I, pp. 232—233). When a period of time, not too short, is taken into consideration, the price of money expressed in terms of wheat will not only illustrate changes in the average price level, but also in the value of wheat itself.

The best discussion of the cash-balance approach is provided by Marget (*op. cit.*, vol. I, chapters XV and XVI especially); also see H. Ellis: *German Monetary Theory,* Cambridge, Mass., (Harvard Economic Studies, vol. XLIV), 1934, chapter IX; and A. Hansen, *op. cit.*, pp. 43—53.

Though Hansen provides a very good analysis of the relation between the quantity theory and the cash-balance approach, we have certain objections to his conclusions: »The pure quantity theory [*i.e.*, that the price level was thought to be a function of the quantity of money, $P = \Phi(M)$] should be distinguished, on the one side from the quantity equation approach (which is not a *theory* but merely a way of posing the problem of money and prices); and on the other side from such variants of the quantity theory as the Marshallian theory which centers attention not primarily on the quantity of money as such but on the shifts in the desire to hold cash» (*ibid.*, p. 48, note 1). In our opinion, the Marshallian approach is not a *variant* of the quantity theory. The former approach is entirely different from the essence of the quantity theory, namely that V is constant, since it deals with changes in the desire to hold cash, *i.e.*, changes in the velocity of circulation of money. The quantity theory deals with money as a medium of exchange only, whereas the cash-balance approach deals primarily with money as a store of value. This is also indirectly pointed out by Hansen in his discussion of the limitations of Pigou's equation: »The symbol k .... reflects the desire for liquidity — in other words, the desire to hold money, compared with the desire to spend it for goods» (*ibid.*, p. 50).

has to know the supply curve of money, which is written $M = \psi\ (p)$. He overlooks, however, that the equation $M = \frac{k\,R}{P}$ is *not* a function denoting the 'demand for money'. The rectangular hyperbola which is called the demand schedule for titles to legal tender, *presupposes* that the total value of M demanded is constant. It cannot be said that the formula $M = \frac{k\,R}{P}$ »enables us to distinguish and to discuss separately the principal elements of which the demand schedule for money is made up»,[12] since a demand function of money must include all those important factors that determine the value of the total demand for money. In its simplest form it reads $M = \Phi\ (p)$. That M can be substituted by $\frac{k\,R}{P}$, has no relevance upon the factors determining the demand for money. Pigou avoids the problem by assuming that the amount of money demanded is given. The formula $M = \frac{k\,R}{P}$ is not a demand schedule in the ordinary sense of the concept; it is a formula merely indicating that *if* the total value of currency demanded is given, then it is irrelevant how much legal tender represents this value, since this value will always be in inverse proportion to their quantity. This is the content of the original quantity theory and not any statement about the demand function for money (further see pp. 171—173).

3. R. G. Hawtrey attacks the problem of the variations in the price level by using the concepts of »consumers' income» and »consumers' outlay». The consumers' income is »what a man has available to spend on his own needs», and the outlay is what he spends. The concept of consumer includes also 'investor', because »investment is one of the purposes on which income may be spent». The difference between consumers' income and outlay is consumers' balances, which, together with outstanding bank credits, form »the unspent margin». It can also be said to equalize the cash in circulation $(F-R)$ and the liabilities of the banks (L), where F represents the total amount of money, R the cash holdings of the banks, and L the assets of the banks less their capital.[13]

---

[12] *Op. cit.*, p. 59.

[13] *Currency and Credit,* London, 1919, pp. 39 and 41; also see note 2, p. 39, in which it is said that »the assets of the bank are equal to their cash reserves and the amount of their other assets». The weakness of the concept of consumers' outlay is, as stressed by

According to Hawtrey, changes in the price level are due to variations in the unspent margin, and are mainly caused by changes in the volume of bank-credits granted. On this basis, he formulates the quantity theory: ».... given all conditions, the prices of commodities are strictly proportional to the number of units of value contained in the unspent margin of purchasing power. The wealth value of the unit is therefore *inversely* proportional to the unspent margin. Here we have in its simplest form what is called the Quantity Theory of money.»[14] This is another way, perhaps a little more intricate, of phrasing the fundamental proposition of proportionality between the amount of money and the value of the money-unit. He includes, however, a feature which is very often thought of as being the principal issue: »The quantity theory, in the form which we have enunciated it, merely equates the unspent margin of purchasing power, which is a total of monetary units, to the command over wealth which the people hold in reserve. It equates, in fact, a total of monetary units to a total of wealth (a potential, not an actual, total of wealth) and so determines the value of the monetary unit in terms of wealth.»[15] The content of the quantity theory is thus thought of as dealing with the determination of the value of the monetary unit. This is a confusion of Davanzati's and Montanari's original theory of the value of money, which actually is what Hawtrey has reformulated here, with the quantity theory.[16] The unspent margin is just another word for the corresponding wealth of the cash in circulation plus the liabilities of the banks (plus

---

Eric Lindahl, that capital investments also are included (»Om förhållandet mellan penningmängd och prisnivå», *Uppsala universitets årsskrift,* Uppsala, 1929, p. 10). As the prices of investment goods have to be included in the price index, it cannot be said to represent the purchasing power of money in the hands of the consumer. R. J. Saulnier in *Contemporary Monetary Theory* (New York, 1938, p. 40), illustrates Hawtrey's theory by letting O represent consumers' outlay, M their unspent margin (having the same import as n in Keynes' equation $n = pk$), and V the income velocity. Then we can write $V = \frac{O}{M}$. Hence $P = \frac{O}{T}$, since $MV = PT$. Both P and T refer to transactions from consumers' outlay. P, then, does not stand for the price level of consumption goods, since consumers' outlay includes outlay both for consumption and capital goods.

[14] *Op. cit.*, p. 34.

[15] *Ibid.*, p. 39.

[16] This was written before the fourth edition of *Currency and Credit* appeared (London, 1950); but it is supported by Hawtrey's own reference to Davanzati in this edition (p. 33), in which the chapter on the quantity theory has been revised. The basic misinterpretation of the quantity theory remains, however.

'hoarding'). Hawtrey differs, however, from his early forerunners by equalizing the total quantity of money, not to an actual, but to a potential amount of wealth.

Hawtrey by no means maintains that the price level moves in proportion to changes in the unspent margin under actual conditions. Instead he proves that the more slowly this margin changes, the faster prices will move during a credit expansion. This assumes, of course, that the credit expansion is not followed by an immediate increase in output. If, by mere chance, a new equilibrium should ensue, it is not considered to be out of the question that prices might have changed in proportion to the increased quantity of the »unspent margin of purchasing power».[17] Even if this did happen, though, it would not necessarily be a proof of the correctness of the quantity theory.

The quantity theory does not belong to the group of theories explaining the variations in the price level. Hawtrey, like most economists, does not make this important distinction. Instead he accentuates the poor practical value of the theory due to its assumptions, which make the application of it to actual price level analysis impossible. He asserts, however, that it is not the quantity of money but the volume of credit that is the important element in the analysis of the variations in the price level. The changes in the quantity of money are the result, not the cause, of variations in the volume of credit. True or not, this does not affect the value of the quantity theory.

4. Interpreting the quantity theory as a theory of the value of money, D. H. Robertson tries to show the similarities between the determination of the value of money and the value of other things. The exchange value of everything depends, when the conditions of demand are given, on the total number of units available. In the case of money, however, there is said to be a very definite and peculiar relation: »*Given the conditions of demand for money,* the relation between its value and the quantity of it available is of this peculiar kind: the larger the number of units available, the smaller, in exactly the same proportion, the value of each unit.»[18] What is this demand for money that is presumed to be given? The assumption has often been made without inquiring as to whether it has any economic bearing on the formulation of the proposition of proportionality. It has been considered so self-evidently justified that nobody ever seriously raised the question

[17] *Ibid.*, p. 44 (1 ed.).

[18] *Money*, London, 1922, p. 32. *Cf.* 6 ed., 1948, p. 31.

of its verity. And yet, the assumption of a given demand for money, irrespective of the ambiguity of term, has no place in this illustration of a proportionate relation. Indeed, it is no assumption of a given demand; it is an assumption that the total value the quantity of money in circulation represents, is given. Hence it follows that the value of the monetary unit must be in an exactly inverse proportion to the number of units. This can obviously be said of the value of any item which forms a unit of a total number, representing a *given* value. It means that we actually have left the field of economics, and instead are presenting a self-evident arithmetic relation. In Robertson's example, however, the ordinary meaning of demand and supply in respect to other things than money has been preserved, which makes the comparison inconsistent. Here the demand *schedules* are supposed to be given. It is mistakenly believed that the proportionate relation, valid only in respect to money, rests upon the specific property of the demand schedule for money; but it does not. It rests upon the assumption that the quantity of money represents a given value. The confusion is mainly occasioned by the interpretation of this proportionate relation as a demand schedule of money.[19] Hence Robertson is incorrect in saying that it is the proposition of proportionality which forms the great difference between changes, due to variations in the respective supply, in the value of money and other things, since there can hardly be any meaningful comparison of these value-relations.

Robertson provides, on the other hand, a very good account of what the quantity theory does not say. Thus it never claimed that *every* change, which is connected with a change in the quantity of money, is the effect of this change; nor does it pretend to give the answer to the causal relations involved.[20]

In order to analyze the factors that presumably determine the value of money, Robertson proposes an equation similar to those of Fisher, Keynes and Pigou. If M represents the stock of money, H its real value, K its period of circulation in terms of finite but indivisible atoms of time called »days», T the volume of output per circulation-period, and P the price level, it follows that $\frac{M}{K} = P \cdot \frac{T}{K}$ or $P = \frac{M}{T}$, that is, the daily stream of money purchases the daily stream

---

[19] Wicksell makes the same mistake in a much more explicit form. See p. 135.

[20] *Op. cit.*, p. 33.

of output.[21] This is true regardless of any equilibrium conditions, since the formula is based upon the same principle as Fisher's equation: The quantity of money paid for the stream of goods equals the monetary value of the goods.

The equation $M = P\,T$ is of the same kind as Pigou's $M = \frac{k\,R}{P}$ or Keynes' $n = p\,k$. It is clarified by Robertson's discussion of the different terms included in the formula, as he writes $H = \frac{M}{P} = T$, which follows from the definitions. Thus $M = T = H$ when $P = 1$. H obviously corresponds to Keynes' k, if the value of the circulation is expressed in consumption-units, to $k\,R$ (when $P = 1$) if it is expressed in units of wheat, and to T when expressed in 'goods'. Robertson's formula signifies that the value of the stock of money, expressed in terms of goods, is equal to the amount of goods exchanged during one 'day', times the circulation period of money. Therefore it is, as in the case of Pigou's and Keynes' equations, impossible to derive from this formula the factors which *determine* the value of money; it only indicates some numerical relations between the quantity of money, its velocity and value, and the amounts of goods exchanged.[22]

5. A. W. Marget has given several examples of how J. M. Keynes in *A Treatise on Money* confused the equation of exchange with the quantity theory.[23] The same mistake is found in his earlier work *A Tract on Monetary Reform,* with the equation $n = p\,k$, in which n stands for the circulating amount of money (and other forms of means of circulation that are kept in cash), p for the price of a so-called consumption-unit, which is a compound of the kinds and articles included in the index number of the cost of living, and k for the amount of consumption-units that people are willing to keep in cash. If consideration is given also to the amount of consumption-units represented by check deposits, k', and the proportion of these potential liabilities kept in cash by the banks, r, then the equation reads

[21] *Banking Policy and the Price Level,* 3 ed., London, 1932, p. 59.

[22] In the first edition of *Banking Policy and the Price Level* (1926) Robertson defined T as »the value [should be volume] of output per finite but indivisible atom of time to be called 'a day'» (p. 60). Then we have $\frac{M}{K} = P\,T$ or $M = K\,P\,T$. Since K is equal to $\frac{1}{V}$, the similarity to Fisher's equation appears.

[23] See Marget, *op. cit.*, vol. I, pp. 19—35.

$n = p\,(k + r\,k')$.[24] Referring to the equation $n = p\,k$, Keynes emphatically announces: »This is the famous Quantity Theory of Money». The blunder is based on a confusion of the fitness of the equation for illustrating the proposition of proportionality with the proposition itself. One might perhaps be inclined to think that it is based on a conviction that the proposition of proportionality is the essence of the quantity theory. As will later be demonstrated, however, Keynes included the proposition of causality also. In spite of this, Keynes well realized that the theory originated with that specific peculiarity of money of having no utility in itself but only as a medium of exchange; he overlooked, however, the limited economic significance of the arithmetic illustration of this phenomenon.

The main difference between Keynes' and Pigou's equations is the unit of value chosen. They have both overestimated the limited use of these identities as means for an analysis of what determines the fluctuations in the purchasing power of money, which is their presumptive purpose. The real problem is to bring out what factors determine the value of p and k. The best application of the equation seems to be for the mere demonstration of the proportionate relation announced by the quantity theory.[25]

Keynes himself was not long satisfied with the definitions of the symbols of the equation $n = p\,k$. He realized that p did not represent the purchasing power of money, and so he redefined P_1 as the price level, weighted with respect to the different objects of expenditure, M as the total volume of cash balances, and C as the corresponding volume

---

[24] *A Tract on Monetary Reform*, New York, 1924, pp. 83—85.

[25] Aftalion considers the advantage of the identity $n = p\,k$, as compared with Fisher's equation, to be its close contact with individuals. The determination of the price level is said to become less objective, less automatic, and more dependent upon the actions of individuals, since changes in the amount of cash will affect the price level directly. But the Keynesian equation as such does not imply that changes in the amount of cash will affect the price level, either directly or indirectly. There can be no conclusion whatsoever of this kind from the identity, $n = p\,k$. On the other hand, $n = p\,k$ is inferior to the equation of exchange, according to Aftalion, for the amount of goods is defined on the basis of the concept of money, while in the equation of exchange the term *transactions* is separated from that concept (*op. cit.*, p. 144). The advantages enunciated of the Keynesian equation by Aftalion do not exist, however, which is indirectly admitted as he points out that Keynes' equation merely states that $n = n$; that is, it is a truism of a more commonplace nature than Fisher's equation. The latter equation contains an identity of a more advanced significance, while Keynes' equation merely expresses the value of the quantity of money being equal to the product of a certain unit of value and the corresponding number of units.

of real balances. The identity then reads $P_1 = \frac{M}{C}$.[26] This equation tells us just as little about *what* determines the purchasing power of money as did its predecessor, $n = p\,k$. It can never be anything but a formula for obtaining the numerical value of P or C (when two factors are given). Keynes' conclusion, that whenever an individual makes a decision which means a diminution in his stock of real balances, *ceteris paribus*, the final proportionate rise in the price level will be exactly in the proportion which the diminution in his stock of real balances bears to the remaining stock of balances,[27] is only a rewriting of arithmetics in economic terms. For the conclusion is based upon the identity, $P_1 = \frac{M}{C}$, and therefore its significance is limited to that of the identity, which does not reveal what will happen if a consumer decides to change his cash- och real-balances. It merely tells us that if, for example, M, the volume of cash balances, is given, then the smaller volume of real cash balances there is, C, the higher is the price level P_1. The formula does not explain *why* C at one time has one value, and at another time another value; therefore it is extremely limited as a foundation of an analysis of those factors determining the variations in the purchasing power of money.

The purpose of Keynes' important *Treatise on Money* was to break with the usual method of analyzing changes in the price level from changes in the quantity of money, and to proceed, instead, from the flow of the community's earnings or money income. Keynes was not the first to make this approach, but his attempt was a definite severing from all theories implying a direct causal relation between variations in the quantity of money and in the price level. It is deplorable that the confusion of Locke's original proposition of proportionality between prices and money with a theory of the fluctuations of the value of money came to dominate the monetary theories for such a long time, thereby hampering any realistic approach to the problem of the variations in the price level. Keynes, however, does not entirely emancipate himself from this barren approach. He makes certain exceptions for a complete rejection of the quantity theory, for example, »in equilibrium — *i.e.* when the factors of production are fully employed, when the public is neither bullish nor bearish for securities and is maintaining in the form

---

[26] *A Treatise on Money*, vol. I, pp. 223—224.

[27] *Ibid.*, vol. I, p.227.

of saving-deposits neither more nor less than the 'normal' proportion of its total wealth, and when the volume of saving is equal both to the cost and to the value of new investments — there is a unique relationship between the quantity of money and the price-levels of consumption goods and of output as a whole of such a character that if the quantity of money were double the price-levels would be double also. But this simple and direct quantitative relationship is a phenomenon only of equilibrium as defined above.»[28]

What makes this statement interesting is the announcement that an increase in the quantity of money will increase prices proportionately under *real* conditions if 'equilibrium' is present. This assumption substititutes the regular prerequisite of other things being equal, simply because 'equilibrium' supposedly implies that there will not be any changes in other factors when the quantity of money is increased. But how do we know? Is there anything that guarantees that an increased quantity of money will *not* affect the equilibrium present, only the price level? Certainly not. Keynes does not furnish any proof of his proposition. He simply assumes that the equlibrium conditions will not be influenced by an increased circulation. This amounts to the same as assuming other things to remain constant, which means that the statement does not refer to what will happen in a real situation, as one would at first be inclined to think, but to the purely theoretical correctness of the proposition of proportionality. Hence it follows that the proposition of causality loses any relevance. Keynes' attractive, but also delusive, formulation is then reduced to the truism of proportionality. This »simple and direct quantitative phenomenon» is *not* a phenomenon of equilibrium, it is a phenomenon of an obvious arithmetic relation.

Keynes criticises the quantity theory for not supplying a satisfactory explanation of the changes in the purchasing power of money, a criticism always expressed when the quantity theory is supposed to claim to be the answer to the solution of this problem. Changes in the price level are said to be occasioned chiefly by differences in planned investment and saving. To substantiate this idea, Keynes formulated his 'fundamental' equations. The activities symbolized in these equations are not directly influenced by changes in the quantity of money, but by the rate of interest. Here Keynes took up some of Wicksell's ideas as they were expounded in *Geldzins und Güterpreise* (1898). These ideas were further developed in *The General Theory of Employment,*

---

[28] *Ibid.*, vol. I, pp. 146—147. *Cf.* p. 228 and vol. II, p. 5. This remark is similar to Schumpeter's (see p. 192, note 23).

Interest and Money, in which changes in the quantity of money were given a new importance, namely, as influencing the rate of interest; in fact, a very old idea clearly enunciated by Locke.

The decisive difference between *A Treatise on Money* and *The General Theory of Employment* is that in the early work the theory of money was treated separately from the general theory of supply and demand.[29] In the later work, Keynes has tried to integrate the monetary theory with the whole framework of his »general theory». Discussing the relation betwen changes in the price level and in the quantity of money, he uses a set of definitions with different elasticities of demand and supply, and distinguishes between conditions of full employment and of less than full employment. Only if there is »perfectly elastic supply so long as there is unemployment, and perfectly inelastic supply so soon as full employment is reached, and if effective demand changes in the same proportion as the quantity of money, the Quantity Theory of Money can be enunciated as follows: So long as there is unemployment, *employment* will change in the same proportion as the quantity of money; and when there is full employment, *prices* will change in the same proportion as the quantity of money.»[30] By this statement, Keynes conceives that he has satisfied »tradition». This he has certainly done as far as concerns the misinterpretation of the theory, and even carried it further by introducing a relation between changes in the quantity of money and in the degree of employment. This reformulation is rather inconsistent in respect to the proposition of the *effects* of an increased circulation under actual conditions without several tacit assumptions, which, as in the earlier discussed formulation of the quantity theory are true only in equilibrium, deprive it of any causal significance and reduce it to a new application of the truism of proportionality. The reformulation implicitly presumes a direct causal relation between changes in the quantity of money and the effective demand, between changes in the effective demand and employment, and between changes in the quantity of money and prices when full employment is reached; that is, the propositions are founded on assumptions, the realistic bearings of which remain to be proved.

Keynes illustrates his opinion of the result of a change in the quantity of money by the formula $e = e_d (1—e_e e_o + e_e \cdot e_o \cdot e_w)$, where e = the measure of the response of money-prices to changes in the quantity of money, e_o = the elasticity of production in reponse to changes

---

29 *The General Theory of Employment, Interest and Money,* p. vi.

30 *Ibid.*, pp. 295—296.

in the effective demand (in terms of money), e_d = the elasticity of effective demand in response to changes in the quantity of money, e_w = the elasticity of money-wages in response to changes in effective demand (in terms of money), and e_e = the elasticity of employment for industry as a whole. Of this formula it is said that since it »gives us the proportionate change in prices in response to a change in the quantity of money, it can be regarded as a generalized statement of the Quantity Theory of Money».[31] Thus Keynes returns to his early identification of the quantity theory with a nonfunctional equation![32] And yet the quantity theory is understood as a statement of the *effect* of an actual increase in the amount of circulation. The equation contains the elasticities of different economic variables which probably will be influenced by changes in the quantity of money in circulation; but it tells nothing of how much they will be influenced or of how they are interdependently related. The equation is mainly an indication of how extremely difficult it is to forecast the effects of changes in the circulation (presuming that it is not an entirely passive factor), and it might intimate that this was not the purpose of the original quantity theory.

6. The emphasis of the Cambridge School on the importance of the variations in the individual cash holdings for the fluctuations in the exchange value of money is fundamentally an emphasis upon the function of money as a store of value. This approach, therefore, is quite different from that of the quantity theory, since it assumes the total quantity of money to be given and deals with the effects of changes in the average time that cash holders want to keep their balances passive (or idle);

[31] *Ibid.*, pp. 282, 285 and 304—305. Tord Palander points out in his article »Keynes' allmänna teori och dess tillämpning inom ränte-, multiplikator- och pristeorien» (*E. T.*, 1942, p. 267 ff.), that the equation should properly be written $e = e_d\,(1—e_o)$ for $e = e_d(1—e_e \cdot e_o + e_e \cdot e_o \cdot e_w) = e_d[1—1e_e\, e_o\,(1—e_w)]$ (1). Keynes' writes earlier $e_p = 1—e_o\,(1—e_w)$ (2), in which e_p is the elasticity of money-prices in response to changes in effective demand (if an earlier definition of e_o as the elasticity of production measured in terms of wage-units is used; see *General Theory,* p. 286). According to this derivation, the formula should be $e = e_d[1—e_o\,(1—e_w)]$. The equation, however, gets the much simpler expression $e = e_d\,(1—e_o)$ if the earlier definition of e_o is not used, that is, if wages are measured in terms of money and not in terms of wage-units as in equation (2). See also Marget's very thoroughgoing discussion (*op. cit.*, vol. II, p. 740 ff).

[32] The same mistake appears in Keynes' discussion of the equation $MV = OP$ and the quantity theory: »Thus if it is practicable to measure the quantity, O, and the price, P, of current output, we have $Y = OP$, and, therefore $MV = OP$; which is much the same as the Quantity Theory of Money in its traditional form» (*op. cit.*, p. 209). This fallacy is also mentioned by Marget (*op. cit.*, vol. I, p. 33 and note 59).

in other words, it deals with the so-called velocity of circulation of money. The desire to keep cash balances is stressed as one of the foremost determinants of the velocity of circulation of money. By changes in the average time of length that cash balances remain passive, *ceteris paribus*, the price level is influenced in the opposite direction. Whereas the original quantity theory provides the foundation for the conclusion that changes in the total quantity of money do not cause any changes in the velocity of circulation of money, the Cambridge School assumes a *given* quantity of money and discusses the effects of variations in the velocity of circulation of money. The Cambridge School represents one of the very first attempts to deal with the function of money as a store of value in its effects upon the price level and appears as an effort to break away from the barren approach based upon the commonly accepted formulation of the quantity theory. The weakness of the Cambridge School lies in the limitation of the discussion to primarily the effects of changes in the velocity of circulation of money on the price level. This weakness is a reminiscence of the great influence of the quantity theory in its generally accepted form.

Keynes' monetary theory is a further development of the basic idea of the Cambridge School. His achievement lies in relating the effects of changes in the quantity of money held as passive balances to changes in the rates of interest, instead of discussing them in relation to their immediate effect upon the price level. This line of thought represents an extension of Wicksell's monetary theory, which was developed as early as in 1898. Keynes, however, seems not to have had a close knowledge of Wicksell's *Geldzins und Güterpreise.* But Keynes went too far and claimed that *all* changes in the total quantity of money exert their influence on the price level by first influencing the various rates of interest. The weakness of this idea is demonstrated in the last chapter of this study (see, especially, p. 232). It seems not to be an overstatement, however, to say that in Keynes' *General Theory of Employment, Interest and Money* the role of money as a store of value is, for the first time, really integrated with a theory of employment and investment. Basically, it is in its function as a store of value that money appears as one of the main obstacles for an economy to reach full utilization of its total resources. If money were only a medium of exchange, that is, a store of value for very short periods only, then the analysis of a monetary and non-monetary economy would fundamentally be the same. Classical economics, which treated money as primarily a medium of exchange, is the best example of this way of looking at the role of money.

CHAPTER VI

SOME FRENCH AND ITALIAN ECONOMISTS ON THE QUANTITY THEORY

In this chapter the views of some representative French and Italian economists will be discussed. As a whole, the difference in their opinions on the content and importance of the quantity theory are rather small, even though one can always find some writers of exactly opposite views. In general the theory has been accepted as theoretically correct.

1. The greatest French economist, and also one of the greatest economists who ever lived, Léon Walras, accepted the proposition, other things being equal, of proportionate price changes as an *effect* of variations in the quantity of money. The same, although inversely proportionate, price changes would follow if the amount of cash holdings per period of time were diminished or increased; that is, changes in the velocity of money will have the same effects as changes in the amount of circulation.[1] These conclusions are based upon a number of nonfunctional 'equilibrium equations', which means that they are reduced to statements of a purely arithmetic character, leaving out any causal relationships.

In his discussion of the influence of changes in individual cash holdings on the price level, Walras appears as one of the founders of the 'cash-balance approach'. It is very improper, though, to denote this view as an extended quantity theory because it is neither a question of changes in the *total* quantity of money, nor an emphasis on a specific peculiarity of money. Partly, it is an extended application of the truism of proportionality. · An analysis, however, of the *causal* relation between changes in individual cash holdings and the price level is of much more economic significance than a similar analysis between changes in the total quantity of money (in circulation) and the price level.

In order to deal with the problem of regulating the variations in the

[1] *Eléments d'économie politique pure ou théorie de la richesse sociale,* Paris, 1896, p. 383.

value of metallic money, Walras formulates an equation similar to those of the Cambridge School. Let Q denote the quantity of metallic money in a given country, p the price of a monetary unit expressed in some other thing, H the total amount of transactions to be carried out during a given period of time, and C the amount of transactions performed without the means of exchange (including all the operations via the clearing-house). Then it follows that $Qp = H-C$.[2] The information provided by this equation is obviously the same as that of Pigou's and Keynes' equations, that is: the total potential value of money equals the value of a certain amount of goods. The formula also lends itself to the same demonstrations of proportionate relations without any implications of causalities. The period of time must evidently be chosen so that H, the total amount of exchanges to be effectuated, minus C, will actually correspond to the value of the quantity of money; that is, it must equal the period of circulation of the quantity of money. If this were not the case, then H would not correspond to the *total* amount of exchanges to be performed during an arbitrarily chosen period of time, but to that amount of exchanges, lessened by C, which will correspond to the value of the quantity of money, the only given factor. As the terms are defined, however, the time period is given implicity. To regulate the value of metallic money, not only the total quantity of money has to be known, but also the quantity of the metal not being coined. This knowledge, though, combined with the equation, still does not provide the solution to the problem.

The verification of the quantity theory requires, according to Walras, equilibrium of exchange, that is, prices correspond to conditions of scarcity; that the value of the commodity which is the means of exchange has the same value as a commodity; and that those participating in the exchange have the cash needed. It also requires equilibrium of production, implying that entrepreneurs make neither profits nor losses. These conditions form the foundation of a system of equations from which it is said to follow that the equilibrium will not be disturbed if prices are n times higher or lower, if only the quantity of money is n times greater or smaller too. Again this is a play with arithmetic relations, pretending that they can be directly transformed, without modifications, into economic relations of some relevance. It is very easy to imagine that if the quantity of money were n times greater or smaller than the actual quantity in a given society, the equilibrium might be completely upset. Thus there is obviously both a certain upper and lower limit

[2] *Théorie de la monnaie,* Paris, 1886, pp. 14—15.

that the quantity of money in circulation cannot pass without occasioning extreme difficulties to the economy. This is a simple indication of the limitations of the economically significant arithmetic conclusions which can be drawn from a system of equations. Yet there are no causal relations involved in Walras' statement, which basically does illustrate the original content of the quantity theory. Walras, however, as well as Keynes, combines the proposition with a statement that lays the emphasis upon an undisturbed equilibrium, thereby only indirectly suggesting the specific property of the means of exchange, which is the fundamental issue. But he also makes the same fallacious inference, which can be exemplified innumerable times in the economic literature, that every increase or decrease of the medium of exchange, *ceteris paribus*, will have the *effect* of a proportionate price-increase or -decrease.[3]

Walras and Clément Juglar are typical representatives of two opposite views which sometimes dominated the debate on the value of the quantity theory: Juglar maintained that the theory is not valid because most payments are performed by clearing and compensation affairs. The quantity of money performs such a small fraction of the total amount of transactions that it is absolutely negligible. Walras, on the other hand, opposed this view and tried to make it as clear as possible that *if* the amount of transactions were given, then prices would be in proportion to the quantity of money in circulation, which could not be said to be unimportant.[4] Walras was primarily basing his argument on the undeniable arithmetic relations indicated by his equation, while Juglar's criticism was founded on the conviction that an *actual* change in the quantity of circulating money would not cause proportionate price changes because of the small share of the total transactions performed with money. Thus both were correct to a certain degree. Their argument is a typical example of the meaningless discussions carried on, assumedly on the correctness of the quantity theory. The participants never could come to an understanding, still less to an agreement, simply because they were arguing over different things.

2. P. Leroy-Beaulieu was very much influenced by Stuart Mill's thinking. This is particularly conspicuous in his treatment of

---

[3] »*Toute augmentation ou diminution dans la quantité de la marchandise monnaie a pour effet une augmentation ou une diminution sensiblement proportionelle dans les prix.*» *Ibid.*, p. 44.

[4] *Ibid.*, p. 20. See Clément Juglar: *Du Change et de la liberté d'émission,* Paris, 1868.

the value of money, using Mill's definition of the demand for and supply of money. At »normal» and constant conditions of credit and when the amount of commodities remains unchanged, prices will, in the long run, increase in proportion to the increase in the quantity of money.[5] In other words, when conditions, except for prices, are such that they cannot be influenced by an increased amount of circulation, only prices will be influenced! The reasons these other conditions would not be affected by changes in the quantity of money, and the specific causal relationships required, are always passed over as if such problems never existed.

Maurice Block, on the other hand, does not render the relationship between changes in the quantity of money and its value any specific peculiarity. The value of money, like that of all other things, is determined partly by the cost of production and partly by the relation of demand to supply. Adopting the definition of the demand for money as the quantity of goods supplied and the supply of money as the quantity of money, Block denies the existence of a strictly mathematical relation between changes in the circulation and the price level, and repudiates the quantity theory because it *does not explain* the causes of price fluctuations.[6]

3. Albert Aftalion distinguishes between three conceptions of the quantity theory. One is called the »popular opinion», namely, that the value of metallic money varies in an inverse proportion to changes in its quantity. This interpretation, which emphasizes the proportionate relation, is considered as not being defensible, since it reduces the content of the quantity theory to the establishment of such an obvious fact that

---

5 *Traité théorique et practique d'économie politique,* 4 vols., 3 ed., Paris, 1900, vol. III, pp. 147—148.

6 *Le Progrès de la science économique depuis Adam Smith,* 2 vols. Paris, 1897, vol. II, pp. 41 and 135. Laughlin characterizes Block as a quantity theorist because he accepted the view that prices were determined by a comparison of the total quantity of money in circulation with the total amount of goods offered (*op. cit.*, p. 304). Another French economist around the turn of the century, A. de Foville, had no objections to the quantity theory if it only implied that prices depend upon the quantity of money paid for the goods exchanged. But in his interpretation it is also said that the value of money will always be equal to the value of all commodities, and that prices will vary in proportion to changes in the quantity of money (*La Monnaie,* p. 141). Thus, entirely separated statements by Hume, Davanzati, and Locke are put together and described as the content of the quantity theory. A. de Foville rejects the theory, as did Juglar, because of the insignificant role the quantity of metallic money plays in the performance of the total amount of transactions.

it has never been disputed. It deprives the theory of all explanatory power and of all characteristics of a theory.[7] Aftalion overlooks, however, that the essence of the quantity theory is not the proposition of proportionality as such, which only serves to illustrate a specific peculiarity of money. This proposition was, by no means, so self-evident when Locke first formulated it as it later became when demonstrated by proper equations. Truly, this interpretation deprives the quantity theory of all reasons for characterizing it as a theory. It became a theory of the value of money when it was misinterpreted as an explanation of why the price level changes, and of how it was going to change.

The second interpretation of the quantity theory, in which the quantity of money includes coins, bills, paper money and deposits,[8] is the interpretation represented by Fisher with the emphasis on the activeness of the monetary factors and on the passiveness of the price level. The dividing line between adherents and critics of this version of the quantity theory is said to be the acceptance or refutation of the proposition of causality. The only justification for the theory that Aftalion can discover is its capability of *explaining* the movements of the price level. Therefore, the equation of exchange should be written $\frac{(MV + M'V')}{T} = P$, so that consideration is given to variations in the amount of transactions also. The left side of the equation will then include only active elements, and the right side the only passive element of the formula. Such a consideration, however, gives a worse relationship between fluctuations in the price level and in the quantity of money (according to an investigation of these relations in France in the early 1920's).

The third form of the quantity theory also implies that the value of money varies inversely with changes in its quantity, but the quantity of money now includes M, M', V, and V'.[9] The essence of this form is the causal relation between the monetary factors and the price level.[10] Therefore, Aftalion maintains, the theory should be called »une théorie qualitative» rather than »une théorie quantitative».[11]

As it is entirely unnecessary to search for proportionate price

[7] *Monnaie, prix et change,* 3 ed., 2 vols., Paris, 1948—50, vol. I, pp. 6—7; *cf.* p. 148; also see the first ed. (1927), pp. 116 and 121—122.

[8] *Op. cit.*, p. 19 (3 ed.).

[9] *Ibid.*, p. 147.

[10] *Ibid.*, p. 149.

[11] *Ibid.*, p. 150.

variations, the proposition of causation, which is regarded as the fundamental content of the quantity theory, remains. But even here Aftalion has found that prices (in France during and immediately after the first world war) have risen more than the amount of circulation, thereby occasioning an increase in one or several of the factors M', V' and V. An increase in the price level is said to have frequently caused an increase in M; indeed, the amount of money is the *passive* factor, presumedly contradictory to the quantity theory. Aftalion explains the chain of causation to be a change first in the rates of exchange, secondly in prices, thirdly in the velocity of money, and finally, in the amount of money.[12]

All these statistical investigations, made in order to prove or disprove the correctness of the proposition of a direct or indirect causal relationship between changes in the quantity of money and in the price level, can never confute the essence of the original quantity theory. Aftalion's research is primarily a criticism of Fisher's basic proposition that the *effect* of variations in the quantity of money will be proportionate price changes. It is very questionable if Aftalion can prove any causal relations, or the passiveness of the quantity of money, by a comparative study of the numerical values of the symbols in the equation of exchange during a certain period of time. How is it decided that an 'original' change in the numerical value of one of the symbols is a cause or an effect?

Aftalion went a little further than Fisher in examining the causal problems involved. He was well aware of the fact that the fundamental causes are not all directly manifested in the different symbols of the equation of exchange. The numerical values of these symbols are merely the results of other elements, which have to be thoroughly analyzed in order to solve the problem. Ultimately, there is the complex economic behaviour of the human beings. To stress the fundamental importance of this factor, Aftalion proposed his »Théorie psychologique de la monnaie».

4. A queer attempt to formulate a precise definition of the value of money was made by François Divisia. Fundamentally, it seems impossible, since the value of money is a relation between individuals and their valuations of prices; yet, he brings forward some points of interest to this study of the quantity theory. He asserts that the only law ever being formulated for the value of money is the quantity theory

[12] *Ibid.*, pp. 123—126 and 140 (1 ed.).

and therefore it constitutes his starting-point. This is apparently a confusion of Davanzati's theory of the value of money and an omission of the cost of production theory (in terms of labor) and the theory of marginal utility. Divisia views the quantity theory as an expression of a century-old observation and refers to Copernicus' remarks on the value of money. It is admitted, though, that it has been formulated deductively too, but then nearly always with reference to actual conditions in order to get affirmation. This hybrid, as he calls these different derivations, is claimed to be due to the lack of a precise definition of the value of money. Such a definition is necessary if the quantity theory is to be an exact law.[13] Obviously, there is no question of any hybrid if a law is derived both deductively and inductively, if only the same definition of the value of money is kept. The hybrid is rather the confusion of quantitative theories of the value of money with the quantity theory. In Divisia's interpretation, the quantity theory becomes a law for the explanation of variations in the value of money. The original quantity theory does not have to dwell on a sophisticated definition of the value of money. It needs only the assumption of a certain value of money.

Divisia proposes the equation $\frac{V g r}{a} = k$, in which k is a constant, V the value of money, g the quantity of money in circulation, and a the activity of transactions. If I denotes the inverted value of money, the equation will read $g r = k a I$.[14] Regarding the difficulties of determining r, he writes $g r = c$, and the equation then reads $V c = k a$. This formula is called »la loi circulatoire» instead of »la loi quantitative», partly because the latter is inexactly formulated in the works of most economists, and partly because it refers to the total and not to the circulating quantity of money.[15] Considering only the quantity of money in circulation as a means of exchange entails that a includes only a certain part of all transactions. Besides, neither the activity nor the measurement of transactions is clearly defined. In order to make the comparison possible, as indicated by the formula, it has to be measured in some form of the monetary unit. Nor is V, the value of money,

[13] *Economique rationelle,* Paris, 1928, p. 263 ff; also see *L'indice monétaire et la théorie de la monnaie,* Paris, 1926, p. 35 ff.

[14] This equation is somewhat similar to Fisher's, but according to Divisia, he had no knowledge of the equation of exchange when he formulated his equation in 1925. See *Economique rationelle,* p. 267, note 1.

[15] *Economique rationelle,* p. 263, and *L'indice monétaire,* p. 36. *Cf.* H. Denis: *Les récentes théories monétaires en France,* Paris, 1938, pp. 42—49.

clearly defined, but it stands probably for some inverted value of the price level. Hence this definition can hardly be said to be more precise than the definitions generally used in formulating the quantity theory. As the quantity theory has been formulated during the last two hundred years, it has referred to »la loi quantitative» and not to »la loi circulatoire», as is correctly pointed out by Divisia.

Jaques Rueff formulates, in order to illustrate the quantity theory, the equation $M V + M'V' = K P Q$, which evidently is an exact imitation of the equation of exchange, except for the constant K.[16] The price level is regarded as being determined by the factors comprised in the equation. He rejects the quantity theory because it is not the *only* law that determines changes in the price level, thus interpreting the theory as an *exclusive explanation* of the fluctuations in the price level. But his attempt to explain variations in the purchasing power of money in terms of changes in the amount of circulation has given rise to the characterization of him as a quantity theorist.[17]

As a whole it can be said that the quantity theory has played a less important role in French than in Anglo-Saxon monetary theory. Generally it has been recognized as theoretically true, but of no value as a practical means of analysis. Angell suggests that while there was more of a deductive research in the Anglo-Saxon countries, the tendency in France has been preponderatingly towards an empirical research of the validity of the quantity theory.[18] This, however, is only true during the period before the appearance of Kemmerer's and Fisher's works. Compared with these works, it can be said that the inductive study in France concentrated more on the question of causation than that of proportionality, which seemed so entirely out of touch with realities.

5. In the historical development of the interpretation of the quantity theory, Davanzati and Montanari have had a very great importance. This is particularly true in respect to the interpretation of the theory as a theory of the ('intrinsic') value of money, of individual prices, and of fluctuations in the price level. Thus they contributed chiefly to the confusion of Locke's original statement and to the prolonged discussion of the quantity theory.

---

16 *Théorie des phénomènes monétaires,* Paris, 1927, p. 47.

17 See, for example, Denis, *op. cit.*, p. 38.

18 *Op. cit.*, pp. 274—275.

Giovanni Pagnini (1765) found Davanzati's monetary theory excellent and even held that no later economist had made any improvements, while Gregorio Pereira, who appeared some years later, accepted Locke's views and ignored Davanzati. Antonio Genovesi (1788) did not pay any attention to Davanzati's or Montanari's writings, but proceeded from Montesquieu's clear exposition of a quantitative theory of money. Pietro Verri, writing about ten years later, accepted the content of the quantity theory as expressed by Hume, but had a somewhat different view of the results on industry of an increased quantity of money. After industry had acquired the additional quantity of money, it would start increasing production, and the result would be a lowering of prices, although not necessarily. There would never, however, be any increase in prices as long as industry got the increase of money. If someone else received it, then prices would rise because there would be no corresponding increase in output. Thus industry only is thought of as being able to raise its production.[19]

During the first half of the nineteenth century the English economists dominated the whole field of economics, placing all other economic writers in the shade except for J. B. Say. In 1813 Cagnazzi formulated his equation $Mc = DC$ (see p. 86), but it did not receive any attention from his fellow-countrymen. Not until the end of the century did some internationally known economists again appear in Italy. One of the outstanding, A. de Viti de Marco, held it self-evident that prices, *i.e.*, the price level, depended upon the relation of the amount of goods to the quantity of money in circulation. This was also the foundation of his acceptance of the quantity theory. But the theory was only valid if the means of exchange were composed exclusively of metallic money, if no credit were used, if there were a free communication between the bullion market and coinage, and if there were a constant supply of goods.[20] Recognizing these prerequisites, he could not think that the proposition of proportionality could be denied if the quantity of money were increased. The prerequisite of a purely metallic currency was necessary in order to get the same percentage increase in prices as in the quantity of metallic money.

Achille Loria rejected the quantity theory and declared that the value of money was determined completely by its cost of production. The amount of money, Q, necessary for the exchange of all the goods

---

19 Monroe, *op. cit.*, p. 217—221.

20 *Moneta e prezzi,* Città di Castella, 1885, pp. 1—3.

in a given society, is determined by the sum of the total costs of the commodities, V, by the velocity of money, v, and by its own cost of production. Hence $Q = \frac{V}{v}$, where Q is the amount of labor that the circulating quantity of money must contain.[21] Accordingly, the *value* of money is not determined by the relation of the quantity of goods to that of money; on the contrary, the *quantity* of money, *ceteris paribus*, depends upon the value of money. Evidently Loria was one of the few consistent adherents of the cost of production theory.

Maffeo Pantaleoni, on the other hand, accepted the quantity theory, but interpreted it primarily as a proposition of an undeniable arithmetic relation. Supposing money to be used solely as a means of exchange and the volume of business transactions to be given, the value of the total quantity of money will be given. And so he drew the same conclusion as Hume did, that if the quantity of money were doubled, prices would be doubled, because the total value of the circulation has not changed.[22] The correctness of the proposition is presumedly proved by the equation $v = \frac{m}{q\,r}$, in which m symbolizes the volume of business transactions, q the quantity of money, r the velocity of money, and v the value of the monetary unit. Pantaleoni, however, is much more careful than Fisher, and, therefore, he does not say that the formula $\frac{m}{q\,r}$ *determines* the value of money. He merely states that it is *expressed* by the formula. Nor does he understand the quantity theory as an explanation of the value of money. Very cautiously he speaks of »the dependence of the unitary value of money on its quantity» as a characterization of the quantity theory, although such a formulation does not indicate anything specific about money.

---

21 *Studi sul valore della moneta,* Torino, 1901, p. 34. One of the most unreasonable critics of the quantity theory was G. Luzzatti, whose criticism goes far beyond Laughlin's (see *Prezzi ideali e prezzi effetive,* Milano, 1892, pp. 3—5). Wicksell even considers his views so fantastic that there is hardly any point in criticising them (*Interest and Prices,* pp. 49—50).

22 *Pure Economics,* transl. by T. B. Bruce, 2 vols., London, 1898, vol. I, p. 231.

CHAPTER VII

THE QUANTITY THEORY IN GERMAN LITERATURE

From the very beginning of the nineteenth century, it is argued, German economists maintained that prices could not be explained by the relations of output to demand. They did not, in contradistinction to the English economists, accept the quantity theory as a means of explaining price movements. Instead they partly applied the law of demand and supply, and partly the cost-of-production theory.[1] This idea seems to be due to a confusion of the theory of changes in the price level with the theory of relative prices. The fundamental difference between the English and German economists of this time seems to be that while the Englishmen had a separate theory for the fluctuations in the price level, the Germans explained all price changes in terms of the theory of relative prices (which was mainly formulated by English economists). Hence, the quantity theory was interpreted rather as a theory of individual price changes than as a theory of the value of money. Some of the German economists, more or less representing this opinion, were L. H. Jacob, Hufeland, Herman Lotz and K. H. Rau.

1. In general the quantity theory is understood as a theory of the value of money, and as excluding the cost-of-production theory. Wilhelm Roscher, therefore, who considered the latter theory as a satisfactory explanation of the value of everything, rejected the quantity theory. It was understood as an explanation of the value of money in terms of the relation of the quantity of money to the amount of goods. This, he held, was refuted by the simple fact that commodities were received and consumed without any exchange of money![2] This evidence, however, can be directed against the quantity theory only as an explanation of relative prices. Roscher's remark must be due to a confusion of relative and absolute prices. As a consistent adherent of

[1] R. Zuckerkandl: *Zur Theorie des Preises,* Leipzig, 1889, p. 176.

[2] *System der Volkswirtschaft,* 5 vols., Stuttgart, 1874, vol. I, § 122.

the cost-of-production theory, he looked upon the quantity of money as a passive factor, determined by the number and volume of transactions to be performed by money, by the velocity of money, and by the number of substitutes for money and their velocities of circulation.

Karl Marx held substantially the same opinion as Roscher, although he emphasized, of course, the amount of invested labor as the decisive element of the value of money, as of everything. Since the quantity of money in circulation is an entirely passive factor in the pricing process, and determined by the velocity of money and the prices of goods, the assumption of (sudden) changes in the amount of circulation causing price changes is inadmissable and must be rejected. Actually, the fact is, claims Marx, that one of the best observed relations in the history of prices is that an increased quantity of money generally went with a decrease in prices and *vice versa*! As a support of his view, he refers to Tooke's and Newmarch's well-known price studies.[3] This seems rather peculiar, since Tooke and Newmarch pretended to prove that changes in the quantity of money *followed* the variations in the price level. The value of irredeemable paper notes, however, is determined by their quantity. Paper money receives its value because it circulates, while coins circulate because they possess value! And the quantity theory is applicable to paper money as it explains changes in its value.[4]

2. A. E. F. Schäffle does not emphasize the conditions on the supply side so one-sidedly as Roscher, but pays due attention to the demand side also in his analysis of the exchange value of money, goods and services. Only in the case of irredeemable paper money has the quantity theory any significance, and then only in so far as it is concerned with the proposition of causation. The theory is comprehended as an explanation of actual fluctuations in the price level. Schäffle distinguishes between the »quality» and the »quantity» theory of money. The quality theory refers to a situation wherein the paper currency has lost its value because of not being redeemable any longer, while the quantity theory concerns a situation in which an additional quantity of money can be absorbed only by an increase of prices. Actual cases are said to be a mixture of these two types of decreasing monetary value.[5]

---

[3] *Till kritiken av den politiska ekonomien,* Stockholm, 1943, pp. 105—106. (Swedish translation of *Zur Kritik der politischen Oekonomie* by R. Wagner.)

[4] *Ibid.*, pp. 125—126.

[5] *Das gesellschaftlische System der menschlichen Wirtschaft,* Tübingen, 1873, § 141.

The line of distinction, however, is not unambiguously drawn, since the quantity of money in circulation is not necessarily related to the character of the currency.

When the cost of production theory is claimed to explain the value of everything, the causal proposition in the quantity theory is generally withheld. Richard Hildebrand denies the causal relation under all circumstances and asserts that there is a confusion of cause with effect. Variations in the quantity of money are exclusively the result of movements in the price level, whether the currency is based on gold or silver, or on irredeemable paper money. He defends his views by saying that the value of money has to be determined *before* it appears on the market.[6] Thus he eliminates entirely the influence of market conditions on the value of money and explains its value solely in terms of the cost of producing it. Yet he also holds that prices are determined by the relation of demand to supply. But if the value of money, that is, its purchasing power, is given, then prices must obviously be given too.

Hildebrand has, in fact, a very strange view of money and its functions. He denies every bit of the importance of the concept of the velocity of money and regards this whole theory as completely barren and purely academic. One reason is that it seems to him impossible to measure the velocity of money. He advances, for example, the idea that the quantity of money required at a certain *point of time* is determined by the number and volume of transactions just at that time, not by the velocity of money.[7] Of course, there is no objection to this argument as such; but it is quite beside the point, since nobody ever seriously alleged that the velocity of money had any meaning at a given point of time. It goes without saying that the concept has to be defined in relation to a given *period* of time; consequently, there are no difficulties in obtaining a numerical value of the 'velocity' of money, if only the necessary statistics are available.

Hildebrand's criticism has influenced other German economists and even so strongly that Karl Kirmaier, in a thesis on the quantity theory, denies the validity of Fisher's equation because it contains a symbol for the velocity of money, which has no equivalence in reality. If it had, it would mean that money is nothing but the visible rate of the turnover of goods. In the equation of exchange, therefore, V denotes the rate of the turnover of goods. If, as is often maintained, an increased

[6] *Die Theorie des Geldes,* Jena, 1883, pp. 110 and 138—139.

[7] *Ibid.*, pp. 43 and 48.

velocity of money will raise prices, then it also has to be proved that it might be possible to pay these higher prices with velocity of money![8]

3. Thanks to his close study of Peel's bank-act, Adolf Wagner also became very familiar with the related discussions of the content and value of the quantity theory. His own conclusion was that just as little as the quantity theory is true of money in general and of paper money in particular, so is it true of the conditions in England at that time.[9] He agreed with the propositions as theoretically correct, but criticised the practical value of the theory, as the assumptions involved would never be realized. At a given point of time, he conceded, the value of money is inversely related to its quantity, so that it would always change in order to 'equalize' the value of the total amount of money offered to the value of the goods supplied.[10] This is thought of as a theory of the determination of the value of money at a given point of time. But is there any determination of the value of money involved here? Evidently not. Since the problem is limited to a certain *point* of time, there can be no question of any *changes* taking place. It is simply an illusion, again based upon a confusion of an arithmetic relation with a process of causation. There is no process of 'equalization', simply because there is no question of any period of time. In fact, the elements involved are all given, and there is no problem in determining any of them. Wagner's way of reasoning is very typical of all those who recognize the quantity theory as logically correct, but deny its correctness when it is applied to realistic conditions. Then the value of the theory is confined to its proposition of causality,[11] which actually is a proposition that tacitly assumes the possibility of a (direct) causal relationship between money and prices.

Carl Helfferich's conception of the quantity theory is another example of its misinterpretation. In his well-known standard work on money, the great weakness of the quantity theory is said to be its *overemphasis* of the influence of the supply of money on its value and

[8] *Die Quantitätstheorie,* Berlin, 1922, pp. 57 and 63. Irrespective of the untenable arguments Kirmaier brings up against the concept of the velocity of money, there has sometimes been a tendency to deal with concept as itself causing an impact. See, especially, H. J. Davenport's criticism of the use of the concept in the article »Velocities, Turnovers and Prices», *A. E. R.,* 1930, pp. 9—19; further, see ch. XIII.

[9] *Die Geld- und Credittheorien der Peel'schen Bankacte,* pp. 60—62.

[10] *Theoretische Sozialökonomik,* 2 vols., Leipzig, 1907, vol. II, pp. 211—212.

[11] *Ibid.,* p. 697 ff.

the ignorance of all those counter-acting forces which exist and decrease the effects of the supply.[12] This weakness, obviously, does not belong to the quantity theory, but to those economists, and others, who used the theory as an explanation of *all* variations in the price level, the so-called 'extreme quantity theorists'. Why the quantity theory ever was understood as *the* explanation of changes in the value of money is only explained by a confusion of the purely theoretical assumptions and propositions of the theory with actual universal laws. Helfferich's main thesis, that there is no reason for giving the supply of money any priority, but that all influencing factors — both on the demand- and supply-side — have to be taken into consideration in an analysis of the fluctuations in the value of money, is not a criticism of the quantity theory, but a general theory of the causes affecting the price level.[13]

4. Joseph Schumpeter is one of the very few who have understood the real purpose of the quantity theory. He firmly emphasizes that its value is not bound up with the assumption of a certain causation or with the proposition of a definite proportionality, but with its clear demonstration of a specific peculiarity of money: the quantity of money has no importance with respect to the amount of wealth. Hence the means of exchange has no value as such, compared with the commodities, but has merely a subservient position. This is the essence of the quantity theory and it cannot be stressed too much. Just imagine, if this had been realized when the theory was first enunciated! Then there would not have been that immense, and mostly meaningless, discussion of the theory as an *explanation* of the value of money and its fluctuations. Instead, the study of these problems would likely have taken other and more fruitful courses, which would have led to significant results. Unfortunately, this was realized rather late and the monetary theory was, for a long time, hampered by this emphasis upon the quantity of money as such in relation to its value, instead of analyzing the causes of the changes in the circulating quantity of money. Certainly, it is admitted that efforts were made, but they did not succeed in breaking the ice until the beginning of this century. But by then, the distorted formulation of the quantity theory had been repeated for over two hundred years!

---

[12] *Das Geld,* 6 ed., Leipzig, 1923, pp. 583—584.

[13] *Ibid.*, p. 608. G. F. Knapp's once so stirring work, *Staatlische Theorie des Geldes* (Leipzig, 1905), does not examine the quantity theory; but it is apparent that the author rejects any fixed relation between changes in the circulation and in prices, and any exclusive causation.

In a proposal aimed at achieving a satisfactory monetary theory, Schumpeter enunciates the equation

$$E = M U = p_1 m_1 + p_2 m_2 + p_3 m_3 + p_4 m_4 \dots . p_n m_n$$

in which E symbolizes the total sum of all incomes — individual, governmental, and all economic associations (not serving any private purposes) — during one year in a closed society, where equilibrium is prevailing. M represents the total amount of money in circulation, including all that serves as money, and U represents the average velocity of money, or, as Schumpeter prefers to phrase it, the efficiency of the quantity of money, during the period assumed. The symbols $m_1, m_2 \dots . m_n$ denote the amount of investment- and consumption-goods, and $p_1, p_2 \dots p_n$ their respective prices. In the case of investment-goods lasting longer than the period in question, the normal quantity of the periodically new supply is considered.[14]

The identity is reminiscent of the equation of exchange, but the symbols included are differently defined and seem to be more ambiguous than those in the Fisherine equation. Thus M includes everything that serves as money, which means that every substitute, for example, an investment- and/or a consumption-good, has to be covered by M. This makes it almost impossible to achieve any measurable value of M.[15] The import of U is quite equivocal, as is evident from its indirect definition. U illustrates that average velocity of 'money' which is necessary in order to make the product of $M U$ coincide with the national income, E, during one year. It is, of course, impossible to determine U before E and M are known. The equation, then, merely serves to obtain the value of U. Obviously, the equation is not appropriate as a foundation for an analysis of causal relations. For example, an increase in M, *ceteris paribus*, may be contingent on either an increased circulation of notes, or an increased bargaining, or a combination of both.

The purpose of the equation is to demonstrate the importance of changes in the total national income in analyzing variations in the value of money, which is defined as the purchasing power of a given unit of

---

[14] »Das Sozialprodukt und die Rechenpfennige», *A. f. S.*, 1917, p. 630.

[15] The concept and definition of M has probably been more criticised than any of the other symbols involved. See, for example, H. Ellis: *German Monetary Theory 1905—1933*, Cambridge, Mass., 1934 (Harvard Economic Studies, vol. XLIV), pp. 126—139; G. Haberler: »Kritische Bemerkungen zur Schumpeters Geldtheorie», *Z. f. V.*, 1925, pp. 645—668; and L. Schönfeld: »Über Joseph Schumpeters Lösung des ökonomischen Zurechnungsproblem», *Z. f. V.*, 1924, pp. 432—477.

income.[16] The equation as such does not reveal the importance of the different factors involved. But it does indicate the decisive change that has taken place: the shift in the approach to the problem, away from the study of purely quantitative monetary relations, to a study of the effects of variations in incomes.

5. Characteristic of German monetary theory has been the great interest in the juridical aspects of the means of exchange. No other country can provide such a number of writings on these questions as Germany. One fundamental reason is the very close connection between the study of economics and of law that prevailed in Germany for a long time. The interest in the quantity theory never became as great as it did in England or in the United States. German monetary writers were primarily interested in analyzing the problem of what *constitutes* the value of money. Instead of two main groups of adherents and critics of the quantity theory there were other groups, distinguished from each other with respect to their views of what constituted the value of money. In Anglo-Saxon literature, where the cost-of-production theory generally was considered to have provided the solution, the discussion centered around the causes of actual changes in the price level.

The different opinions in German monetary theory have been fairly equally distributed. Among the nominalists, who denied the existence of any value in money whatsoever, Bendixen, Elster, Knapp and Liefman may be mentioned as prominent representatives. Their opponents, the metallists, included, among others, Diehl, Knies, Lotz and Menger. The latter ardently maintained that money in itself has to have a value, whereas the nominalists considered the value of money to be based on a reflective imagination only. A third group defended the so-called functional theory of the value of money. It included several outstanding economists, like Helfferich, Simmel, von Wieser and Soda.

There have also been several substantial contributions to the theory of the fluctuations in the purchasing power of money. It is very significant that they are seldom founded upon an application of the quantity theory. Friedrich von Wieser was one of the first to formulate an income theory, which was later extended by Schumpeter. Its contrast to the quantity theory was especially underlined by Liefmann, who, together with Kerschagl and some others, formed this group. Bendixen

[16] *Op. cit.*, p. 651.

and Elster approached the problem from another angle and tried to fuse the income theory and the principles of the Banking School together, whereas Othmar Spann, and above all, Ludvig von Mises, recommended a historical and institutional explanation of the changes in the price level. S. P. Altmann and Heinrich König emphasized the variations on the commodity side and denied that the equation of exchange could give any answer to the problem of the fluctuations in the price level. Neisser, on the other hand, showed a great conformity to the cash-balance approach and was also noticeably influenced by the Cambridge School. This is also true of Friedrich von Hayek. Besides this he makes the suggestion of 'saving' the quantity theory by defining the quantity of money as the product of MV, the so-called effective quantity of money.[17] The problem, however, is not one of 'saving' the quantity theory, but of giving the monetary factors their proper place in the analysis of the purchasing power of money and its fluctuations. A satisfactory explanation, according to Hayek, has to take the whole problem of business cycles into consideration.[18]

---

[17] Friedrich von Hayek: »Reflections on the Pure Theory of Money of Mr. J. M. Keynes», *Economica*, 1931, pp. 270—295.

[18] The summary is based upon S. P. Altmann: *Zur deutschen Geldlehre des 19. Jahrhunderts* (in G. Schmoller: *Die Entwicklung der Volkswirtschaftlehre,* Leipzig, 1908, vol. I); K. Diehl: *Die Entwicklung der Wert- und Preistheorie im 19. Jahrhundert* (in G. Schmoller, *ibid.*); Ellis, *op. cit.*, chs. VIII—XI; Hoffman, *op. cit.*, and Kirmaier, *op. cit.*

CHAPTER VIII

THE QUANTITY THEORY IN SCANDINAVIAN LITERATURE

The analysis of the discussion of the quantity theory in Scandinavian literature will be limited, almost exclusively, to this century. There is no work previous to the turn of the century, except for Wicksell's *Interest and Prices* (first published in 1898), that is of any particular interest here. On the whole, the early economic literature is rather insignificant and mostly eclectical. There can be no comparison with the extensive writings on the continent or in Great Britain. Although the substantial contributions to economic theory were made rather late, they have had a strong influence on the present development.

1. Knut Wicksell has provoked more discussion as to whether he was an opponent or adherent of the quantity theory than perhaps any other economist.[1] It is easy to understand, from the fact that there never was any common and unified definition of the content of the theory, that there must have been many different answers to the question. The discussion of *Interest and Prices* from this viewpoint is a striking example of how the essence of a very important book is lost in a discussion of a subsidiary question.

In his first work on the relationship between changes in the rate of interest and in prices, Wicksell thinks of the quantity theory as a theory according to which (average) prices are (indirectly) regulated by the relation between the total amount of goods exchanged and the total volume of money in circulation. But he does not stress this *regulation* of prices as the essence of the theory. Instead he maintains that it »marks a decided theoretical advance, by bringing into prominence

[1] Marget mentions that he has amused himself by »collecting a very extensive list of instances in which the '*Interest and Prices*' of Wicksell was discussed primarily, if not solely, from the standpoint of the 'quantity theory' or 'anti-quantity theory' reasoning which its argument was supposed to embody» (*op. cit.*, vol. I, p. 24).

the purely formal or conventional character of the value of money — or rather, of the function of money — in antithesis to the 'mercantilist' conception.... of money as possessing a more or less unchangeable value of an intrinsic kind, which in the course of exchange is merely compared with the value of other commodities».[2]

This is nothing but a clear restatement of Locke's fundamental idea, which provides the basis for the formulation of the quantity theory. Wicksell makes the very significant distinction that it is not the *value* of money but the *function* of money that is of consequence. Since the sole function of money is to circulate goods and services, then the conclusion is that changes in monetary purchases, if the volume of transactions is constant, must cause proportionate price changes; *i.e.*, since the function of money as solely a medium of exchange (within relatively short periods) is the only function considered, the velocity of money will not be influenced. *This is the conclusion that follows from the original quantity theory.* It has never been brought out more clearly than by Wicksell in the following statement: »...the whole dispute on the conclusions of the quantity theory turns ultimately on this last point: whether the velocity of circulation of money is of autonomous or merely subordinate significance for the currency system.»[3]

In criticising the quantity theory, Wicksell accentuates that its limitation is due tc its assumptions, which hardly have any consistency with facts. These assumptions are said to be: 1) everybody is holding cash balances; 2) the velocity of money is constant; 3) an almost fixed proportion of all business is performed by means of money; and 4) the supply of precious metal used as a medium of exchange can be clearly differentiated from the part employed for other purposes. Only when these given conditions are present is the quantity theory valid.[4]

It is rather clear that these assumptions are not quite consistent with Wicksell's statement about the real issue in this controversy. But it must then be added that the criticised assumptions appear in a more rigid form in *Interest and Prices* than in the later *Lectures on Political Economy*, in which the real issue is best stated. Furthermore, and this is very important to notice, when Wicksell speaks of the velocity of money he generally, and particularly in the second assumption above,

---

[2] *Interest and Prices,* p. 38; also see *Lectures,* vol. II, p. 144, and »Mål och medel i nationalekonomien», *E. T.*, 1904, p. 466.

[3] *Lectures,* vol. II, p. 143—144.

[4] *Interest and Prices,* pp. 41—42.

includes both 'real' velocity of money (V) and 'virtual' velocity of money (most nearly corresponding to Fisher's $\frac{M'V'}{M}$). In the Wicksellian sense, therefore, the velocity of money will not remain constant when the quantity of money, *i.e.*, coin and bank notes, increases or decreases. Consequently, he refuted the proposition that variations in the quantity of money would cause proportionate price changes. »Notes *i.e.*, bank notes, provide in themselves the basis for a more or less elastic system of credit, and they circulate with a velocity which is more or less variable. It is for this reason that it was never possible for even the older supporters of the Quantity Theory to provide a satisfactory demonstration of the exact relationship which they held to exist between the price level and the quantity of notes (and coin).»[5]

In spite of these clear statements of the fundamental idea of the quantity theory, Wicksell also formulated the theory in a way which has not contributed to a clarification of this controversy: »The special peculiarity of the Quantity Theory consists in the proportionality required between the quantity of money and commodity prices.»[6] This is considered to be tantamount to saying that the elasticity of demand for money is equal to unity, which Wicksell illustrates by drawing a 'demand' curve for money, distinguished from other demand curves by being a rectangular hyperbola asymptotic to the two axis.[7] The quantity theory then appears as a special case of the general law of demand and supply. But it is quite obvious, and Wicksell would probably be the first to recognize it, that the proportionality between changes in the quantity of money and prices is a subsidiary question. The fundamental idea is that the velocity of money will not be affected. Only in the case of a constant volume of transactions would the quantity theorist affirm that prices will vary in exact proportion. Thus this possibility actually appears as a *special* case of the quantity theory. The formulation that the elasticity of the 'demand' for money is equal to unity might perhaps be viewed as another formulation of the thesis of a constant velocity of money.

---

[5] *Ibid.*, pp. 69—70.

[6] *Lectures,* vol. II, p. 141.

[7] *Cf.* Pigou's discussion, p. 104. This 'demand' curve will be discussed in chapter X, pp. 170—173.

Wicksell's treatment is very similar to the one by Taussig, who also spoke of the elasticity of demand for money as distinguished from other elasticities of demand (see p. 80). Say, on the other hand, thought that *all* elasticitities of demand were equal to unity, and therefore also that of money (see p. 50)!

It has been alleged that Wicksell aimed at the rehabilitation of the quantity theory by proving that a change in the amount of circulation will cause a corresponding change in the price level.[8] Ohlin mentions in his introduction to the English edition of Wicksell's *Interest and Prices* that Wicksell always insisted that his explanation of the price variations »did not mean more than an amplification of the old quantity theory».[9] None of these views, however, seems to be accurate, at least not in the light of that interpretation of the content of the quantity theory that Wicksell really fostered. Certainly, Wicksell never aimed at the rehabilitation of the quantity theory. His purpose was to achieve a satisfactory theory of the variations in the purchasing power of money. The well-known explanation, that they were caused by a difference between the so-called natural rate of interest and the bank or money rate, is not necessarily bound up with changes in the total amount of money. On the contrary, he emphasized that a difference in these rates of interest will primarily cause a change in the amount of credit, *i.e.*, of circulating bank deposits, while the quantity of money, *i.e.*, coins and banknotes, might just as well remain constant. The result will be an increase in the total money purchasing power (by means of an increase in the virtual velocity of money), which will raise the price level since no immediate increase in the total supply of goods is likely to be forthcoming.

To speak of an amplification is somewhat better, but it still is not quite accurate, partly because Wicksell dit not build his explanation upon the quantity theory, and partly because the latter theory is *no explanation* of the variations in the price level. The relation between the two theories consists in the acceptance of the fundamental idea that variations in the value of money are determined by changes in the relation of the total quantity of money to the total amount of transactions. There is no foundation for the intimation that Wicksell denied the influence of changes in the supply of commodities on the price level because this would be contrary to the

---

[8] See, for example, J. Pedersen: *Pengeteori og Pengepolitik,* København, 1944, p. 284. See also his article »Wicksells Theorie des Zusammenhangś zwichen Zinssatz und Geldwertschwankungen», *A. f. S.*, 1933, pp. 129—150, in which Wicksell's cumulative processes are closely analyzed. All those who share Pedersen's view constitute probably the main group of the great number of names, connected with this controversy, that Marget allegedly has succeeded in collecting (see note 1, p. 133).

[9] P. viii. Ohlin refers, as evidence, to Wicksell's preface to the German edition of his *Vorlesungen*, II: *Geld und Kredit*, 1922.

quantity theory.[10] The absurdity of such an idea was forcefully stressed by Wicksell himself: »In the foregoing I have merely wished to point out the folly of supposing that circumstances in which, as in the case of concrete commodity prices, there is an essential relation between two things — goods and money — can ever be satisfactorily explained from the point of view of the changes undergone by only one of them.»[11] Furthermore, he emphasized that it was fully consistent with the quantity theory that increased production, if it were not counteracted by an increased velocity of money, tends to lower prices; indeed, it is very likely, since the velocity of money can increase up to a certain limit only.[12]

This last remark is not identical with the basic idea of the quantity theory, for Wicksell builds his structure on the concept of a virtual velocity of money. Actually, his main viewpoint is opposed to the essence of the quantity theory, as he maintained that »not only does an addition to the amount of material money act as a *cause* of easier credit but an increase (actual or virtual) in the velocity of circulation comes about as an *effect*».[13] It is to the upper limit of this possible increase in the velocity of money Wicksell refers in the preceding statement. If this limit were reached, he evidently would agree with the essence of the quantity theory, which thus would have relevance in the Wicksellian theory as a *special* case. This again indicates that these two theories must be founded on the same basic idea, which is also clearly pointed out by Wicksell in the preface to his *Interest and Prices.* There he states that his approach is an attempt »to follow up the logical consequences of the fundamental conception which had given rise to the Quantity Theory»;[14] and this fundamental idea is the same idea which forms the foundation of the equation of exchange. The quantity theory implies that the effect of an increase in the quantity of money, if the amount of transactions remain the same, must be a corresponding price increase, *because* the velocity of money will *not* be affected; whereas Wicksell maintained a price increase, because both the

[10] See J. Pedersen, *loc. cit.*; also see p. 283, in which Pedersen suggests that Wicksell tried to restate the quantity theory in terms of the income theory approach. Such an interpretation seems to be based upon a misunderstanding of the essence of the quantity theory. *Cf.* A. Hansen's remark: »The quantity theory concerned itself with prices, not with incomes» (*op. cit.*, p. 83).

[11] *Lectures*, vol. II, p. 159.

[12] *Ibid.*, p. 155.

[13] *Interest and Prices,* p .XXIV.

[14] See pp. XXIII—XXIV.

velocity of money and the quantity of money were changed. From this point of view one might, perhaps, speak of an amplification of the quantity theory. Wicksell, accordingly, would argue that the price increase will be greater than what a 'quantity theorist' would admit.

The following statement is, therefore, in complete accordance with what has been said: »The Quantity Theory is correct in so far as it is true that an increase or relative diminution in the stock of money must always *tend* to raise or lower prices — by its opposite effect in the first place on rates of interest.»[15] It cannot be emphasized enough that this statement does not imply that the quantity theory *is* correct. Its basic idea, that the velocity of money is of autonomous significance, may be entirely wrong — and Wicksell definitely refused it, at least as long as *short*-run effects were considered; but the conclusion that changes in the quantity of money, if not opposed by other simultaneous changes, will cause corresponding price changes, cannot be denied, if proper assumptions are made.

The last quotation is of great importance, because it displays another fundamental difference between the two theories, namely in respect to the question of causation. The quantity theory has always been criticised from this viewpoint, and so also by Wicksell. These critics have then forgotten that the question of causation is only of subsidiary relevance to the essence of the quantity theory. From its point of view, it is of no consequence *how* prices are raised or lowered as an effect of changes in the quantity of money, since the issue is the relation between these (latter) changes and the velocity of money. The adherents of the quantity theory have therefore remained satisfied by pointing to the equation of exchange (either in words or algebraically), or some similar equation, as adequate evidence of the correctness of their *causal* proposition, thereby exposing themselves to the confusion of causal and arithmetic relations.

2. In a study of the relation between fluctuations in the gold production and the price level during the period 1850—1910, Cassel came to the conclusion that »*the chief causes of the secular variations of the general price level are to be found in changes in the relative gold stock,* and that the quantity theory is correct in so far as the general price-level, although influenced in addition by other factors, is *directly*

---

[15] *Ibid.*, p. XXVIII.

proportional to the relative gold stock».[16] This idea was first presented in an article in 1904,[17] but Cassel made no reservations — in spite of all criticism — in the last revised edition of *The Theory of Social Economy*.[18]

Cassel proceeds from Sauerbeck's index figures for international wholesale prices, according to which the 'general' price level in 1850 and 1910 coincided. Therefore, he characterizes the total amount of gold in these two years as 'normal'. In 1850 the world's total stock of gold is estimated, in conformity with Lexis' calculations, to be 10 billion reichsmarks, and in 1910 to be 52 billion reichmarks. Consequently, the stock of gold has multiplied 5.2 times, corresponding to an average increase per year of $\sqrt[60]{5.2} = 1.0279$, *i.e.*, 2.79 per cent. The concept of a *normal* increase in the gold stock is now introduced. It refers to such a »uniform increase in the gold stock which, after the elapse of a certain period, leaves the price-level unaltered».[19] The stock of gold, referring to any such period, is called the *normal* gold stock. Thus the level of prices was the same in 1850 and 1910, in spite of the increase in the international gold stock by 42 billion reichsmarks during that period. Price variations, therefore, caused by changes in the stock of gold, must have been due to deviations in the actual gold stock from the 'normal' gold stock, because a yearly increase of 2.8 per cent was necessary to keep the price level stable in the continual economic expansion of the world. If the actual stock of gold is computed in percentage of the 'normal' stock, a direct comparison of this quota, called the 'relative goldstock', can be made with the price level, recalculated with 1850 as the basic year. The comparison gives a very good correspondence — if yearly price fluctuations are disregarded — well justifying, according to Cassel, the conclusion of a causal relationship.

The simplest and most direct objection — an objection which was made by Professor F. Brock (Uppsala) immediately after Cassel first published his investigation [20] — is, of course, that Cassel completely neglects the importance of silver as a means of exchange! This is surprising since silver played a much more important role as a medium of exchange than gold during the greater part of the period

[16] *The Theory of Social Economy,* transl. by S. L. Barron, 2 vols., London, 1932, vol. I, p. 472.

[17] »Om förändringar i den allmänna prisnivån», *E. T.*, 1904, pp. 311—331.

[18] See, especially, *Teoretisk socialekonomi*, 2 ed., Stockholm, 1938, p. 442 ff.

[19] *The Theory of Social Economy,* vol. I, p. 470.

[20] See Wicksell: *Lectures,* vol. II, p. 145.

investigated. As far as we know, Cassel never replied in writing to this serious criticism, only to J. T. Phinney's criticism in the early thirties. Phinney pointed out that Cassel's investigation rests on three assumptions: 1) the possibility of selecting two years, separated by a certain minimum period of time, at which the price level is the same, 2) the possibility of determining what the 'normal' quantities of gold were for the years selected, and 3) a demand for gold increasing at a constant rate during the whole period.[21] Phinney criticised sharply all three assumptions, especially the third, which he divided into three sub-assumptions; namely, that the rate of growth of trade has remained the same, that the standard policy has not undergone any violent changes, and that the rate of increase of the gold supply and of the means of exchange has varied in the same way.[22] Of Phinney's main objections the last two are obviously the most serious ones.

Let us momentarily disregard the most fundamental criticism that has been raised, that the amount of silver used as a medium of exchange has been neglected, and turn to Cassel's conclusion that the quantity of gold in 1850 and in 1910 can be characterized as normal, *because* the price level is the same at the two instances. It goes without saying that the position of the price level in these cases might just as well have been occasioned by other factors, represented, for example, by Fisher's symbols V, V', M' and T.[23] Cassel, who repeatedly stresses that one

[21] »Gold Production and the Price Level: The Cassel Three Per Cent Estimate», *Q. J. E.*, 1933, p. 649.

[22] *Ibid.*, p. 678.

[23] F. von Hayek points out that Cassel's and Fisher's opinion of *general* price changes as being caused by variations in the amount of money is based upon an argument that goes in a circle. They *presume* that the quantity of money should adapt itself to changes in the volume of transactions, so that the price level would remain constant. If it does not, but remains the same, then the quantity of money becomes, in a very peculiar way, the *cause* of the variations in the price level (*Geldtheorie und Konjunkturtheorie,* p. 154).

A. Amonn expresses about the same opinion, but phrases it a little differently. He asserts that Cassel's explanation of the secular changes in the general price level by variations in monetary factors rather presupposes the correctness of the quantity theory than proves it (»Cassels System der theoretischen Nationalökonomie», *A. f. S.*, 1924, p. 327).

Cassel's main argument has recently been scrutinized by L. Dupriez, who restates most of the early criticism, and adds the influence of political action, social pressures and public opinion on the development of the price level (»Central Banking Policy and Long Trends in Prices», in *Money, Trade, and Economic Growth.* In Honor of J. H. Williams, New York, 1951, pp. 243—252). A more detailed analysis is given in his *Des mouvements économiques généraux,* Louvain, 1947, chs. XV—XVI).

has to select *objective* factors which can be regarded as primary causes, actually bases the investigation on his own, rather subjective, opinion that the gold stock of two different years can be characterized as normal when prices stand at the same level. If the criteria is accepted, it follows that of any two, or more, years selected, which have the same price level (in the period 1800—1910), it can be said that their stocks of gold are normal. The presumption is only that the years chosen are not so closely related, so that the figures of their price levels cannot be considered as independent of each other; that is, there shall be no direct relation between their different price levels. Let us apply, therefore, Cassel's method to some other years and look at the result.

The index figure of the year 1829 is 132 and of 1868 also 132. The relative gold stock of these two years should then be the same, provided that the price level is not rapidly increasing or decreasing concurrently. The average price level during the period 1828—32 and 1867—71 is respectively 134 and 131 and there are no rapid changes in the price level in either period.[24] Thus the years selected well meet the requirements. In 1829 and in 1868 the gold stock was respectively 8242 and 19829 billion reichsmarks.[25] The actual stock of gold in 1829 then, has multiplied 2.4 times. But $\sqrt[39]{2.4} = 1.023$. The figure should, of course, have coincided with Cassel's, if his method had been objectively correct. The time period of 39 years is of sufficient length for such a computation. Cassel's figures for the relative stock of gold in 1830 and 1870 should have been about the same, since the price levels only differ by 7 units (respectively 128 and 135) and the price development is relatively stable in the preceding and succeeding years, but they are respectively 1.17 and 1.43. It is quite clear that Cassel's method is entirely arbitrary.[26]

[24] The figures of the price level in 1828, '29, '30, '31, and '32 are respectively 135, 132, 135, 137 and 130, which gives the average 134; in 1867, '68, '69, '70, and '71 they are respectively 133, 132, 131, 128 and 133, which averages 131. In 1833 the figure is 125, which gives an average of 132 for the period 1829—33. The difference between the average price level in these two periods has no importance. The figures used are taken from the Swedish edition (1938) of *The Theory of Social Economy.*

Cassel demonstrates in his reply to Phinney that a miscalculation of 6 units in one of the price levels he has compared merely means that the error in the computation of the normal factor of growth will be $\sqrt[60]{1.06} = 1.001$.

[25] The figures have been obtained from Cassel's by interpolation.

[26] B. Nogaro criticises Cassel for his assumption that only variations in the quantity of money in respect to the number of transactions can influence prices. He also

Even if Cassel had taken into consideration the amount of silver used as a means of payment, the objection still remains that the greatest part of the transactions was performed by other means of payment. Why study only one of them, gold, in an examination of its relation to the price level, and from this compute a factor of growth in the stock of gold necessary in order to maintain a stabilized *general* price level? Why assume a constant relation between the stock of gold and the other media of exchange? Cassel maintains that even if the total amount of the means of payment is taken into consideration, changes in the stock of gold will affect the price level, since there is a certain relation between the bills and the gold reserve of a bank. But why should its effect be just proportionate? Cassel's conclusion that 'the chief causes of the secular variations of the general price level are to be found in changes in the relative gold stock', is based upon a study of the *arithmetic* relation between prices and the stock of gold, not upon an investigation of the causal relationships involved. Actually, he can never prove any causal relationship merely by a comparative study of purely arithmetic relations between the quantity of gold and the price level at different times. In fact, if he proves a proportionate relation in every year, all causation is excluded. The proposition, maintained by the so-called quantity theorists, that changes in the relative gold-stock will cause (proportionate) price changes, still remains to be proved. It seems very strange indeed, that although recognizing the influence of other factors in the price level, Cassel compares the *total* variations in the price level with changes in the relative gold stock only. This criticism is no denial of a relation between fluctuations in the supply of gold and the price level, only of the way of its demonstration and the conclusions.

Cassel repeats his inadmissable conclusion, based on a purely *proportionate* relation, of a *causal* relationship between changes in the quantity of money and in the price level, in the discussion of these relationships under a paper currency. Thus he states that if an increase in the general price level of 50 per cent can be proved *simultaneously*

points out, as has been demonstrated above, that it is sufficient to select another period in order to find an entirely different factor of growth (*La Monnaie et les Phénomènes monétaires contemporains*, Paris, 1935, pp. 278—293). See also J. Lescure (»Prix, Monnaie et Credit», in *Economic Essays in Honour of G. Cassel*, London, 1933), who mentions that although economic progress requires an increase in the quantity of money, this increase is independent of the increase in the stock of gold (p. 395), and K. Shibata: »An Examination of Professor Cassel's Quantity Theory of Money», *Kyoto University Economic Review*, 1932, pp. 52—84.

with an increase in the relative amount of circulation of 50 per cent, then it can be maintained, provided the habits of payments and the amount of trade are constant, that the *cause* of the price increase is exclusively due to the augmentation of the circulation.[27] Fundamentally, this is the same logical mistake that Hume made, confusing simple arithmetic relations with causal relationships, although it is illustrated somewhat differently.

Generally, Cassel has been considered as a rather pronunced quantity theorist, implying that he explained changes in the price level as caused primarily by changes in the amount of circulation.[28] He flatly denied, however, that he had proceeded from any form of the quantity theory in his discussion of the currency problems during the first world war. On the contrary, he did not regard the increased circulation in itself as the cause of a corresponding, proportional increase of the price level. The real cause was the artificially created addition of new purchasing power, whereas the quantity of money that remains in circulation is determined by the price increase.[29] It is evident, though, that Cassel is far from consistent in his statements. Apparently, he meant to distinguish between an increase as such of gold and of paper money, and the causal relation in respect to price fluctuations. In asserting, in one instance at least, that the amount of paper money added to a given circulation was the effect of the price increase, he even agreed with Tooke's fundamental view. Yet these two men represented two different opinions of the causal relationship between money and price variations.

Cassel evaluated the quantity theory according to its ability to *explain* actual variations in the price level. Hence he considered its assumptions of other things being equal as 'absolutely inadmissable',[30] because changes in the amount of circulation may influence other factors

---

[27] *Dyrtid och sedelöverflöd,* Stockholm, 1917, p. 21.

[28] A. Östlind, who has studied Cassel's monetary discussions and recommendations very closely, characterizes Cassel as being more influenced by the quantity theory than any other contemporary Swedish economist. Östlind himself, however, does not clearly distinguish between the quantity theory and the equation of exchange. He speaks of 'imputing great importance to the equation of exchange at the explanation of the price development' (referring to Cassel) as synonymous with accepting the quantity theory (*Svensk samhällsekonomi 1914—1922,* Stockholm, 1945, pp. 71—72 and 77). The equation of exchange is obviously 'neutral' to any *explanation* of the price development.

[29] See »Riksbanken och dyrtiden», *E. T.*, 1917, p. 291. *Cf. Dyrtid och sedelöverflöd,* p. 20. This explanation was very much the same as Wicksell's.

[30] *The Theory of Social Economy,* vol. II, p. 459.

than the price level. Curiously enough, he himself did not include this possibility in his great examination of the relationship between gold and price variations.

3. In modern Swedish, as in international monetary theory, it is often stated that the quantity theory no longer has any place in the analysis of the fluctuations in the price level. Modern theorists consider the quantity of money to be of little importance. The main interest has been directed to a study of the streams of consumption and investment expenditures, the variations of which have a direct influence on the purchasing power of money. Fisher's equation has gradually lost its significance as a starting point for an analysis of these changes, and other, presumably more suitable, equations for a direct study of the influence of income variations, have been enunciated.

Erik Lindahl interprets the quantity theory as an explanation of changes in the price level, and renounces the theory since these changes cannot be satisfactorily explained by referring to simultaneous changes in the quantity of money. He accentuates that a general theory of the variations in the price level has to follow other tracks — appropriately with modern monetary policy as a starting point — than those showing the development of the quantity theory,[31] and formulates the following equation, which resembles Schumpeter's: $E(1-s) = PQ$. E stands for the total nominal income, s for the fraction of it being saved, P for the price level of consumption goods and services, and Q for the quantity of these items during a given period of time.[32] The validity of the equation requires a closed economy, a free currency, no cash holdings and only one bank, the central bank. The typical feature of this formula is the absence of a term for the quantity of money. It is an indirect illustration of the shift in emphasis to those factors which are of importance in a realistic analysis of the fluctuations in the purchasing power of money. Furthermore, it recognizes the desirability of defining the price level not as representing a rather meaningless average figure, but as a figure that indicates the purchasing power of money in the hands of the consumer.

Bertil Ohlin accentuates very strongly that variations in the amount of money in circulation and of check balances are of secondary importance in respect to demand and supply, which are the primary factors in the pricing process. The quantity of money has significance

[31] »Om förhållandet mellan penningmängd och prisnivå», *op. cit.*, p. 18.

[32] *Studies in the Theory of Money and Capital,* London, 1939, p. 142.

only in so far as changes in its quantity influence the liquidity and the policy of the private banks, or lead to special monetary actions by the central bank.[33]

In an article on the Stockholm School and its relation to the quantity theory, Ohlin tries to demonstrate how the realistic sequence analysis, used by the Stockholm School, of the causal relations, leads to the rejection of the quantity theory. Variations in the amount of the means of exchange are only one of several factors that influence the liquidity of the banks, of the entrepreneurs, and of the individuals and thereby, under certain circumstances, the demand for goods and the development of prices.[34] Ohlin's interpretation, however, of the quantity theory is formulated in a very specific way, which gives it a somewhat different content from the so-called general opinion. Thus he writes that it »cannot be said that the obstacle to price increases is the creation by the central bank of a scarcity of the medium of exchange, an idea which seems to be the very essence of the quantity theory».[35] This is, rather, a description of the fundamental idea of the Currency School (see p. 62). The common interpretation of the quantity theory, including the propositions of causality and proportionality, does not imply that all price increases are made possible only by an increased amount of money. Hence it is not in the power of the central bank to check all price increases; and the power to diminish the amount of circulation is very limited. Furthermore, the assumption of other things being equal is far from applicable, and thus the strict relation between money and prices is excluded. Finally, it does not follow from the proposition of an increased quantity of money leading to price increases, that a scarcity of money will impede price increases, whatever their causes may be. Then other causal relationships have to be presumed which are not involved in the proposition commonly considered to be the essence of the quantity theory.

In conformity with his interpretation, Ohlin characterizes the opinion of economists, influenced by the quantity theory, in the following way: »Variations in the quantity of money are considered as the most important causal factor in a process of increasing prices, and behind these variations lies the credit policy.»[36] The quantity theory has then become a theory that provides an *exclusive* explanation of the most important

---

[33] *Bidrag till expansionens teori* (Statens offentliga utredningar, 1934: 12), Stockholm, 1934, p. 47.

[34] »Stockholmsskolan kontra kvantitetsteorin», *E. T.*, 1943, pp. 39 and 43.

[35] *Ibid.*, p. 46.

[36] *Ibid.*, p. 27.

cause of actual fluctuations in the price level. The explanation of the fundamental cause of the variations in the circulation is also covered by this broad generalization of the theory. It is questionable, however, if this characterization is accurate. On the whole, changes in the quantity of money are considered a passive factor when the original cause is ascribed to the credit policy; then there is no direct causal relation maintained between money and price variations. The causation is rather the reverse. It seems very difficult to find any economists who would embrace both opinions simultaneously. Both Cassel and Wicksell, for example, who made the banking policy responsible for the development of the price level, regarded variations in the circulation as the effect of price fluctuations, primarily caused by a restrictive or non-restrictive credit policy.

Ohlin explains, by employing the symbols and relations of the equation of exchange, that there are still economists who accept the ideas of the quantity theory. Referring to the fact that every price increase, which involves an increase in the product PT, also necessitates an increase in M, since the velocity of money can be regarded as fairly constant, he infers that this might be the reason that the fundamental cause — changes in the credit policy — is overlooked. Actually Ohlin himself embraces here the essence of the quantity theory — although not according to his interpretation — by affirming that »the velocity of money can be regarded as fairly constant». If the price increase or the increase in the quantity of money is the original cause, it has no direct relevance. For the basic idea of the quantity theory — that changes in the quantity of money will not influence the velocity of money — does not say anything exclusive about the causal relation money-prices. The most often drawn conclusion from this basic idea by *assuming* a change in the quantity of money, does not deny the possibility of price increases as the original cause. But since the quantity theory is a theory based upon a specific peculiarity of money, it is quite natural that the conclusions drawn primarily concern the *effects* of changes in the quantity of money, treated as original causes.

4. One of the prominent Danish economists, Jörgen Pedersen, expounds the quantity theory as a proposition of proportionality, *ceteris paribus*, between variations in the quantity of money and prices, in which the price level is the dependent and the amount of money the independent variable.[37] In algebraic terms the idea corresponds

[37] *Op. cit.*, p. 131.

to the formula $P \cdot k = f(M)$ in which k is a constant, symbolizing all those other factors which have to remain unchanged. Accordingly, whenever it is established that the amount of money in circulation and prices have changed, but other factors have remained the same, the additional or diminished quantity of money is the cause, and the price variation is the effect. This idea of the absolute passiveness of the price level does not belong, as been pointed out earlier, to the quantity theory, not even to its commonly accepted formulation.

Theoretically viewed, Pedersen considers the quantity theory self-evident. He must then refer to the arithmetic relation only, excluding all causation and the idea of the passive price level. It is very doubtful, however, if this is his intention. Rather, he seems to be the object of the common confusion of arithmetic relations with causations. He rejects the quantity theory primarily because price changes never are uniform and never occur instantaneously, which is necessary if the relations of exchange are to remain the same. Its proposition is deemed practically irrelevant, since the important question is: What actual changes will follow from variations in the amount of money? It would be better still, we think, to say that the important thing is to investigate the role that the quantity of money and its variations play in the economic relations, without postulating anything about cause or effect.

If the quantity theory, in its commonly accepted version, is going to have any practical bearing, then, proposes Pedersen, it should be formulated in the following way: »The price level — although not from day to day, but in a little longer run — varies in proportion to the quantity of money.»[38] This is similar to Fisher's thesis with the emphasis on both proportionality and causality.

The attempts being made to 'save' the quantity theory by introducing the concept of hoarding — meaning that part of the individual's cash holdings which is not used, nor deposited in any bank — are also criticised, partly because of the difficulty in determining the amount of money being hoarded, and partly because the size of this inactive amount of money is determined by the total quantity of money.[39] These objections, though, do not invalidate the proposition that an increase in the total quantity of money will cause proportionate price changes to the same extent as it also leads to an increase of the circulation, thereby allowing for an increased 'hoarding'.

---

[38] *Ibid.*, p. 133.

[39] *Ibid.*, p. 138.

To replace the quantity theory, Pedersen propounds an income theory, based upon an equation identical with Schumpeter's:

$$I = (p_1 q_1 + p_2 q_2 + \dots . p_n q_n) + (p'_1 q'_1 + p'_2 q'_2 + \dots . p'_n q'_n) = P'Q',$$

in which $\Sigma\, p\, q$ equalizes the value of all consumption goods marketed, $\Sigma\, p'q'$ the value of the increase in capital equipment, and I the total income during the period chosen. If a proportionate relation between I and P' could be proved, the enunciator presumes, then one might say that »the quantity theory is valid when the quantity of money is defined as the total income».[40] This means that the essence of the quantity theory is completely lost, and is substituted by a truism — built directly upon the general law of demand and supply — which has no direct bearing on a monetary economy.

Erling Petersen, a Norwegian economist, has made an effort described as »an attempt to combine the theoretical advantages of the income theories of money with the empirical advantages of the equation of exchange approach».[41] He rejects the rigid form of the quantity theory, mainly because of the required passiveness of prices — considered to be »the corner stone of *the* quantity theory»[42] — and the non-correspondence between variations in M and P, demonstrated many times by statical investigations. This non-correspondence is due to what is called the reflection-phenomenon, which renders any proportionality between changes in money and prices impossible, because their variations must cause variations in the velocity of money, V, and in the amount of transactions, T. Hence, it is inadmissable to assume other things being equal if it is not proved that there can be independent changes in M and P.

Introducing the so-called elasticity-principle, Petersen undertakes to provide a more realistic account of the causal relations involved. Every change in one of the factors in the Fisherine equation must be matched by a change in one or several of the others. The magnitude of these induced changes depends upon the elasticity coefficients of the different factors in respect to the active factor. The rapidity by which a factor will change is divided into an active and a passive element. The last-mentioned is a function of the velocity of change ('acceleration')

---

40 *Ibid.*, p. 140.

41 *Macro-Dynamic Aspects of the Equation of Exchange,* pp. 107—108.

42 *Ibid.*, p. 108.

of the factors, multiplied by the respective coefficients of elasticity.[43] The main purpose of this approach, emphasizing the value of the different coefficients of elasticity, is to bring out the extent to which every factor dealt with in the general monetary analysis varies with every other factor involved.[44]

Instead of the equation of exchange as an analytical means, Petersen proposes a rather complicated formula, called »the double equation of the industrial circulation», which focusses attention on the importance of the rates of change in incomes and cash holdings for the fluctuations in the value of money.[45] As it presupposes a closed economy, and excludes financial transactions and government activity, it cannot be satisfactorily used for an analysis of the different forces acting upon the price level during a business cycle without further extension. There are no theoretical obstacles to this, though the equation then becomes still more complicated.

By applying the principle of elasticity to the factors in the double equation of the industrial circulation, the formula might be used as a basis for a dynamic, monetary theory. A computation, however, of the elasticity-coefficients of the different factors involved appears to be extremely difficult to perform. Will it be possible to compute some figures of any relevance for the problems encountered? Of what practical use will they be for predictions of the reactions and the magnitudes of the factors involved? Petersen is well aware of the practical difficulties that will be concomitant with statistical investigations of these coefficients. His purpose has been rather to suggest a theoretical principle than a program of research, thereby illustrating the great number of variables which has to be taken into consideration.

---

43 *Ibid.*, p. 20 ff; also see *Den moderne kvantitetsteoris gyldighet for pengeverdiens bestemmelse*, Oslo, 1933, pp. 62—63.

44 »Fra kvantitetsteori til elasticitetsteori», *E. T.*, 1944, p. 130.

45 *Macro-Dynamic Aspects*, pp. 33 ff. and 95 ff.

CHAPTER IX

SUMMARY

The self-evidency of the law of demand and supply must have been realized as soon as barter began to take place, and its applicability to all kinds of commodities must also have been readily understood. In this early traffic, gold and silver had no special position, but constituted commodities fully comparable to others. Hence the law of demand and supply also applied to them.[1] But as their durability, divisibility, and scarcity distinguished them from other commodities, their fitness as a common medium of exchange was realized. Gradually, they began to hold a more specific position in respect to other commodities as they became the commonly accepted means of exchange; and so the idea developed that their value was something intrinsic and given, not subject to any changes. Variations in the relations of exchange, *i.e.*, in prices, were ascribed to the conditions on the commodity side, while the value of money was thought to be constant. This development of thought refers primarily to that of European monetary theory. It is very interesting, indeed, that in the old Chinese writings on economics, the value of money was not considered constant. On the contrary, the possibility, and sometimes the desirability, of influencing its value was stressed both by Confucius and his disciples. There are several explanations for this notable circumstance. First, gold and silver played a very small role as common means of exchange. Other metals were used, mainly copper, whose functions as commodities were more clearly realized; accordingly, fluctuations in their value were easily conceivable. Secondly, the frequent counterfeiting — one of the great problems of the government — also counter-influenced any idea of a constant value in the means of exchange. Finally, the early Chinese economists' way of comparing the total amount of commodities with the quantity of money, made them presume

[1] In cases where the exchange relation of money to goods was fixed by law (or by other regulations), demand and supply could have no direct influence on the media of exchange. As W. Carlile suggests, this might have been the case in many old economies (*Monetary Economics*, London, 1912, p. 144).

the possibility of influencing the exchange-relations by variations in both the magnitudes. This approach also deterred them from maintaining any exclusive causal relationship between changes in the quantity of money and prices. They declared that fluctuations in prices depended upon variations either in the amount of circulation or in the amount of commodities. It is very significant that in Confucius' principles of money, the medium of exchange is said to be a commodity which did not possess any specific property in respect to value, distinguishing it from other commodities. Naturally enough, there was no attempt to formulate the quantity theory.

Xenophon is a representative of the idea that the value of money is fixed, not because of any intrinsic and constant value, but because the demand for money is unlimited. Consequently, an increase in the amount of money would not influence its value, even if other things remained the same. He particularly stressed the different position of money, especially of silver, in regard to other commodities, for example gold, to which the law of demand and supply applied without exception. This very idea of placing the medium of exchange in a special position with regard to its value, fostered the opinion that money had an intrinsic and constant value, and that price-variations were to be explained exclusively from conditions on the commodity side. Though this idea gradually gained ground, especially in economies where prices were rather stable over long periods, it was not entirely dominant.

During the Roman era, it was thought that the value of money was influenced by changes in its quantity. This is easily accounted for as the idea was promoted by the results of the significant variations in the amount of circulation that took place, particularly during Paulus Æmelius' reign. The writings of Julius Paulus, the Roman lawyer, do not touch upon the problem of the variations in the value of money. He was essentially concerned with the legal position of money. There is no ground whatsoever for the common belief that he founded the quantity theory. His writings have apparently been confused (and also misinterpreted) with the fact that some Romans realized a connection between variations in the quantity of money and its value. Although there is no evidence of any such observations in the writings of the Canonists, some of the Scholastics, for example Henry of Ghent and Antonine von Florence, pointed out the influence of the 'supply' of money on its value. But these statements are exceptions. On the whole, the idea that the value of money held a special position prevailed up to the beginning of the sixteenth century. Although this was primarily due to the circumstance that prices generally were rather stable, it was commonly ascribed to something specifically inherent in the medium of exchange.

The most explicit statement of the relation between the quantity of money and its value before Bodin's famous observation, was made by Copernicus. He even went so far as to assert that the value of money depended entirely upon the limitation of its quantity, in spite of the monetary metal being silver. In the contemporary Saxon controversy of the monetary reforms, the same causal relation was recognized, but was not thought peculiar. When Bodin, therefore, pointed out that the most important cause of the great price increase in the middle of the sixteenth century was the considerable influx of precious metals from America, he was far from the first to recognize this causal relation. But he was the first to employ it in the explanation of this extraordinary price increase which puzzled his contemporaries.[2] Almost all explanations prior to Bodin's observation tried to trace the causes to the conditions on the commodity side, fundamentally because of the great influence of the idea of a constant monetary value. Malestroit, however, also expounded the causes in reference to circumstances on the monetary side. But there was a significant difference betwen his and Bodin's explanation. Malestroit did not admit that the value of money had been influenced by the great influx of precious metals. He manifested a pronounced aversion to explaining the fluctuations in the value of money in terms of demand and supply. Instead, he explained the basic cause to be the depreciation of the monetary unit. The idea of an intrinsic and constant value of money could then still be maintained, since only the amount of the precious metal contained in the medium of exchange had been purposely diminished and caused a corresponding price increase.

Malestroit's explanation was doomed to fail in the light of the overwhelming evidence that supported Bodin's view, which, although not immediately, but gradually and finally, became commonly accepted. This obvious reluctance to approve of Bodin's explanation was based primarily on the common belief of a constant value of money,

[2] Bodin de Saint-Laurent mentions Noël du Fail as the first to refer to the influence of the American supplies of the precious metals in his book *Bolivernes et contes d'Eutrapel,* published in 1548 (*Les idées monétaires et commerciales de Jean Bodin,* Bordeaux, 1907, pp. 34—35). In Germany there were some contemporaries, for example Georg Agricola and Sebastian Frank, who remarked on the great influence of the abundant supply of precious metals from America, although not in connection with the explanation of the price increase (see Roscher, *op. cit.*, §§ 116 and 120); further, see p. 15, note 25.

fundamentally due to the experiences of a rather stable price development which fostered the idea of money as having an intrinsic and given value. Hence all price variations were explained in terms of changing conditions on the commodity side, which meant that price variations were looked upon as changes in the relative prices of the commodities. This is rather understandable as long as the medium of exchange kept the same stamp and coinage, and since fluctuations in the value relations between money and goods were indicated by numerical changes in the commodity prices. But when it was obvious that a general price change was occasioned by circumstances on the monetary side, then it was explained as being caused by an actual change in the stamp and coinage of the monetary unit itself.

The effect of Bodin's commonly adopted explanation became, without overstatement, detrimental to the progress of a realistic monetary theory. Although his merit was that he convinced not only the economists, but also the businessmen and statesmen, that the value of the precious metals, and hence the monetary metals, was subjected to the same law of demand and supply as all other commodities, the result was that he also laid the foundation for a belief that all general price variations were caused by changes in the quantity of money.[3] Had the tendency before been to explain all general price changes as due to circumstances on the commodity side, the rule now became to place all the causes on the monetary side.

It seems quite natural that Bodin has been often characterized as a quantity theorist, since his explanation of the changes in the value of money as owing to variations in its quantity might be described as a quantity theory of the variations in the value of money. Admitting this, however, he was certainly not the founder of this idea, but the first to make it widely known and accepted. But this idea is not identical with Locke's statement, which aimed at the illustration of a specific property of money as the medium of exchange. Here is where the confusion started, because Locke's proposition, when it was taken up by other economists, was reformulated in the same terms as used by Bodin, and so the proposition of causality was imposed on it. It is obvious that Bodin did not aim at pointing out a specific peculiarity of money.

[3] *Cf.* Monroe, who speaks of the price revolution as eventually stimulating »an important advance in the theory of the value of money; the influence of supply, which hitherto had been little attended to, now being given its due weight» (*op. cit.*, p. 72). But he also mentions that it gave rise to a tendency in the following hundred years to emphasize almost exclusively the supply of money (p. 101).

On the contrary, he claimed that the exchange value of coins obeyed the same law of demand and supply as all other commodities. There is no more reason for denoting the application of this general law to the means of exchange as a quantity theory of money than there would be to speak of a quantity theory of commodities. If the designation is accepted, then it may be correct to say that this interpretation of the quantity theory is merely the application of the law of demand and supply to variations in the value of money.

As the tendency later developed — to explain all general price fluctuations in terms of variations in the quantity of money — the idea of an *exclusive* causal relationship was added to Bodin's original 'quantity theory of the variations in the value of money'. It is interesting and significant that this extension of Bodin's theory received its theoretical support from the incorrect reephrasing of Locke's statement. This meant the complete mixture of two entirely different propositions. The misformulation of Locke's statement — that changes in the quantity of money, *ceteris paribus*, will *cause* proportionate price changes — then became the commonly adopted formulation of the 'quantity theory of money'. It contained two propositions: one of causality, and one of proportionality. Since the proposition of causality goes back, it is held, at least to Bodin's famous reply to Malestroit, he was made the founder of this version of the quantity theory, supposedly extended by Locke's proposition of proportionality.

Concomitant with the early development of the quantity theory, there were other monetary theories, which have been characterized as the quantity theory of money and confused with the quantity theory ascribed to Bodin and Locke. These theories aimed at explaining the exchange value of money, whereas Bodin's explanation referred to *variations* in this value. We have called these theories, distinguishing them from Bodin's monetary theory, *the quantitative theory of the exhange value of money,* and *the quantitative theory of individual prices.* These theories originated in Davanzati's monetary theory. As a result of the confusion of his ideas with Bodin's and Locke's he also has been described as the founder of the quantity theory.

When Davanzati explained the value of the monetary unit by equalizing the total quantity of all precious metals used as money to the value of the total amount of goods, he did not pretend to have enunciated a new theory of the value of money. He merely thought of this equalization as being actually made 'by the consent of all nations'. It was not an explanation of any intrinsic value in money. The different things derived their value from the wants they could satisfy, or, as he also said, their utility. Money had no direct utility, since it could not satisfy any immediate wants, and hence had no real value. But its fictitious value was derived from its property of being exchangeable for other goods. This was made possible only by a common consent that the *total* quantity of money was exchangeable for *all* goods. Hence it follows that the greater number of monetary units there is, the smaller will the value of one unit be, if the amount of commodities is the same. This simple conclusion is obviously based on the same arithmetic relation that Locke used in his illustration. Davanzati, however, never drew this conclusion. Furthermore, there is a fundamental difference in their approach. According to Davanzati, an increased amount of commodities would raise the *total* value of the quantity of money, since it then equalized a greater amount of value. In conformity with Locke's view, however, there would be no effect on the total value of money, since his demonstration supported the idea that money as such had no value.

From the illustration of the proportionate relation between the quantity of money and the value of the monetary unit, to which Davanzati's monetary doctrine easily lends itself, it was falsely concluded that an *increase* in the quantity of money, *ceteris paribus*, would *cause* proportionate price changes. Hence Davanzati was claimed to have laid the foundation of Locke's quantity theory. The incorrectness of such an interpretation has been pointed out above. The only conclusion Davanzati drew was that 'the parts follow the whole'. By this he laid the foundation of a quantitative theory of relative prices which was later elaborated by Montesquieu. It explained individual prices in terms of a quantitative comparison between the group of commodities in question, the total amount of commodities, and the quantity of gold.. This explanation of individual prices (in terms of the quantity of money) then became confused with certain pronouncements, particularly by Hume, that prices, implicity referring to *average* prices, were determined by the quantity of money in circulation. And so that quantity theory ascribed to Bodin, Davanzati, Locke and Hume, was sometimes criticised for its alleged pretension to explain individual prices. The criticism was mainly based upon Montesquieu's interpretation of Davanzati's quantity theory, which actually was a quantitative theory of individual prices.

Montanari improved Davanzati's doctrine of the exchange value of money by comparing and equalizing only the circulating quantity of money with the amount of goods exchanged. His purpose was the same as Davanzati's, to explain the exchange value of money. The comparison was not made in order to explain *variations* in the value of money. It is obvious, however, that Montanari's comparison cannot explain the value of money, since it has to be based on some kind of a unit of measurement. The choice of this unit actually becomes the explanation. This was overlooked by both Davanzati and Montanari.

Now it is but one step to Locke's well-known declaration that prices are in proportion to the quantity of money. Locke did not proceed, as might have been expected, from Davanzati's approach. This is quite evident from the different purposes of their statements. And he did not explain the value of money in terms of a quantitative comparison, but declared that human beings had decided to put an imaginary value upon money; this is quite important to remember. His statement that 'the exchange value of money in any country is the present quantity of the current money in that country in proportion to the present trade' (see p. 28) became the foundation for explaining those factors that *influence* the value of money, though it originally was an emphasis and an illustration of his fundamental idea that the quantity of money, as such, was of no importance for an isolated economy; in other words, gold and silver serving as money do not add to the wealth of a country. This was not, as far as can be judged from his writings, a conclusion drawn from the statement that prices are in proportion to the quantity of money. Rather, it was realized from the circumstance that money, merely serving as the medium of exchange, does not constitute any wealth in itself; and it was directed toward all those mercantilists who regarded the quantity as such of the precious metals, and not the relative amount of them (in comparison to other countries), as part of the wealth of a nation. The mercantilists' view was mainly based upon an acceptance of the old idea of the monetary metal as possessing an intrinsic value.

Locke's view, that the quantity itself of money has no value, substantiated by his proposition that prices will always be in proportion to the quantity of money (*ceteris paribus*), is the fundamental idea of the original quantity theory. The proportionate relation between money and prices merely serves to illustrate this idea, which emphasizes a specific peculiarity of money. Obviously, it is not a theory of the exchange value of money; nor did Locke speak of it as the quantity theory of money. On the other hand, it might legitimately be called a theory of the 'intrinsic' value of money, simply stating that money as such has no value. Originally, it was such a theory, opposing the mercantile idea of the value of money.

It is very significant that Locke did not speak of a determination of the exchange value of money by a comparison between the quantity of money and goods. As has been pointed out above, such a determination is logically impossible. It is also quite obvious that the exchange value of money is not determined by any quantitative comparison of total categories. Hume, however, was not so careful in his statements, and hence he was very often severely criticised. But he was never criticised for his most fallacious conclusion — built upon Locke's statements of proportionality between money and prices — namely, that *changes* in the quantity of money, *ceteris paribus*, will *cause* proportionate price variations. This effect cannot be maintained without *presuming* that a direct causal relationship is possible between variations in the quantity of money and prices. Hence, nothing concerning causation can be proved by Hume's illustration. In the case of Hume's affirmation, it is very likely that he merely wanted to emphasize the proportionate relation, whereas the causal relation was taken more or less for granted. This is where Bodin's role in the development of the quantity theory again comes in, as the tacit assumption of a causal relationship was primarily based upon the common recognition of the great influx of precious metals during the sixteenth century as the *cause* of the great price increase. The assumption was adopted without any clarification as to how the chain of causation worked. But it was also thought that the causation itself was theoretically proved by Locke's and, above all, by Hume's statements. Hence the proposition of causality was the least criticised. The most peculiar feature in this development of the quantity theory is that the theoretical demonstration of a primarily proportionate relationship came to be thought of as a *support* of the idea that *actual* price variations were exclusively *caused* by changes in the amount of circulation. It was entirely neglected that this formulation of the quantity theory was based upon the assumption that the amount of circulation increased or, although very rarely, decreased. The repeated emphasis upon increases in the quantity of money, was, of course, historically substantiated.

Hume's formulation of the mathematically necessary relation between variations in money and prices became the accepted formulation of the quantity theory. It now contained two propositions: one of proportionality and one of causality. Instead of interpreting it as an illustration of a specific peculiarity of the medium of exchange, contrasted with the mercantile view, it became a theory of the variations in the exchange value of money. This quantity theory of money was understood as a theory of the *variations* in the general price level as being caused primarily by changes in the *quantity* of money. This appelation might be more adequate than the characterization of Locke's original statement as a quantity theory of the value of money, although in both theories the emphasis is on the role that the quantity of money plays; but in Hume's formulation the quantity of money is given an active role, whereas in Locke's formulation its fundamental insignificance is stressed.

If Hume's statements had been more carefully analyzed, it might have become clear that he constantly emphasized the subservient role of money as a means of exchange. His illustrations of the proportionate relation between money and prices were always meant to indicate that money as such had no value. It is therefore very likely that he unintentionally included the proposition of a direct causality. This is also sustained by the fact that he did not maintain that an *actual* increase in the quantity of money would cause proportionate price variations. On the contrary, he became famous for his explanation that an actual increase of the circulation would not lead to proportionate price variations. But the first outstanding economists to criticise the quantity theory, Cantillon and Steuart, interpreted it as a serious statement of the result of a real increase of circulation. Cantillon might be said to have started the perpetually repeated criticism that other things will not remain constant. Instead of inquiring: what is the purpose of this assumption — to which the answer must be: to illustrate a specific property of money — the effects of changes in the quantity of money were thoroughly analyzed. From one point of view this was undoubtedly commendable, as he threw light on all those different channels through which money circulated. But his emphasis upon the different and unpredictable changes in demand, resulting from an increase in the quantity of money, did not divert, or even weaken, the view of these quantitative variations as being an active factor. Rather, he further accentuated the emphasis on the activeness of the monetary factors by adding that changes in the velocity of money would have the same effects as changes in the quantity of money. The readiness with which this idea was accepted was very likely due to the convincing power, by using the same way of reasoning as Hume used in formulating the quantity theory, of its demonstration. Hence both the causal and the proportionate proposition were held as theoretically correct, when the formulation actually was a description of a simple arithmetic relation in economic terms. Including Cantillon's proposition in Locke's and Hume's statements, the so-called *extended* quantity theory of money appeared (*cf.*, p. 182).

Steuart tried in vain to convince the economists that mere changes in the quantity of money would not have any effect upon prices if they did not have any on demand. In fact, it was not even possible to increase the circulation without a corresponding increase in demand. But the idea that variations in the quantity of money had an immediate and direct effect on prices had been so commonly accepted — fundamentally because of the supposedly clear, theoretical evidence provided — that he did not have any perceptible influence towards a more realistic attitude of the prevailing monetary theory. On the other hand, neither Steuart, nor Cantillon, made any effort to understand the purpose of Locke's and Hume's doctrine, but attacked it, in conformity with the prevailing interpretation, as a theory of the variations in prices.

Montesquieu's influence on the misinterpretation of the quantity theory as partly a theory of individual prices can hardly be overestimated. Because of his great prestige — he was often cited by other economists — this view won some adherents. But he also stressed the proportionate relation between money and prices, and in such a clear way that he very likely directly influenced the first equations which were enunciated towards the end of the eighteenth century and which aimed, more or less, at expressing this relation.

In rejecting the explanation of individual prices as being determined by the quantity of money given in exchange for the different commodities, and Steuart's price theory, Adam Smith formulated the cost of production theory, which was thought of as a complete theory of all relative values. Hence he also rejected the interpretation of the quantity theory, according to which the value of money (coins) was determined by the quantitative relation between the total amount of goods exchanged and the quantity of money in circulation. These are not the only interpretations of the quantity theory which puts it in opposition to the cost of production theory. Locke's original statement denied the existence of any value as such in the means of exchange. According to Adam Smith, the relative value of everything was determined by its cost of production, mainly by the amount of labor invested. If he had been consistent with his value theory, then he would have denied the essence of the original quantity theory.

Since Adam Smith looked upon the amount of circulation as a passive factor, determined by the demand for money and its cost of production, he could not reconcile his views with the assumption of a sudden increase in the quantity of coins, followed by a proposition of its effects. Then it was easier to make the experiment of thought in respect to (inconvertible) notes, as their cost of production could be neglected. And so the idea arose that if you accepted the cost-of-production theory, the quantity theory could be intelligibly discussed only in reference to notes. Adam Smith's answer was that an increased quantity of notes would be matched by a corresponding decrease of coins. Consequently, the total amount of circulation would remain constant; and this was consistent with his idea that the quantity of money was a passive factor.

In view of this development of the interpretation of the quantity theory, it is amusing to reflect upon the animated discussion of Ricardo's position. All peremptory affirmations that he discussed the quantity theory in respect to inconvertible paper money only, overlook the historical development of the quantity theory and its purpose. It is surprising that no thorough comparative analysis of the development of the quantity theory has been made. Then it would have been clear how entirely different Locke's and Hume's approach was from Ricardo's. This has escaped observation, because they used the same arithmetic illustration. And so all three have been characterized as pronounced quantity theorists.

Ricardo, like Adam Smith, held that the quantity of coins constituted a fixed value, whereas Locke and Hume thought that it only represented a certain value and had no intrinsic value. Consequently Adam Smith and Ricardo said that an increased quantity of coins meant an increased amount of value, while Locke and Hume would have asserted that there had been no actual augmentation in value. But Ricardo, primarily influenced by the contemporary monetary conditions in England, went farther than Adam Smith and discussed the corresponding relations of an inconvertible paper currency. In doing so he applied Locke's and Hume's argument, which referred to coins only, to irredeemable paper money. Instead of saying that the quantity of circulating coins represented a given value, he said that the quantity of paper money, substituting the coins, represented a given value. Hence changes in the number of inconvertible notes could not influence the total value they represented, only that of each single paper note; that is, prices must be in accordance with the quantity of irredeemable notes.

The purpose of Ricardo's illustration was not to support his opinion that paper money as such had no value. That was too obvious to need demonstration. Nor did he want to emphasize the proportionate relation. The object was to prove a direct causal relation between variations in money and prices. This theoretical demonstration of the necessary arithmetic relation, under the circumstances presumed, was then used as a *support* of his explanation that the fundemental *cause* of the price increase in England during the period 1797—1819 was the 'surplus' of paper money made possible by the restriction of its convertibility. Ricardo's great authority shifted the interpretation of the quantity theory to an explanation of the causes of general price fluctuations under a regime of inconvertible paper money, although it is not difficult to quote instances in which he asserted that the effect of an increased quantity of coins would be also a proportionate change in prices. These instances, however, must be ascribed to inconsistencies mainly caused by an eagerness to uphold weak arguments, particularly in his discussion with Mr. Bosanquet.

The acceptance of the quantity theory promoted a simplified way of reasoning in the discussion of the causes of the variations in the value of money. The frequent use of total categories and the discussion of the results of merely numerical changes in their magnitudes, constituted a great obstacle to a realistic analysis. The best example of this superficial view, which is a direct consequence of the misunderstanding of the original quantity theory, was provided by James Mill. His discussion of the effects of changes in the rapidity of circulation and in the total amount of goods on the value of money, formed an extended application of the arithmetic illustration indicating the quantity theory. As it was used also to prove different causal relationships, where general price variations were always treated as the effect of other changes, it supposedly proved the theoretical correctness of the idea that the price level was an exclusively passive factor. This idea became so commonly accepted that Tooke's attack on its correctness had rather little influence. His criticism of the explanation of the causes of the great price increase in the beginning of the nineteenth century did not have such convincing power as might have been expected in view of his and Newmarch's very comprehensive study of prices. The reason was not only that he had Ricardo, with all the latter's authority, as the leader of the opposite view, but also that the adherents of this view considered the correctness of the causal relationship maintained as being theoretically proved by the proposition of the quantity theory. If it then could be statistically proved that prices and the amount of circulation had increased (proportionately) in an actual case, the cause must be the increased quantity of money. Since the explanation referred to a period with an inconvertible paper currency, those adherents of the cost-of-production theory who accepted the proposition of the quantity theory as the answer to the problem of the enhanced prices, were still consistent.

Tooke's criticism was not directed towards the quantity theory as such, but towards the idea that it could be used as an explanation of real price changes without a specific investigation of all the complicated causes involved. His attitude was, very correctly, that the only way to get an accurate answer was to investigate the causes of the individual price changes, although he did not always differentiate clearly between changes in relative and average prices. Since he and Newmarch found that the price increases had preceded the increases in the circulation, they claimed that the quantity of money was a passive factor. They have generally been characterized as anti-quantity theorists, mainly because they disavowed the quantity theory as a correct explanation of a real increase in the general price level.

Another example of how the content of the original quantity theory changed, is the characterization of the dividing line between the Currency and the Banking School as being the acceptance, or the rejection, of the quantity theory. Such a characterization lays the emphasis exclusively on the acceptance of the causal relationship, while Locke, the founder of the quantity theory, emphasized the proportionate relation.

The incompatibility of the quantity theory as an explanation of the variations in the value of money with the cost-of-production theory was particularly stressed by Senior. The main difference appeared to be that while the quantity theorists maintained that the quantity of money determined the value of money, the adherents of the cost-of-production theory asserted that the value of money, *i.e.*, coins, determined the amount of circulation. Senior especially criticised the assumption in the quantity theory of a suddenly increased circulation without an explanation of the cause. There can only be one reason, he claimed, for an increase in the quantity of money, and that is cheaper costs of production. Hence changes in the circulation must necessarily be the effect of other changes. It was not realized, either by Senior or the adherents of the quantity theory, that the assumption fundamentally served to *illustrate* a proportionate relation only. In the case of Senior, it is quite understandable, as he explained the value of money in terms of its cost of production; but it remains a strange fact that the 'quantity theorists' always assumed an increased circulation and stated the effects, never inquiring into the causes. It has partly been explained from the support that this view received from experience and partly by the confusion of arithmetic relations with causal relations. Still, it cannot give the whole answer. It must also be due to the simple fact that if a false theorem is repeated enough times, it will finally be taken for granted, and nobody will question its correctness.

As a rule, most adherents of the cost-of-production theory denied the causal proposition; but the greatest part of the criticism was directed towards the proposition of proportionality. The first objection was, of course, that other things will not remain constant. Even if due consideration were taken of changes in other factors, yet there would be no proportionate price variations, a steadily growing group of critics maintained. This increasing criticism was induced by the development and the greater use of other means of exchange. The concept of the quantity of money gradually became more dubious. Although Hume mentioned that changes in the volume of credit will have the same effects on prices as variations in the quantity of money, the influence of credit on prices was mostly disregarded. As it became more and more recognized that the quantity of actual money constituted only a part of the total purchasing power, even the 'theoretical adherents' of the quantity theory admitted that an increase of the quantity of money, *ceteris paribus*, would not increase prices proportionately. The most outstanding exponent of this gradual change was Stuart Mill. In his description of the application of the quantity theory as belonging to the 'simple and primitive state of things' only, the value of the theory was made dependable upon its ability to explain real changes in the value of money. This was only possible when the total amount of the medium of exchange corresponded to the total amount of money, *i.e.*, coins (and notes). In a 'modern' society, however, so many other means of exchange were used that the quantity of money could not be said to regulate general prices. They were regulated by the total amount of purchasing power.

Mill's influence gradually led to a decline of the role of the quantity theory and a shift away from the immense interest in the effects of changes in the quantity of money towards a common realization that the 'pure' quantity of money merely represented a minor part of the total purchasing power, which, in comparison with the total supply, was said to determine the development of the price level. But in 1911, a new, and probably the last, effort was made to rehabilitate the quantity theory. Fisher's attempt came as a great surprise, since he tried to prove the validity of both the proposition of causality and, in the long run, the proposition of proportionality. He met Mill's criticism of the quantity theory by saying that even though the quantity of money in circulation constituted only a certain part of the total means of exchange, there was still a direct relation between changes in the quantity of money and in the price level, because of a fairly constant ratio of bank reserves to bank deposits, and of cash holdings to check transactions. Fisher went even farther than any other 'quantity theorist' by not assuming other things being equal, but maintaining that these other things, that is, the velocity of money and the amount of transactions, will not be influenced — except for transition periods — by variations in the quantity of money. One necessary assumption that Fisher omitted here and perhaps tacitly presumed, was the existence of full employment. Without this assumption it was very easy to criticise his proposition. The reason Fisher made his statements so affirmative and was so serious about them in spite of their incurring criticism was that his approach was fundamentally built upon Locke's original proposition that money as such had no value, a proposition to which Fisher most unreservedly agreed. His great mistake, which he shared with many economists, was that he did not make the distinction between the proportionate relation as such of the quantity of money to prices and the effect of changes in the quantity of money. In that respect the equation of exchange was a deceptive formula as it convinced him, not only of the theoretical validity of his proposition of a direct causal relation between variations in the quantity of money and prices, but also of the correctness of his interpretation of the statistics, applied to the formula, as revealing the same causal relationship. His interpretation of the quantity theory, however, was a restatement of Locke's original idea that money is mainly a medium of exchange. Hence his conclusion that changes in the quantity of money will not influence the 'velocity' of circulation of money — the essence of the quantity *theory.*

Fisher's basic purpose was to determine those forces which determine the purchasing power of money. Because of the indisputable correctness of the equation of exchange and because it contained a term symbolizing the relative value of money, he erroneously concluded that the other factors included in the equation *determined* the value of money.

Unfortunately, the criticism of his equation was not directed towards the possibility as such of enunciating similar formulas from which conclusions could be drawn as to what causes determine the purchasing power of money, but merely towards the ambiguity of some of the symbols involved, primarily of T and V. But the idea of including the quantity of money was not questioned seriously. Other attempts, made in order to formulate equations which would provide a foundation for the analysis of fluctuations in the value of money, also included a term for the quantity of money — a reminder of the great influence the quantity theory once had held and still partly kept.

The enunciators of the Cambridge quantity equations did not succeed in renouncing the great influence of the quantity theory. Both the formulas and the discussion of their implications were very much open to the same criticism as the equation of exchange. Actually, the equations differed very slightly from Fisher's equation. Instead of equalizing the real and potential wealth that the total quantity of money had exchanged during an arbitrarily chosen period — although long enough to necessitate a symbol for the rate of turnover of money — to the corresponding monetary transactions, the Cambridge quantity equations equalized the total quantity of money to the potential wealth it represented. Since the total quantity of money equalized the sum of all cash holdings, it indicated the total amount of potential wealth that people were willing to keep in cash at a certain price level. The emphasis upon the effects on the price level of the decisions to change this amount of potential wealth distinguished the cash-balance approach from Fisher's or, as it also has been characterized, the quantity-theory approach. While the 'quantity theorists' related variations in the price level to changes in the quantity of money, asserting that the 'velocity' of money could be regarded as institutionally determined, and hence, fairly constant, the adherents of the cash-balance approach explained the variations in the price level primarily in terms of changes in the 'velocity' of money. The latter's demonstration of this relationship suffered from the same confusion of arithmetic relations with causal relations as Fisher's illustration of the theoretical correctness of the quantity theory. But their emphasis on the importance of the decisions to keep a certain amount of potential wealth in cash gave an intelligible meaning to the concept of a demand for money.

The fundamental reason for the isolated existence of monetary theory, which kept it separated from economic theory almost since its beginning and through the first decades of this century, has been the dominant influence of the quantity theory. Its adherents made the variations in the price level purely a study of the changes in the amount of circulation, leaving out the influence of variations in consumption, investment and employment. Partly they were justified by their tacit assumption of full employment. Wicksell's idea of explaining fluctuations in the price level in terms of a discrepancy between the bank rate and the 'natural' rate of interest was taken over by Keynes and further developed into a business cycle theory. The variations in the purchasing power of money were ascribed to a discrepancy between (planned) investment and saving, while the quantity of money was regarded almost exclusively as a passive factor. This meant a decisive break with earlier monetary theory, but not until the appearance of Keynes' *General Theory of Employment* was his monetary theory made an integral part of a 'general economic theory'. Variations in the quantity of money were again considered to be of importance, although in a different causal relation from the one the quantity theory maintained. They were now directly related to the monetary rates of interest. The demand for money was defined — in striking contrast to Stuart Mill's famous definition — as a demand for cash, mainly influenced by changes in the rate of interest. This new interpretation of the significance of variations in the quantity of money marked the end of the dominance of the quantity theory and the beginning of a new theory, in which changes in the quantity of money were treated as part of a monetary theory integrated with a general theory of employment. Naturally enough, Keynes went to the extreme in his emphasis upon money as a store of value — in contradistinction to the quantity theory which stresses only money as a medium of exchange — and claimed that *all* changes in the quantity of money would primarily influence the rates of interest. A synthesis, therefore, of the role of money *both* as a medium of exchange *and* as a store of value is suggested in the second part of this work, which also is a demonstration of the fundamental idea behind the quantity theory. Before this is done, however, a classification of all the various interpretations of the quantity theory will be undertaken.

CHAPTER X

THE FUNDAMENTAL CONTENT OF THE QUANTITY THEORY AND ITS VARIOUS MISINTERPRETATIONS

Content and purpose of the original quantity theory

1. The history of the quantity theory is a history of a theory which was basically misunderstood and therefore confused with other ideas. The misunderstanding rested partly on a confusion of the indicators of economic changes with the causes themselves, and partly on a confusion of arithmetic relations with causal relations. The extended duration of this confusion has been possible because of a lack of knowledge of the fundamental content and purpose of the original statement that gave rise to the commonly accepted formulation of the quantity theory. This statement is Locke's well-known proposition that prices are always in direct proportion to the quantity of money. The simple content of this statement is best illustrated by Fisher's equation $MV = PT$, since Locke recognized the role of the velocity of money. He merely said that if the quantity of money (in circulation) were, for example, five times as great (with the same velocity of money and number of transactions), prices must be five times higher. This proposition is obviously a truism as it is based on a self-evident arithmetic relation. It was induced by a comparison of the total quantity of money with the total amount of goods, implicitly — in contrast to Davanzati — with due regard to the velocity of money.

Locke's comparison rested upon one fundamental assumption, namely, that the (total) quantity of money was the only means of exchange. This tacit assumption was seriously criticised first by Tooke. But the importance of the assumption for the incurred limitations of Locke's proposition was not recognized. Locke was evidently correct in his assumption as long as he dealt with macro-economics in an isolated economy. Then money has only the role of being a standard of value and a medium of exchange, while it would be meaningless — disregarding the industrial use of the monetary metal — to characterize the quantity of money as representing a potential wealth of the economy as a whole. Locke would be the first to admit, however, the importance of the relative quantity of money in international trade.

The purpose of Locke's proposition was to support his view that money, as a means of exchange, had no value in itself. This emphasis upon the specific peculiarity of the means of exchange was primarily directed toward the prevailing mercantile view that money, *per se*, constituted (the most important) part of the wealth of a nation. But it was not, as has been proposed, directed towards the mercantile *policy*.[1]

Locke, still subscribing to the ideas of mercantilism, did not face any dilemma by formulating the quantity theory, for he differed from most mercantilists in his argument for a policy promoting an export surplus by emphasizing the importance of the *relative* quantity of money. This distinction did not interfere with the goal of making the nation powerful by means of an export surplus.[2]

The commonly accepted, theoretical version of the quantity theory

2. Hume's unfortunate formulation — based on fallacious conclusion — of Locke's statement, introduced the proposition of causality, thereby

[1] See, *e.g.*, J. Davidsohn who speaks of the quantity theory as 'the great weapon' in the fight of the widespread belief in money and of the policy which was founded on this belief, that is, mercantilism (*op. cit.*, p. 199). Only the first part of this statement seems correct, since the whole mercantile policy was fundamentally based upon the realization of the advantage of having *relatively* more precious metals than other countries, even if many of them did confuse money with wealth. Therefore we question the following remark by Viner: »With regard to the theory of international exchange, Mercantilism contained one great and fundamental fallacy. This was its failure to take account of the apparent contradiction between an acceptance of the quantity theory and the advocacy of the accumulation of the precious metals» (*op. it.*, p. 39). The acceptance of the basic idea of the quantity theory merely meant that the arguments for the mercantile policy had to be improved.

Davidsohn goes even so far as to characterize the quantity theory as »not only an integral part of economic liberalism, but historically viewed — its very starting point» (*op. cit.*, p. 209). The starting point for economic liberalism; as well as for the entire movement of liberalism, was, of course, the demand for freedom. H. P. Willis, on the other hand, considers the formulation of the quantity theory as being »based simply upon the mercantilist ideas regarding money» (*J. P. E.*, 1896, pp. 421—422). This false conclusion might be based on the circumstance that the quantity theory was used by some mercantilists as a device for realizing their desire 'to sell dear and buy cheap'.

[2] This view is supported by E. Heimann's interpretation of the mercantilists' conception of money (*History of Economic Doctrines,* 2 ed., London and New York, 1947, p. 30).

transforming the truism into a theory. And so the quantity theory was given its commonly accepted version, namely, that *if* the quantity of money is increased (or decreased), *ceteris paribus*, prices will vary in direct proportion. The theoretical correctness of this formulation has never been questioned. It has been overlooked, however, that its theoretical verification rested merely upon the arithmetic relation pointed out by Locke. Consequently nothing could be proved deductively as to the proposition of causality.[3]

The common version of the quantity theory *postulates* that the quantity of money is used exclusively as a means of exchange, that it is the only means of exchange, and that there is a direct causal relation between changes in the quantity of money and in prices; it *assumes* that the quantity of money is increased (or decreased), but that all other things, primarily the velocity of money, the amount of transactions, and the structure of demand and supply — except prices — remain constant; and it *predicates* that prices will change in the same proportion as the amount of circulation. These are the full implications of the commonly accepted, theoretical version of the quantity theory. In general, it has been neglected that this formulation rests upon the postulate of money as the only and exclusive means of exchange and of a direct causal relation between changes in money and prices. This makes Hume's formulation just as much a truism as Locke's, since it does not *prove* any causality; that has to be assumed. Hence it contains fundamentally the proposition of proportionality only, which was the main purpose of Hume's formulation. The aim was not to formulate a theory of the variations in the exchange value of money, but to illustrate the specific property of money as a means of exchange.

The interpretation of the common version of the quantity theory

3. The purpose of Locke's and Hume's statements was misunderstood, and they were interpreted as a theory of the variations in the exchange value of money. Bodin's explanation of the great price increase of the sixteenth century was interpreted as a direct application of the law of demand and supply to metallic money, and was taken as an evidence of a direct causal relation between variations in money and prices. Locke and Hume merely seemed to point

[3] *Cf.* Hawtrey's telling remark: »The hypothesis [of the quantity theory] supposes a *different* price, not a *change* of price» (*op. cit.*, 4 ed., p. 41); also see G. Myrdal: *Monetary Equilibrium*, London, 1939, p. 12.

out that, if other things remained the same, the value of money varied in inverse proportion to its quantity. The quantity theory, therefore, appeared as a special case of the general law of demand and supply.[4] This speciality has also been crudely expressed by saying that the elasticity of the demand for money is equal to unity (see pp. 80, 135 and 173).

A. The idea of the quantity theory as a simple application of the law of demand and supply to the value of money was definitely established by Stuart Mill's famous definition of the demand for money as synonymous with the supply of goods and of the supply of money as synonymous with the total quantity of money in circulation. To speak of an application, however, of this law to the exchange value of money is very deceptive, because it presumes the existence of some standard of value. If the unit of this standard of value happens to correspond to the unit of the medium of exchange, then the value of this unit of exchange must be constant; that is, changes in the price of a given commodity must be looked upon as purely changes in the exchange value of the commodities in question, not in the means of exchange. This is quite evident from the fact that prices are not denoted in order to measure any relation of exchange between the medium of exchange and the commodities, but between the various commodities. A price has meaning only in relation to some other price, and changes in this price are mainly indications of changes in the demand for and/or supply of the commodity in question and in its cost of production.

An isolated exchange of only two commodities does not require any given standard of value. The determination of the exchange value of money, by comparing the total quantity of money in circulation with the total amount of goods to be exchanged, is similar to transactions in an isolated exchange. The untenability of such a determination is not only

[4] See, for example, Gide and Rist: »La même loi qui réglait la valeur des marchandises [la loi de l'offre et de la demande] s'appliquait aussi à la monnaie. Elle aussi a une valeur courante déterminée par la quantité en circulation sur la marché et par les besoins de l'échange — c'est la célèbre théorie quantitative — et une valeur naturelle déterminée par le coût de production des métaux précieux» (*Histoire des Doctrines Economiques*, Paris, 1913, p. 425); and B. Nogaro: »La théorie est essentielle l'application de la loi de l'offre et de la demande à la monnaie» (*Le Rôle de la monnaie dans le commerce international et la Théorie quantitative*, Paris, 1904, p. 77); also see the latter's *La monnaie et les phénomènes monétaires contemporaines*, Paris, 1935, p. 209. Aftalion shares this opinion also (*op. cit.*, 3 ed., p. 4), which seems to be especially prevalent among French writers. P. Einzig, an English economist, affirms that the »quantity theory of money is in substance a sophisticated application of the old supply and demand theory» (*Primitive Money*, London, 1949, p. 401).

that the law of demand and supply has no real application to an isolated exchange, as long as no common standard of value is used, but also that there is no question of exchanging the total amount of goods for the total quantity of money. Stuart Mill, in his famous definitions of the total demand for and supply of money, simply transformed money, as a means of exchange, into a commodity having a demand as such. It merely means that the total of a homogeneous group of commodities, that is, money, is exchanged for the total of a heterogeneous group of commodities. Such an 'isolated exchange' excludes any relation of exchange expressed in a common standard of value, and reduces the whole argument to a play with definitions without any realistic content. If more money were given in exchange, it would only mean that the quantity *per se* of money had changed; still, nothing could be said of the relations of value.

The total demand for money, M (in monetary terms), consists of two main parts: the demand for money as a means of exchange, M', and the demand for money as a store of value, M''. M' can be divided into three parts: one which is influenced by changes in the rate of interest, M_1, and which is the smallest part;[5] a second which is primarily a function of the level of real income, M_2; and a third, which is a function of the value of money, M_3. In fig. 1, the demand curves of M_1 and M_2 are perpendicular lines, while the demand curve of M_3 is a curve falling to the right. There is no reason to expect the elasticity of this curve to be equal to unity. It is very likely that the slope of this curve is 'underelastic' (*i.e.*, $\frac{dx}{dy} < 1$), because of the strong influence of the nominal value of our cash holdings on our demand for cash. The horizontal summation of these three curves gives the total demand curve for money as a medium of exchange, M'.

The dotted curves represent the proposition of the original quantity theory, that is, the arithmetic relation between variations in the quantity of money and the price level, presuming that money is the exclusive means of exchange and that other things remain constant. They illustrate, for example, the relation between M and P in Pigou's equation $P = \frac{kR}{M}$, if k and R remain constant. The form of these curves is obviously that of a rectangular hyperbola, that is, their point-elasticity

[5] See, for example, Lloyd Mints: *Monetary Policy for a Competitive Society,* New York, 1950, p. 35.

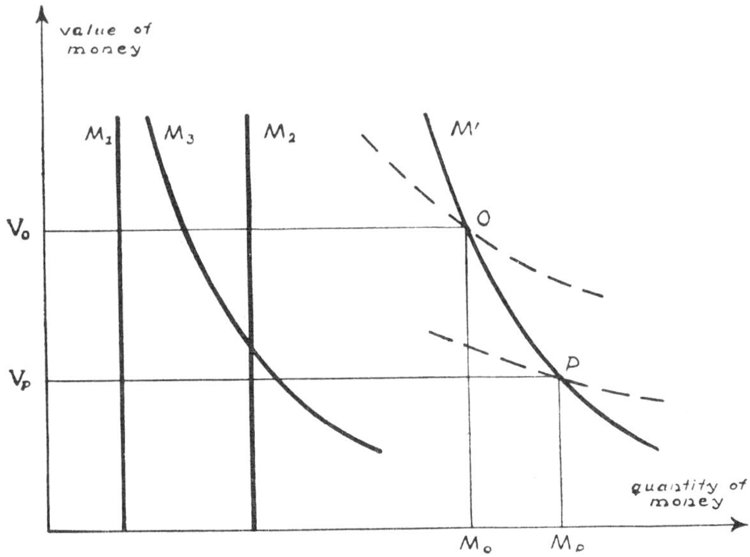

Fig. 1.

is equal to unity. This, however, has nothing to do with the elasticity of the demand for money. Suppose that the total demand for the medium of exchange at a given value, V_o, corresponds to M_o units. This demand will represent a certain amount of potential wealth, which might be measured in wheat, as proposed by Pigou, or in consumption-units, as Keynes preferred. This would be at the point O of the demand curve for money (as a medium of exchange). But if we wanted to illustrate the inversely proportionate relation between the quantity of money and its value with a given demand for money (in real terms) in order to stress the function of money as the means of exchange, we would draw the rectangular hyperbola that passes through O (indicated by the dotted curve through O). Then, it is quite evident that we have left the demand curve for money, and are merely moving along a curve that illustrates the fundamental proposition of the original quantity theory. To characterize this hyperbola, as done by Pigou (see p. 101), as the demand curve for titles to actual legal tender is to confuse the concept of the demand for money. The proposition of the original quantity theory contains only an undeniable arithmetic relation. *If* the quantity of money had been double as great as M_o, *ceteris paribus*, and the value of money consequently half of V_o, that would have been no indication of an increased demand for money. It is merely a hypothesis to illustrate a specific property of the means of exchange. The curves in fig. 1 would all have been the same, if only the scale-unit of the horisontal and of the vertical axis had been halved and doubled, respectively.

Similarly, if the demand for money as a medium of exchange at a lower value, say V_p, corresponds to M_p, the arithmetic relation between variations in the quantity of money and its value, *ceteris paribus,* is illustrated by the dotted hyperbola going through the point P. Evidently, we can draw a rectangular hyperbola through every point of the demand curve for money, M', always illustrating the proposition of proportionality of the quantity theory at varying levels. Of course, there is a theoretical possibility that the demand curve, M', would be a rectangular hyperbola, and thus coincide with a dotted curve illustrating the proposition of the quantity theory. Indeed, if cash holders were perfectly rational in their economic behavior, the demand for money as a function of the price level, M_3, would be illustrated by a rectangular hyperbola. But the total demand curve for money, $M_1 + M_2 + M_3 = M'$, then would not be a rectangular hyperbola. Since all statistical investigations have shown that there is no exact proportionate relation between variations in the total amount of money and the price level, this might indicate that the elasticity of the demand for money, as a function of the price level, is unity, although the probability is extremely small.

B. The basic content of the quantity theory is generally considered to be the proposition of causality. The problem then is whether changes in the quantity of money have an independent importance, and whether or not they will influence prices primarily. A positive answer to this question is found in Fisher's interpretation and defense of the quantity theory. The causal relation, which in Hume's formulation rests upon a tacit *assumption*, now becomes the fundamental proposition. This interpretation of the quantity theory emanates from Bodin's famous observation, even if the causal relation was pointed out earlier. This theoretical formulation of the quantity theory is built upon Locke's and Hume's statements about the proportionality, whereas the practical application rests upon Bodin's interpretation of a real price increase. The question, therefore, which naturally presents itself is: Is the correctness of Bodin's observation due to the specific property of the means of exchange, pointed out by Locke and Hume? The answer must be: Not necessarily; either reference is made to their statements or to the commonly accepted, theoretical formulation of the quantity theory. Only if it can be proved that the increase in the circulating quantity of money occurred first and that no other simultaneous changes occurred, except in prices, will Bodin's observation be in complete conformity with Locke's and Hume's statements.

A very common interpretation of the quantity theory, built upon the idea of a (direct) causal relation between the quantity of money in circulation and the price level, considers the main content of the theory to be that it »makes the quantity of money in circulation the determinant of the price level».[6] This notion must be described as a misinterpretation, since the theory, not even in its commonly accepted, theoretical version, makes the quantity of money the determinant of the price level. Such a conclusion is logically impossible to draw from that version, as it is based upon the *assumption* of a change in the quantity of money, thereby implicitly assuming the price level to be a passive factor. Since the exchange value of money is a relation between money and goods, one of them cannot be described as *the* determinant of that relation (*cf.* Wicksell's criticism, p. 137). All those factors influencing this relation must evidently be characterized as the determinants of the price level. That the commodity side could ever be left out as one of the determinants might be explained by the circumstance that the quantity of money could vary much easier than the amount of goods. But this does not justify the conclusion that the quantity of money is the determinant. Nor does it follow from the name of the theory, as Heimann maintains, which merely indicates that the quantity theory deals with the quantity of money.

C. Parallel with the emphasis on the proposition of causality goes an interpretation of the quantity theory as an *explanation* of changes in the price level. Also this interpretation neglects that the formulation of the quantity theory rests upon the tacit presumption of a causal relationship between changes in the quantity of money and prices, and that it *assumes* the quantity of money to increase and other things to remain constant. Hence the theory can serve as an explanation only if all these prerequisites are present. To explain the fluctuations in the

---

[6] Heimann, *op. cit.*, p. 29. A similar interpretation is offered, among others, by R. F. Harrod, who asserts that according to the quantity theory »the price level depends on the quantity of money available for active trade» (»Mr. Keynes on Traditional Theory», *Econometrica*, 1937, p. 75). A. Hansen speaks of the *pure* quantity theory, *i.e.*, that the price level was thought to be a function of the quantity of money (*op. cit.*, p. 48).

price level in terms of the quantity theory is merely one of many possible explanations and one which has to be proved by a real investigation of the relevant data. Even if a direct proportionality is demonstrated between the quantity of money and prices, the chain of causation is not given. The problem is not solved by referring to the quantity theory, since it removes the problem by assuming all relevant relations, except one, to be constant.

This interpretation of the quantity theory, naturally enough, turned it into a business cycle theory.[7] The weakness of this approach is the assumption that changes in the quantity of money always have an independent meaning. This is mainly due to a confusion of the indications of certain changes with the causes of these changes. It also has to assume the nonexistence, or at least, the irrelevancy, of other causes. Furthermore, the adherents of this approach will not be able to explain those business cycles which occur without any or with very slight price increases. Thus they assume that business cycles necessarily go with price changes. The only thing the quantity theory can 'explain' is why variations in the quantity of money and prices have to be proportionate, if its assumptions are fulfilled. Theories, however, are not enunciated in order to prove truisms.

In accordance with Keynes' monetary theory, a business cycle theory can be formulated upon the effects of changes in the quantity of money. This approach is completely different from that above, since the chain of causation goes via variations in the rates of interest, and since the effects might be limited to variations in employment and output, without any significant price fluctuations.

Implications of the explicit and implicit assumptions of the common version of the quantity theory

4. The extremely limited significance of the quantity theory as a proposition of the effects of changes in the quantity of money is due

[7] H. P. Willis points out that the interpretation of the quantity theory as an explanation of variations in prices also made the theory an explanation of »all the phenomena which accompany these variations» (*op. cit.*, p. 417); also see M. Palyi: »Die Quantitätstheorie», *Handwörterbuch der Staatswissenschaften,* 4 ed. (Jena, 1925), p. 1147. A. Michaelis: *Die Quantitätstheorie als Grundlage der Konjunkturforschung* (Jena, 1929) and A Spiethoff: »Die Quantitätstheorie insbesondere in ihrer Verwertbarkeit als Haussetheorie» (in *Festgaben für Adolf Wagner,* Leipzig, 1905) are two attempts to use the quantity theory as a business cycle theory and they are both open to the criticism advanced above.

to its many implicit and explicit assumptions. This limitation is further accentuated by the ambiguity of the concept of money. In the early days of the quantity theory, money referred exclusively to coins. Circulating notes were thought of as representing a corresponding, actual amount of bullion. Together they were regarded as the only means of payment. The purpose of Locke's statement was to emphasize that the precious metals used as the means of exchange do not constitute any wealth. But even in respect to that development of the quantity theory, which primarily originated in Bodin's famous observation, the explanation referred to coins. The combination of Bodin's and Locke's views, plus the introduction of the *ceteris-paribus* premise, made the quantity theory appear as a special case of the general law of demand and supply applied to coins.

The formulation of the cost-of-production theory caused confusion as to what kind of money the quantity theory referred to, as well as to the interpretation of the theory. The consistent adherents of the cost-of-production theory accepted the quantity theory as an explanation of the value of inconvertible paper money, and rejected all other applications.

The tendency to understand the quantity theory as an explanation of general price variations and the recognition of the extensive use of other means of payment entailed a broadening of the concept of money. It was sometimes said to include everything that served as money. This gave rise to an endless discussion, which underlined the vague import of such a definition, but also dwelt frequently on distinctions without differences. Therefore, some economists preferred to use money as implying coins and bank notes only, whereas deposits subject to check transactions, bills and other means of payment were distinguished as credit. The sum of all circulating money and credit-means constituted the total amount of purchasing power, the variations of which would cause corresponding price fluctuations at a given supply.

Fisher, in his rehabilitation of the quantity theory, defined money as everything which »is generally acceptable in exchange for goods».[8] Variations in the quantity of money would then influence the price level, partly directly, and partly indirectly by affecting the amounts of deposits subject to check. When it was more commonly realized that changes in the quantity of money were to be looked upon as often the effects of other and more fundamental changes, the interest in the quantity theory declined.

[8] *Op. cit.*, p. 8.

The most criticised assumption of the quantity theory is the *ceteris-paribus* premise, which was used as early, at least, as 1735, by Bishop Berkely (see p. 38, note 29). The content of this premise has varied from time to time and also between contemporary writers. Its purpose has always been to justify the proposition of proportionate price changes. It is very significant, because it partly reveals the meaning of his statement, that Locke never used this assumption. His proposition, that prices always are in proportion to the quantity of money, refers to a given point of time and does not involve the effects of changes.

Several of Locke's successors, for example, Hume and Montesquieu, equalized the total quantity of money to all goods. The proposition of proportionate price changes then required the sole assumption that the total amount of goods remained the same. As the velocity of circulation of money became commonly recognized, the assumption of other things being equal also included the constancy of the velocity of money. Sometimes, the velocity of circulation of money was the only factor assumed to remain constant. Accordingly, price variations were said to be directly proportionate to changes in the quantity of money and inversely proportionate to changes in the amount of goods. The reformulation was performed in order to make the theory more suitable for the explanation of general price variations.

The different uses of the *ceteris-paribus* premise often indicated a different application of the quantity theory. Ricardo, for example, merely assumed the 'real' value which the paper money represented, to be constant. The more the illustrations resembled purely arithmetic examples,. the less presumptions were needed. If the theory implied that every price would change in exact proportion, then it had also to be assumed that the structure of demand and supply remained the same. Stuart Mill, however, underlined that even though average prices must change proportionately, if the quantity of goods remained constant, changes in the structure of demand will cause different price fluctuations for various commodities. These attempts to minimize the number of factors supposed to be constant, aiming at giving the quantity theory a realistic content, actually changed its content, unnoticeably, into a mere *ex-post* statement which could be illustrated by a simple equation of the Fishcrinc type.

Marshall criticised the quantity theory for not giving an account of those factors which were included in the *ceteris-paribus* premise. This criticism was frequently repeated before the theory was illustrated by the help of equations, typically enough, since it was then more clearly realized which factors that had to remain constant. The time element in this proposition was diffused when equations were employed in proving its correctness. The fundamental difference between an equation, for example, $MV = PT$, which is based on a logical combination of concepts, and the quantity theory as a prognosis, was disregarded.[9] Instead, it was presupposed that the whole content of the quantity theory could be demonstrated by an equation of this type. The *ceteris-paribus* premise was thus reduced to the assumption that V and T remain unchanged.

The advantage of using the equation of exchange is the disclosure of the vagueness of the commonly accepted formulation of the quantity theory. It clarifies the implications of the assumption of other things being equal. In the analysis of Fisher's illustration of the quantity theory (see p. 88 ff.), it was particularly emphisized that it is incorrect to say that changes in M cause corresponding changes in P, if V and T are constant. Since the equation is void of any causal relationships, all references to it will only exemplify arithmetic relations. Fisher's illustration, which reduces the quantity theory to a proposition of proportionality, eliminates its character as a prognosis. The *ceteris-paribus* premise then refers to the constancy of certain numerical values only. Consequently, the factors included in the presumptions are not enough if the quantity theory is designed to be a prognosis.

The attempts to illustrate the quantity theory by dint of Fisher's equation, clearly bring out the necessity of including an assumption of a direct causality between variations in the quantity of money and prices. This has repeatedly been ignored, partly because Bodin's statement gave rise to the impression that there existed such a direct relation, and partly because the different equations, which usually originated in the old idea of comparing and equalizing the total quantity of money to all the goods, were fallaciously interpreted as justifying the proposition of causality.[10]

---

9 This dualism is a reflection of the dualism which faces the content and form of economic science as a whole. The 'tension' between the study of open sequences of evolution in time (which the verification of the common version of the quantity theory requires) and closed relations of logical concepts of a general and timeless kind (which the equation of exchange exemplifies) has been particularly stressed by J. Åkerman. See, for example, »Det ekonomiska framåtskridandets problem» in *Studier i Ekonomi och Historia.* Tillägnade Eli F. Heckscher, Stockholm, 1944, pp. 319—320.

10 Le Branchu is one of those very few who speak of the following three elements as constituting the quantity theory: 1) the exclusive causality, 2) the proportionality, and 3) the 'automatism', that is, the variations in the price level follow immediately those in the quantity of money (»La théorie quantitative», *R. E. p.*, 1934, p. 1243).

It seems unquestionable that the *ceteris-paribus* premise reduces the common, theoretical version of the quantity theory to a proposition of proportionality only. Since a (direct) causal relation has to be presumed, the proposed effect of changes in the quantity of money becomes a platitude. The point of interest cannot be *that* prices are affected, but *how* they are affected. Because of the presumptions, they must vary in the same proportion. This is obviously a truism. Hence it is very improper to denote these propositions as constituting a quantity *theory* of money, since it is no real theory. As this version of the quantity theory is formulated, its content is actually reduced to the illustration of the same specific property of money as Locke indicated in his statement. This might also be indicated by the frequent confusion of Fisher's equation with the quantity theory.[11]

To make the quantity theory an intelligible theory requires the abandoning of the *ceteris-paribus* premise. This is what Fisher did. Irrespective of the weaknesses of the theoretical arguments, his inductive study intends to prove that the 'velocity' of circulation of money and the amount of transactions will not be affected, except temporarily, by changes in the quantity of money. The essence of this interpretation of the quantity *theory* is that the velocity of money has an autonomous meaning. But even if this were correct, and a certain arithmetic relation could be proved between the quantity of money and prices at different points of times, still, this would not provide sufficient ground for the conclusion that there also is a certain causal relation between changes in the quantity of money and in prices.

A classification of the different forms and formulations of the quantity theory

5. The numerous interpretations of the quantity theory can properly be divided into two main groups: one lays the emphasis on the idea of causality, and the other on the idea of proportionality. There is a

[11] There are, of course, no difficulties in formulating an equation illustrating the idea that changes in the quantity of money, *ceteris paribus*, will cause corresponding price changes. The proposition of proportionality requires (using the symbols of the Fisherine equation) that $\frac{T}{V}$ is a constant, k, and the causal proposition that prices are functionally related to the quantity of money. Hence one can write $P \cdot k = f(M)$. This causal relation, however, has no 'time-dimension' and the equation cannot prove the actual effects of changes in the quantity of money. Any such proposition has to assume the possibility of a (direct) causal relation in time.

third group also, which is not directly related to these two groups, but in which the quantity of money is given an important role, so that the theories of this group have sometimes been confused with the usual quantity theory. This latter group contains the 'quantitative' theories of individual prices and of the exchange value of money. It might also include the 'quantity' theory of the monetary rate of interest.

A. The first group contains the greatest variety of heterogeneous opinions. The simplest form is the idea that there is a causal relation between changes in the quantity of money and its value. This idea goes back at least as far as to the Chinese in 500 B.C., who used it in their recommendations for *influencing* the price level. It is sometimes characterized as the *naive, primitive, crude,* or *mechanical* form of the quantity theory.[12] This causal relation constitutes the foundation of either a *prognosis* or an *explanation* of the variations in the price level, or of *recommendations* for monetary policy. The natural application of the idea as both a prognosis and a recommendation was later put into practice by Copernicus. Bodin's use of the idea as an explanation of a general price increase at first gave rise to a second form, in which an *exclusive* causal relation was maintained. The implication was that at simultaneous increases in the quantity of money and in the price level, the relation was always that of cause to effect respectively. In a circulation of coins and/or convertible notes this explanation seemed self-evident, since there would be no reason, *ceteris paribus*, to increase the production and/or the import of bullion if prices had increased. A third form,

---

[12] See, for example, Kirmaier, *op. cit.*, pp. 33—34. It might also be denoted as the simplistic form, but Baudin, who differentiates between four groups, uses this appellation for describing the idea that variations in the quantity of money will cause proportionate price variations (»la forme simpliste»). The second version is called »la forme mathématique»: variations in the quantity of money and in its velocity of circulation will cause proportionate variations in the price level; the third is »la forme causale»: the movements in the price level are exclusively caused by variations in the quantity of money, but no proportionality is necessarily required; and the fourth »la notion quantitative»: general price fluctuations are due to variations in the quantity of money, although not exclusively and not necessarily proportionate (*La monnaie et la formation des prix*, pp. 512—513). M. Palyi, on the other hand, characterizes the idea of comparing the total quantity of money with the total amount of goods, and the assertion that a given fraction of the quantity of money would correspond to the same fraction of the goods (treated as a homogeneous group), as a *nominalistic* opinion, or also the naive or mechanical opinion, (*op. cit.*, p. 1148). F. von Hayek identifies the attempts to explain the business cycles from the variations in the price level with the naive quantity theory (*op. cit.*, pp. 53—54).

developed from this view, is the opinion that *all price increases* can be explained in terms of an increased quantity of money.[13]

When general price decreases were also experienced, a fourth form was enunciated: *all variations* in the price level are caused by changes in the (circulating) amount of money, or to put the same point in other words: the quantity of money determines *exclusively* the value of money.[14] Consequently, the price level is an entirely *passive* factor. The acceptance of the latter idea *per se*, however, is no subscription to the preceding exclusive explanation of the fluctuations in the price level. They might be explained in terms of changes both in the quantity and in the 'velocity' of circulation of money, and in the amount of transactions, or by only one or a combination of two of these factors. Accordingly, it is incorrect to denote the adherents of this idea as quantity theorists as they also might contend that the quantity of money is a passive factor. By *extreme* quantity theorists is sometimes meant those who unreservedly accept this fourth form of the quantity theory.

Admitting the influence of changes in the amount of transactions (and, to a minor degree, in the velocity of circulation of money) the fourth, rigid form has been somewhat modified. Thus one group which maintains that the variations in the price level are chiefly caused by fluctuations in the quantity of money, can be distinguished. This group comprises three forms: one that does not differentiate between various kinds of currency, a second according to which the explanation refers only to a convertible or metal currency, and a third, which implies its applicability to irredeemable paper money only.

There is also another, still more modified group, covering those forms which assert that the quantity of money is one of the main causes influencing the price level. The most modified group merely maintains

---

[13] This form constitutes the fourth group in Marschak's classification, which reads: 1) prices will increase in proportion to the increase of the quantity of money; or 2) they will increase, but not proportionately; 3) the increased quantity of money *may* be the cause of a price increase; 4) it *is* the cause of *every* general price increase; 5) it is *always the cause* and never the effect of the decreased value of money; and 6) its sole effect is a deterioration of the value of money (»Die Verkehrsgleichung», *A. f. S.*, 1924, p. 345). There seems to be no real difference between group 4 and 5, since the latter statement is a necessary corollary of the fourth. It is merely a difference in phrasing the same idea. The first, second and sixth groups evidently involve a prognosis, while the other groups involve an explanation of the changes in the price level.

[14] This formulation is used by A. Pose as a description of the quantity theory (»Esquisse de l'évolution de la théorie quantitative», *R. H. é.*, 1926, p. 153; also see pp. 162—163).

that the quantity of money may play an active role, more or less dominant, in relation to the price level.[15] Although the adherents of this group can hardly be called quantity theorists, they are characterized as such if they happen to explain an actual price increace in terms of an increased quantity of money. Then there is but one step to that comprehensive group of 'anti-quantity theorists' who consider the quantity of money an exclusively passive factor.

B. The formulations of prognoses based upon the causal relation were, of course, concomitant with the recognition of this relationship. Thus the Chinese maintained that an increase or decrease of the circulation would raise or lower prices. The same idea occurs in Copernicus' writings, but Locke (although not consistently) and Adam Smith contended that a decrease in the quantity of money would lead to a corresponding decrease in the amount of transactions, not to a lowering of prices. When the misinterpretation of Locke's idea of proportionality was combined with the idea of causality, the commonly accepted, theoretical version of the quantity theory appeared. Being a proposition of what will happen under very restricted circumstances, it was later reformulated: variations in the quantity of money will *tend* to cause proportionate price variations in the long run. Also this form, which represents Fisher's view, is sometimes called a *modified* quantity theory. The same attribute is also applied to that version which gives consideration to parallel fluctuations in the amount of transactions, that is, the causality and proportionality is maintained between M and $\frac{PT}{V}$.

The proposition that variations in the 'velocity' of circulation of money have the same effect as those of the quantity of money, is frequently denoted as an *extended* quantity theory.[16] Since a change in the total

---

[15] Denis calls this opinion the quantitative idea: »l'idée quantitative, *c'est-à-dire l'idée suivant laquelle la variation de la quantité de monnaie exerce* parfois *une influence* dominante *sur la mouvement des prix*» (*op. cit.*, p. XIV). This idea is said to be the primary and fundamental concept of monetary theory.

[16] There is no unanimity in using these different appellations. Thus, what is here called an extended version of the quantity theory is characterized as »la forme mathématique» by Baudin (see p. 180, note 12), and by Kirmaier as the modified quantity theory. Kirmaier also speaks of the mechanical quantity theory, implying only a mechanical relation between money and price, of the theory of proportionality, and of that theory, finally, which expresses the relation between the circulation and the transactions by an equation and from this tries to elicit numerical conclusions concerning the variations

quantity of money and in the velocity of circulation of money appears as a change in the quantity of money used during the relevant period of time, consistency requires that the effects must be the same in both cases. There is no possibility of determining whether an increased amount of purchases during a given period is due to an increased quantity or velocity of circulation of money until the end of the period. Therefore, the cash-balance approach has sometimes been treated as merely an extended form of the quantity theory. This is particularly true when the quantity theory is formulated as a prognosis. In inflationary times this form has been used as an explanation of the price increase — especially with reference to the equation of exchange — if the additional quantity of money has not been sufficient to account for the whole price increase. This coalescence of two entirely different ideas is fundamentally due to the misinterpretation of the original quantity theory. The very name itself, if it is to have any justification, must be an emphasis upon the quantity as such of money. In Locke's statement, which we consider to be a correct formulation of the basic idea of the quantity theory, the emphasis is upon the insignificance, in point of principle, of the *quantity* of money. The proposition that general prices will always be in proportion to the circulating amount of money, is an *illustration* of this idea. The extension of this illustration to the relation between changes in the velocity of circulation of money and the price level has entirely overlooked the fundamental idea based upon the quantity theory, namely that variations in the quantity of money will not affect the velocity of circulation of money. If this 'extended' formulation, which cannot be described as an extension of the quantity theory, includes the *ceteris-paribus* premise, the import of the prognosis is reduced to a proposition of an undeniable, arithmetic relation in economic terms which has no purpose. It is merely playing with words. Such a simplification of the cash-balance approach is misleading. Its purpose was not to relate the velocity of circulation of money to proportionate price variations, but to emphasize that changes in the desire to keep cash-holdings (in real terms) meant changes in the velocity of circulation of money, which would influence the price level. In so far it was an objection to Fisher's method of treating the velocity of circulation of money as wholly institutionally given.

---

in the value of money (*op. cit.*, pp. 33—34). His four groups are rather a classification of the historical development of the interpretation of the relation between money and prices than of the formulations of the quantity theory.

C. The quantity theory has also been understood as the explanation of the exchange value of money. The interpretation originates in Davanzati's equalization of the total quantity of money with the total amount of goods. Hence the exchange value of the monetary unit was thought of as being determined by the number of units with a given amount of goods. As has been pointed out (see pp. 19, 33 and 54), this reasoning is untenable; for if there were one single exchange of the total quantity of money for the total amount of goods, there would be no exchange relation in terms of any standard of value. It would be the same thing as an isolated exchange of two commodities. Such an exchange relation could, of course, be expressed in the relative weights of the commodities, but nothing could be said of their relative values. Since there is no 'macro-exchange' of all commodities for all money, but only a 'micro-exchange', that is, every single commodity is exchanged for a certain amount of monetary units, the exchange value of money must be determined in some other way; and since no exchange value could be originally determined without a real exchange, the exchange value of money must have been determined in that way. The unit of measure was then some unit of weight as the names of some means of exchange still indicate. Consequently, a comparison of the total quantity of money with the total amount of goods must be based on some standard of value, which means that the exchange relations are settled also.

Nor is another conclusion that was drawn from Davanzati's comparison, namely that the quantity of money and the total amount of goods *determine* the price level, correct. In Fisher's equation, for example, the symbols M, V and T, do not *determine* the price level, P, since all their numerical values are interrelated; but changes in the activities they represent will *affect* the price level, if they are not counterbalanced by other changes. This way of comparing aggregative quantities was further employed by Locke, Hume and Montesquieu, and fostered the idea that the quantity of money determined the exchange value of money. The quantity theory then appeared as a contrast to the cost-of-production theory, according to which the quantity of money was determined by its value. This interpretation, which really is a quantity theory of the value of money, has been accepted more in its application to an inconvertible paper currency. The impossibility, however, of determining the value of money in this way, remains.[17]

[17] L. von Mises stresses that the quantity theory as such does not constitute any theory of the value of money, but that it must be based upon some general theory of value

These interpretations also provided the background for the early attempts to coordinate the general theories of money and prices. Using the cost-of-production theory or some other theory, as an explanation of relative prices, the quantity theory was thought of as supplying the equation which would determine the multiplicative factor and hence absolute prices. But then the quantity of money must be shown to be determined independently of the value of money.[18]. As mentioned above, however, the quantity of money is interdependently related to prices and the number of transactions, and there are no exclusive causal relations. Besides, the multiplicative factor is institutionally determined. Treating general prices as a function of the quantity of money, *ceteris paribus*, and presuming an exclusive, causal relation, this version of the quantity theory would only be able to explain certain changes in the price level.

Though the quantity of money has been most often related to general prices, it has also been related to individual prices. This form of the quantity theory has been characterized as a quantitative theory of individual prices. It might be worth remembering that the quantity theory was criticised from this standpoint as late as the beginning of this century (see p. 78).

(*Theorie des Geldes und der Umlaufsmittel,* München, 1924, pp. 110—111). W. C. Mitchell's title of the article »The Quantity Theory of the Value of Money» is significant (see p. 000, note 00), and M. Palyi begins his description of the quantity theory in the following way: »Wie jede Geldwerttheorie stellt sich auch die Quantitätstheorie . . . .» (*op. cit.*, p. 1147).

Wicksell speaks of the cost-of-production theory as an *element* of the quantity theory, because it provides the reason for the changes in the quantity of money (*Lectures,* vol. II, p. 149).

[18] See Rosenstein-Rodan's article »The Coordination of the General Theories of Money and Prices» in which he points out that the difficulty in determining quantitatively the supply of money (because the velocity of money was left undetermined) was not realized at first (*Economica*, 1935, p. 258). G. Myrdal affirms that the quantity theory has »to prove that there is a certain *causal* connexion between the two, such that, *ceteris paribus*, the price level is determined by the amount of means of payment. For otherwise the quantity theory does not provide the missing link in the theory of prices. The multiplicative factor (in the quantity theory, the 'price level') has to be given as a function of the amount of means of payment, which in its turn has to be determined in some other way than by relation to the 'price level'» (*op. cit.*, 12; also see pp. 13—17). Though Myrdal is correct that the quantity theory does not provide »the missing link» in the theory of prices, his argument seems to be basically wrong. He, as well as many other economists, does not draw the distinction between a change in a *given* price level, caused by variations in the amount of the means of payment, and the determination itself of this given price level. No missing equation can supply the answer since it is institutionally conditioned (*cf.*, note 43, p. 93).

Locke has been said to be »the parent of twin quantity theories»: one for the relation between money and prices, and the other for the relation between money and interest.[19] Almost every theory in which the quantity of money plays an important role is thus called a quantity theory. But if the rate of interest is considered as merely the price of the right to use money, then there is no specific reason for denoting the determination of this price as a quantity theory, since it is a simple application of the law of demand and supply. Indeed, it is very interesting that Locke contended that only decreases in the quantity of money (as capital) would influence the rate of interest, since the demand for money (both as capital and as a means of exchange) could never be satisfied. Hume pointed to the distribution of property as decisive for the rate of interest, because it influenced the supply of money. Montesquieu also recognized the importance of the supply of money, while Ricardo, on the other hand, firmly asserted that the rate of interest was independent of the quantity of money, except for temporary influences. His opinion was substantially shared by Tooke.[20] Since Locke related the total (circulating) quantity of money (because of his confusion of money with capital) to the rate of interest, his interest theory is evidently closer to the quantity-theory approach than the Keynesian, in which only a certain part of the circulation is said to influence the rate of interest. In any case, it is misleading to name it a quantity theory of money, even though it might be contended that the idea of a causal relation between money and prices still remains, but works indirectly and via changes in the rate of interest.

D. The correct formulation of the basic idea of the quantity 'theory' as indicating a specific peculiarity of money has few variations. In Locke's original statement, that prices are always in proportion to the quantity of money, money refers to metallic money. Therefore, it has been asserted that the quantity theory applies only to a metallic standard of value. But this argument is based on an implicit assumption of a certain causal relation and does not invalidate the applicability of Locke's proposition to all means of exchange. The fundamental idea still is, that whatever media serve as means of exchange, they have no value as such, and do not add to the wealth of nations. If this formulation

---

19 Keynes: *General Theory,* p. 343.

20 See *The Works of Ricardo,* pp. 220—221 and 284, and Tooke: *An Inquiry into the Currency Principle,* p. 124, and *A History of Prices,* vol. III, p. 245, vol. IV, p. 200, and vol. V, p. 345.

is to be called a theory, then it is merely a theory of the nonexistence of an 'intrinsic' value of money. The application of this theory to paper money reduces it to a platitude, since nobody would argue that notes as such have any value. The idea of proportionality can also be phrased: If other things remain the same, money and prices *vary* in the same proportion, and direction.[21] Such a formulation is evidently limited to the arithmetic relation between money and prices. Hence no causal relations are involved. But since this formulation most often implies a causal relation, although no exclusiveness in that respect, it is better not to use it, especially if the purpose is to stress the proportionate relation only.

It is obvious that Locke's original idea cannot be termed a *theory*. Nor did Locke aim at formulating any theory of the effects of changes in the quantity of money. But his argument can very well furnish the foundation of such a theory, namely that money is fundamentally a medium of exchange only. Hence changes in the quantity of money, *ceteris paribus*, must imply corresponding changes in the quantity of the medium of exchange. This is merely another way of saying that changes in the quantity of money will not affect the velocity of circulation, or the rate of turnover, of money. Changes in the quantity of money will thus cause corresponding changes in the amount of monetary purchases. This is the *theory* of money that can be formulated upon Locke's original idea. To characterize this formulation as a quantity theory of money appears rather inadequate, as it reveals nothing about its basic content. It would be more adequate to denote it the theory of money (as a medium of exchange) in its relation to changes in the quantity of money. The much debated question about the relation of changes in the quantity of money to prices then appears as only of secondary interest. If the total supply of goods and services remain the same, average prices will vary in conformity with the increase or decrease in monetary purchases. Such a coincidence must then be described as a *special* case of the theory of money (as a medium of exchange) in its relation to changes in the quantity of money. This special case, however, must be distinguished from the illustration, *e.g.* (by using the equation of exchange), of the specific peculiarity of the medium of exchange, which does not contain any causal propositions. It is very curious, indeed, that this special case, which has no practical relevance, has been debated for centuries, and has been the object of the most elaborate statistical investigations, mainly undertaken in order to prove who was wrong or who was right

[21] This formulation is suggested by G. Åkerman; see »Inflation, penningmängd och ränta», *E.T.*, 1921, p. 162.

in their propositions about the effects of changes in the quantity of money. It is unnecessary to say, that monetary theory did not make any substantial progress by these so futile discussions, which very often appeared as matters of prestige rather than as matters of truth.

Say's law, Keynes' General Theory, and the Quantity Theory

6. Say's law of markets — that supply creates its own demand — has two purposes: to prove that general over-production is impossible and that the use of a general means of exchange does not influence the fundamental economic relations. Money is only a veil, concealing the fact that the real exchange is not money for commodities (and services), but commodities for other commodities. This idea dominated the whole orthodox economics. From its point of view it did not make any difference as to whether money existed or not. It did facilitate the operations of exchange, but fundamentally it did not change anything. Money appeared as a standard of value and as a means of exchange; its property of being a store of value had no influence on the economic system. This view was in full conformity with Locke's statement that prices are always in proportion to the quantity of money. Of course, the conclusion was drawn that changes in the quantity of money would only influence prices, but not the state of general equilibrium. If, for example, demand should diminish because of an increased 'hoarding', average prices would decline, but the general equilibrium would still remain and no unemployment would result. Those commodities and/or services not being purchased by the hoarders would be purchased by other people, who, thanks to the general decrease in prices, could increase their quantity demanded. If, on the other hand, there were a shift in demand from one product to another, the change in relative prices would merely cause a reorganization of production, which was a purely technical question, causing only temporary unemployment. Thus the theory of money was a theory of price levels, and the orthodox economists, implicitly or explicitly, accepted the quantity theory as it was stated by Locke and Hume.

The logical outcome of Keynes' criticism of classical economics is a refutation of the quantity theory, that is, of treating money as purely a means of exchange. Since changes in the circulating amount of money mean changes in the total demand, the fundamental economic relations will be affected. There is nothing that automatically makes the system work towards a state of equilibrium at full employment. The orthodox theory, that there is only one state of equilibrium — that of full employment, in which all prices, *i.e.*, the prices of commodities and services, wages, rates of interest and rents of land, exactly conform to the existing relations of demand and supply — was 'proved' to be inadequate in explaining actual conditions, where 'equilibrium' existed at less than full employment. In fact, the general equilibrium in orthodox economics was said to be a special case, the realization of which appeared to be a fortunate coincidence.

The difference between Say's law, which is the foundation of classical economics, and Keynes' *General Theory* can be illustrated by a simple diagram.

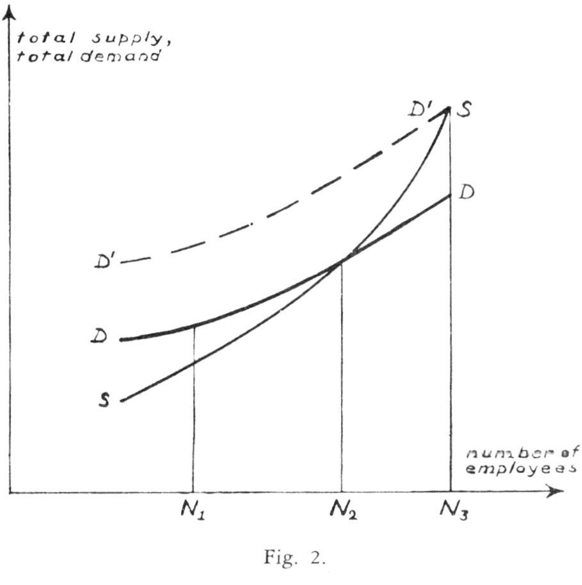

Fig. 2.

In fig. 2 the curve $S-S$ signifies the total supply of, and the curve $D-D$ the total demand for goods and services (measured in real terms) with various numbers of employees in a closed economy. It is reasonable to assume that within relevant ranges, increased employment results in an increased output and demand. But with decreasing employment it might well be argued that the declining demand does not follow the same curve as when employment is rising, since human beings will tend to increase consumption, at a given increase in income, more than they will reduce it at a corresponding decline in income. For the sake of demonstration, however, this does not make any difference. Furthermore, it is assumed that an increase in the number of employees means an increase in the total amount of real wages, and that there is a fixed correlation between variations in employment and output.

In conformity with Keynesian economics, the point of equilibrium, where the total demand corresponds to the total supply, is the same point on the horizontal axis at which total planned investment matches planned saving. But there is no reason that this point should automatically correspond to that point which denotes full employment, N_3. Experience shows that the demand and supply schedules might intersect before full employment is reached. This is denoted by N_2, which thus illustrates a state of equilibrium at less than full employment.

Some further explanation of the relative position of the curves might be required. Suppose that the total amount of supply and demand were measured in monetary terms. Then the supply curve would characterize the development of the total national income as employment increased (at a given price level). At relatively low levels of the total national income, it is very likely that the total demand will exceed the national income — the monetary difference made possible by using 'hoarded' money, deposits, loans or consumer's credit, exceeding the total amount of planned saving. The sum of these items is detoned by that part of the perpendicular at N_1, which falls between the two curves. The difference in real terms is matched by a decrease in stocks. The effect will be an increase of production and employment. This will continue until the point, where the two curves intersect, is reached. If production and employment rise beyond this equilibrium point, the total supply will exceed the total demand; that is, saving will exceed planned investment, the difference being equalized by increased stocks. As a result, production and employment will decrease to N_2.

The fundamental difference between Keynesian and orthodox economics is now easily demonstrated. For according to Say's law there is, simply, no discrepancy between the total demand and supply curve, since his law actually means that the two curves coincide in their whole extent (illustrated by the 'double' curve SD—SD in fig. 3). Accordingly, there are no problems of equilibrium at less than full employment. Every point on Say's curve would represent an equilibrium point. The number of employed would always correspond to full employment, implying that all those who want to work are employed. If the total supply and demand are measured in monetary terms, then an increased (and realized) desire to hold cash (with a given quantity

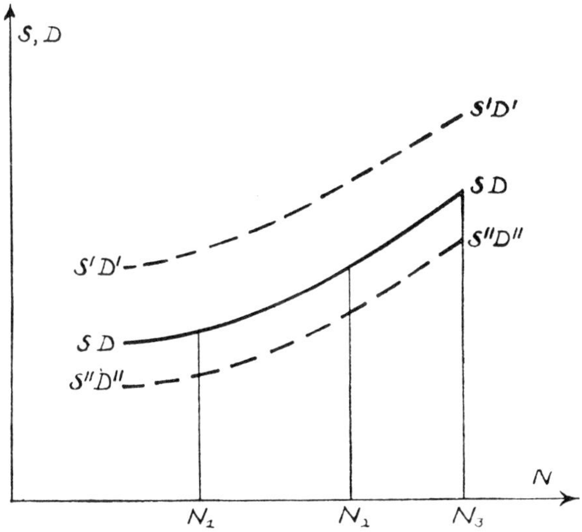

Fig. 3.

of money) would merely mean a parallel shift downwards of the curve SD—SD (indicated by the dotted curve $S''D''$—$S''D''$ in fig. 3), with no effects on output and employment. Increased savings are always met by increased demand for savings and might lead to reorganizations of production, but with no effect on total supply. An increased quantity of money would only lead to a parallel shift upwards of 'Say's curve' (indicated by the dotted curve $S'D'$—$S'D'$ in fig. 3); if, on the other hand, total demand and supply are measured in real terms, nothing would happen to the curve SD—SD. This is the necessary result of the role ascribed to money in orthodox economics.[22]

In Keynesian economics, increases in the quantity of money will always affect production and employment except for one case: at full employment. Although Keynes mainly emphasized their effects on the rate of interest, their chief effect will be on total demand. Increases in the quantity of money, for example by 'dishoarding', budget-deficit spending, and/or open-market operations, will cause an upward shift of

[22] *Cf.* Calvin B. Hoover's remark that Say's law of markets will be operative also in 'statized', *i.e.*, fully collectivized, economy. This means that our discussion above can just as well be interpreted as a comparison between a »Keynesian economy», *i.e.*, an economy in which equilibrium at less than full employment is possible, and a fully collectivized economy (»Keynes and the Economic System», *J. P. E.*, 1948, pp. 394—396).

the demand curve *D—D* in fig. 2, whereas 'Say's curve' will remain unaffected (if demand and supply are measured in real terms). This upward shift will continue until the Keynesian demand curve intersects the supply curve at that point from which the perpendicular crosses the horizontal axis at N_3, indicating full employment (illustrated by the dotted curve *D'—D'* in fig. 2). Thereafter, further increases in the quantity of money will not influence the demand curve. If demand is measured in monetary terms, the equilibrium point will move straight upwards in conformity with the corresponding point on the demand curve *SD—SD* in fig. 3. This is the only case where the application of the quantity theory, implying a proposition of causality and proportionality, has any relevance, and where orthodox and Keynesian theories agree. But it must be remembered that it only refers to *increases* in the quantity of money. If it is decreased, the Keynesian equilibrium point will move down the supply curve, while the orthodox equilibrium point will remain unaffected.[23]

Orthodox economics cannot be blamed for the lack of integrating monetary theory within its general theory. Rather, one might praise the consistency of the system. Money, simply, did not constitute an integral part of the system; it was something added 'afterwards' in order to facilitate the working of the system without influencing its basic relations. This view received its first clear-cut statement by Locke, but the convincing power of its correctness was provided by Say's law of markets, and further illustrated by the accepted version of the quantity theory. This emphasis upon money as chiefly a means of exchange is the fundamental reason that monetary theory remained outside the scope of economic theory for such a long time. Variations in the price level were not a function of the working of the system itself, but were explained in terms of changes in the (relative) quantity of money; nor, could they be any indicators of changes in the total demand, which was determined by the supply of commodities.

---

[23] *Cf.* also Schumpeter's remark: »It should, however, be noticed that, for a point of equilibrium, one of the relations subsisting between aggregative quantities may be expressed by what is known as the *equation of exchange* or even in terms of the 'quantity theory of money', which is formally correct for such points and only for such points. In fact, it is simply a condition of equilibrium» (*Business Cycles,* 2 vols., New York and London, 1939, vol. I, p. 44). The relations between the aggregative quantities *M*, *V*, and *T* can, of course, always be expressed by the equation of exchange, regardless of any equilibrium; but the 'quantity theory' is correct only for an equilibrium point, implying *full employment,* and if it is formulated as a proposition of the effects of an increased quantity of money, used as a medium of exchange (*cf.* pp. 110—111).

The merit of the quantity theory is its clear illustration of the fact that money as such does not constitute any wealth; but in this lies also its great weakness. It focussed attention on money as a pure means of exchange, which led to a neglect of its function as a store of value, representing potential purchasing power. In a monetary system of disequilibrium, caused by a discrepancy between total demand and supply, or in a system of equilibrium at less than full employment, this function of money is one of the basic reasons for these unsatisfactory conditions. An adequate economic theory must make the role of money as a store of value an integral part of its framework. Every analysis of the effects of changes in the quantity of money must consider the function of money both as a medium of exchange and as a store of value. An attempt to synthesize the analysis of these two functions is provided in the second part of this study.

PART II

CHAPTER XI

THE QUANTITY OF MONEY AND ITS DIFFERENT FUNCTIONS

1. Money will be understood to include coins, bank (and treasury) notes, and demand deposits (so-called bank money). A second definition of money as including everything which is generally accepted as a means of payment is not applicable in this case, for checks are not accepted generally but only between certain individuals and institutions for certain payments. From the viewpoint of monetary theory, however, the first definition seems to be the best one and is also most often used. The total quantity of money within a given society, M, will then be equal to the total quantity of coins and bank notes, and deposits subject to check (so-called demand deposits), minus those quantities which function as a reserve against circulating media of exchange.[1] The quantity of money thus defined does not correspond exactly to Keynes' definition of M, since he also included overdraft facilities.[2] This will not be done here, however, because it makes the concept of the total quantity of money rather vague.

No sharp line can be drawn between money and near-money, and the definition is merely a matter of convenience for the purpose of this analysis. It should be mentioned that the original quantity theory only referred to coins (or bank notes covered by 100% reserves). A realistic analysis, however, of the effects of changes in the quantity of money of a present society must also include deposits subject to check. When time deposits are turned into demand deposits, whether at a certain price or not, they should be included also. Here the line of distinction immediately becomes obscure. This is also true in respect to all those near-moneys represented by government bonds, treasury bills, first-rated

[1] For a more detailed discussion of different definitions of money, see L. Currie: *The Supply and Control of Money in the United States* (Harvard Economic Studies, vol. XLVII), Cambridge, Mass., pp. 10—24; also see Ellis, *op. cit.*, pp. 105 and 128—129.

[2] See *General Theory*, p. 167, note 1, and p. 196; also see Pigou: *Keynes' General Theory. A Retrospect*, London, 1950, p. 9, where attention is drawn to this circumstance.

securities, *etc.*, which at certain transactions are perfect substitutes for money.[3] There is no need, however, for the purpose of our discussion, to dwell on these questions, since they will be of no importance for the ideas.developed in chapter XIV.

2. The most important function of money is to serve as a generally accepted medium of exchange, that is, a commodity which is accepted by everybody in exchange for any commodity or service. It will serve as a perfect medium of exchange, other things being equal, only if the time interval between its reception and its spending is relatively short. This is the basic purpose of the usage of money.[4] The longer the period becomes between the reception and the spending of money, the more it becomes a store of value and the less it appears as merely a medium of exchange. No sharp line of distinction can be drawn between these two functions from the viewpoint of an individual cash holder. If money is to be a medium of exchange (and a standard of value), it also must be a store of value between the reception and spending of it. But in this fact lies also the basic dilemma. For it is quite obvious that from a social point of view, money is fundamentally a medium of exchange and it is meaningless to speak of it as a (potential) store of value.

Classical doctrine treated money mainly as a medium of exchange, simply because it dealt primarily with money from a social point of view. The acceptance of the basic idea of the quantity theory, which emphasized the role of money as a medium of exchange, is then merely the logical outcome. The very name of Fisher's well-known formula, the equation of *exchange*, is a direct indication that money is dealt with only in its function as a medium of exchange. Fisher deals with total aggregates, and he is undoubtedly correct in that every increase in the quantity of money used *only* as a means of exchange, *ceteris paribus*, must occasion corresponding changes in the price level.

If money functioned solely as a means of exchange, then it could be looked upon as merely the oil which makes the economic system operate more smoothly (Hume), or as a shunting locomotive at a railway station (N. G. Pierson), or as a veil (Say and Pigou). The theory of money would then only have to be added after the analysis of the

[3] For a short but concise discussion of this question, see E. C. Simmons: »The Relative Liquidity of Money and Other Things», *A. E. R.*, 1947 (Supplement), pp. 308—311 (reprinted in *Readings in Monetary Theory,* Philadelphia, 1951).

[4] *Cf.* the following, very pertinent, characterization by Halm: »It is the very essence of money to be re-spent» (*Monetary Theory,* 2 ed., Philadelphia, 1948, p. 66).

'fundamental' economic relations. Such a treatment of the functions of money, however, leaves out the function of money as a store of value, which actually seems to be one of the roots of the *imperfection* of the working of the economic system. That no real attempts were made before the appearance of Keynes' *General Theory,* except for Wicksell's, to integrate the monetary theory with the economic theory is primarily due to the fact that the function of money as a store of value was considered to have just as little influence on the economic system as that of being a medium of exchange, that is, actually none. For changes in the quantity of money 'hoarded' were merely interpreted as changes in the quantity of money as a medium of exchange, and with the same results, that is, causing corresponding changes in the price level. The total economic activity could not be influenced; only minor adjustments would take place. It was perfectly correct from a social point of view, for then money loses its function of being a store of (potential) wealth. But the total economic activity is the result of endless individual actions. And from the individual's viewpoint, money as a store of value is of fundamental importance.

3. It is not surprising that Keynes, in his attempts to provide a realistic theory of money to be integrated with a 'general' theory, went too far in his emphasis on money as a store of value, thereby making the same mistake as the mercantilists. He stated in italics that »*the importance of money essentially flows from its being a link between the present and the future*».[5] This is not quite correct, for the importance of money essentially flows from its being *a link in the exchange of one commodity or service for another.* Because of the imperfections of market conditions[6] and the very fact that every process of exchange (with money) will always require some time, money must also be a store of value over short periods. A short period means that length of time which is required, because of market imperfections, for money to function fundamentally as a medium of exchange. When money is primarily looked upon as a link between the present and the future, then its main function has become that of being a store of value.

There are three main reasons the function of money as a store of value played such an important role in ancient times: (1) the great imperfections of the commodity market, (2) the still greater imperfections

[5] *General Theory,* p. 293.

[6] For example, that willing borrowers and lenders cannot be brought in touch with each other; further see Halm, *op. cit.*, p. 73, note 6.

of the credit market, and (3) the lack of distinction between money, *i.e.*, coins, as a medium of exchange and as a commodity.[7] If money has a value as a commodity, then it will represent a store of wealth also from the viewpoint of society as a whole. Since this factor can be neglected under present conditions, it follows that money is a store of value only from the viewpoint of an individual cash holder, and only under certain conditions as will be pointed out below.

In contrast to Keynes' statement above, we quote Wicksell, who emphasizes that »the function of acting as a *store of value* is not essentially characteristic of money».[8] This is easily demonstrated if we assume that everybody simultaneously refrained from spending ten per cent of his cash holdings, held, *e.g.*, for consumption expenditures. The result would then be, *ceteris paribus*, a corresponding decrease in the price level of consumption goods. Consumption in real terms, consequently, would be the same as before, and nothing would be saved. If everybody later on increased his consumption expenditures on the same day by ten per cent, then average prices — other things remaining the same — would increase by the corresponding amount. Consumption would still be the same in real terms. Accordingly, the money withdrawn has not acted as a store of value, for the cash holder is not better off in any respect. Money has only functioned as a medium of exchange.

If we assume, instead, that only one cash holder diminishes his cash balances for consumption expenditures by ten per cent, then there will be an infinitely small decrease in prices on consumption goods. As a result, all other cash holders will be a little better off and they will increase their consumption in real terms by as much as our cash holder has diminished his own. But our cash holder does not succeed in diminishing his consumption by ten per cent in real terms. Because of the slight price decrease, he also gets a little more from his remaining expenditures as compared with what they purchased for him before the withdrawal of some cash (or slowing down of the rate of turnover of his cash holdings). Consequently, nothing is saved (in real terms) from a social point of view. But in this case, the withdrawn money will act as a store of value for the individual cash holder, although not as a perfect one. When he increases his consumption expenditures by ten per cent on a future day, then — other things remaining the same —

---

[7] Wicksell speaks very pointedly of »the *ancient function* of money as a means of storing value» (*Lectures*, vol. II, p. 24; italics added).

[8] *Ibid.*, p. 8.

there will be a very slight increase in prices, so that the total consumption of the other cash holders is diminished by exactly the same amount as is was earlier increased. Owing to the slight price increase, as well as to the original price decrease, the cash holder does not first decrease and then increase his consumption expenditures by quite ten per cent in real terms. Hence, money, even from the individual cash holder's point of view, is not a perfect store of value.

On the other hand, the cash holder does not directly store anything in real terms by slowing down the rate of turnover of his cash holdings. In as much as he has temporarily diminished his consumption in real terms, so much it is increased when he increases his spendings in the future. But he certainly has to pay a price for his increased liquidity, namely the amount of goods by which he diminishes his consumption, thereby letting the other consumers increase their consumption in real terms to a corresponding degree. What actually takes place is a redistribution of total income (in real terms) as long as our cash holder prefers an increased liquidity. Society as a whole will not be better off, unless the redistribution of income makes it possible to increase the productivity of the benefiting cash holders more than it diminishes that of our cash holder.

The fundamental fact which has been demonstrated is that money is not a perfect store of value without certain assumptions. If, in our case, the cash holder wants to diminish his consumption expenditures (by slowing down the rate of turnover of his cash holdings) by, say, ten per cent in *real* terms, then he has to diminish his monetary outlays by approximately eleven per cent. Money will act as a perfect store of value only if the price level remains stable. This requires that as soon as somebody is diminishing his stream of expenditures, someone else's has to be increased by the same amount. Accordingly, the policy of keeping the price level stable, *ceteris paribus*, appears to be extremely difficult since it requires a perfect money and credit market, which could eliminate the fluctuations in the circulating quantity of money.

It should be added that money will serve as a store of value also from a social point of view, if we are dealing with one nation as compared with other nations, that is, in respect to international trade. This was, indeed, the basic idea of the mercantilist policy, the purpose of which was to obtain more precious metals than other countries. What was true for an individual cash holder, was then also true for a single nation. The seeming dilemma was that the increased imports of precious metals tended to raise prices, thereby making it gradually more difficult to achieve an export surplus (*cf.* Viner's remark, note 1, p. 168). If the imports of precious metals primarily served to build up a cash reserve, then there was no inconsistency in the mercantilists' reasoning, for that meant a building up of the potential purchasing power of the nation in the international market. The critics of these mercantilist ideas, therefore, in formulating the quantity theory, looked upon money mainly from a social point of view in a closed economy. In such an economy, money has but one main function, that of being a medium of exchange. But those quantity theorists, for example, Locke and Hume, who also regarded money as a store of value from a social point of view, could, without being inconsistent, be adherents of the mercantilist views.

It cannot be said that classical economics disregarded the function of money as a store of value, and that Keynes' *General Theory* is the only attempt to give due consideration to this function and to its effects upon the economic system. On the contrary, the existence of so-called hoarding has been a well-known phenomenon since ancient times. The fundamental difference between the classical doctrine and the Keynesian theory lies in the treatment of the *effects* of changes in various cash holdings. For the early and the classical economists, following the basic idea of the quantity theory, the effects would be the same as those from changes in the quantity of money as a medium of exchange, that is, only prices would be affected. They (*e.g.*, Locke, Hume and Ricardo) admitted, however, that the rates of interest could be influenced also, but only temporarily. Keynes, on the other hand, maintains that changes in the quantity of money (held primarily as a store of value) will lastingly affect the rate of interest, thereby influencing the whole economic activity. In so far as Keynes is dealing with equilibrium situations at less than full utilization of all resources, he should not attack the classical view since it only concerned equilibrium situations at full utilization of all resources.

4. The third function of money is that of being a standard of value. This function is not necessarily related to that of being a general medium of exchange. It was not a distinguished property of money at first, but was imparted to it later on. In early days, the commonly accepted medium of exchange, whether a goat, a cow or an ox, was not also necessarily the standard of value. This meant that every medium of exchange had to be estimated in respect to a given standard goat, cow, or ox. That these animals happened to be chosen may be explained by

the circumstance that they once were the most *marketable* commodities.[9] These media of exchange could never simultaneously become the standard of value, since various units of the same kind always differed more or less from one another. Therefore, they were gradually replaced by the precious metals, because of the latter's superior qualities as media of exchange. Those qualities are, primarily, their small costs of transportation as compared with their high value of exchange, their divisibility into small pieces, their homogeneity, their indestructibility (almost), and their relative scarcity.

With the evolution of the coinage of precious metals, constituting either a given standard of value or a given multiple of it, the third function (in the short run), or perhaps more properly speaking, property was automatically given to money. It is widely recognized that if the medium of exchange also serves as a standard of value, it becomes highly desirable that its value is kept constant. This has not been possible, partly because the monetary authorities never had the power to eliminate all influences due to changes in the relative quantity of money in circulation, and partly because even the existence of these possibilities is not enough to keep the price level stable. It should also be borne in mind that the function of money as both a medium of exchange and as a store of value makes it extremely difficult to predict anything reliable about the effects of changes in the quantity of money.

5. The monetary controversies have circled very much around the emphasis given money as either a medium of exchange or as a store of value in the analysis of the effects of changes in the quantity of money upon the price level. Thus the Fisherine approach continued the emphasis — taken over from the quantity theory — on money as purely a means of exchange, whereas the cash-balance approach, by pointing out the importance of changes in individual cash holdings, *i.e.*, in the rate of turnover of money, was again an attempt to emphasize the role of money as a store of value. Keynes' main contribution to monetary theory seems to lie in his accomplishment of a differentiation

[9] See, for example, T. Greidanus: *The Value of Money*, London, 1932, p. 199 ff. Adam Smith's remark that the choice of a common standard »will naturally at first be the commodity with which they [*i.e.*, men] are best acquainted» seems to give the basic reason (*Lectures*, p. 183). The chain of causation may then be that because these animals were more marketable, men were more acquainted with them; and so they were selected as the standard of value. The reason for their great marketability was probably, as convincingly explained by Adam Smith, the little expense of keeping the cattle since the whole country was considered as one great common.

between cash holdings kept for transactions purposes, *i.e.*, money kept as a medium of exchange primarily, and cash holdings kept for speculation purposes, *i.e.*, money kept primarily as a store of value. It is no coincidence that he went to the mercantilists in order to sustain his ideas. The main difference is, however, that whereas the mercantilists emphasized money as a store of value from a social point of view, Keynes emphasized this role from the viewpoint of the individual cash holder.

The main purpose of monetary theory can perhaps be characterized briefly as an analysis of the function of money as a medium of exchange and as a store of value in their effects upon the function of money as a standard of value, thereby providing a basis for actions of monetary policy aiming at regulating the value of money according to given principles.

CHAPTER XII

VARIOUS CASH HOLDINGS AND THEIR RELATION TO THE RATE OF INTEREST AND THE PRICE LEVEL

1. Cash holdings can be distinguished according to the different functions of money. Thus, money is held as a medium of exchange, the so-called transactions balances; and it is held as a store of value, the so-called precautionary and speculative cash holdings.[1] Money, though not according to our definition, can also be held in order to keep the value of money stable; that is, the monetary authorities can keep a reserve which is used only in order to offset changes in the demand for money. In the following analysis, the cash holdings, because of the third function of money, are assumed to be zero. This seems to be a justifiable assumption, since we will not deal with a free currency system based on a precious metal. Hence, there is no reason for the monetary authorities to keep any cash reserve for stabilizing the value of money since they can print and destroy money at will.

2. It is evident that there is no way of telling exactly which part of the total quantity of money belongs to the *transactions* cash holdings until the end of a given period.[2] The quantity of money which has

[1] This way of looking at the different demands for money is mentioned by E. Petersen (*Macro-Dynamic Aspects*, p. 93).

[2] A. Hansen mentions that there is no way of separating statistically active and idle (passive) cash holdings without rather arbitrary assumptions (*op. cit.*, p. 56). This is undoubtedly true in respect to available statistics, and it refers just as much to the Keynesian separation of cash holdings according to the motives for keeping them as to our classification. From a purely theoretical point of view, however, there are no obstacles. Nor are there any practical obstacles, in point of principle, to distinguishing between active and passive cash holdings.

The symbol used in the following discussion, M_T, is also used by Hansen, although not in exactly the same sense. He includes, as Keynes did, cash holdings, because of the precautionary motive, under M_T, whilst we will include that part only which will actually be used during the relevant period. This is due to the fact that we differentiate fundamentally between used and unused (active and passive) cash holdings, not between the motives for keeping cash.

been used for at least one transaction during the relevant period constitutes the transactions cash holdings and is denoted by M_T. M_T will be called the *active* cash holdings as distinguished from the *passive* cash holdings.[3] They might also be classified as circulating and noncirculating money, respectively. Then it must be clearly emphasized, however, that the definition is connected with a certain period, since all money sooner or later will circulate. As this appelation is more apt to give rise to confusion than to clarification, it will not be used.

Ex ante, M_T is the total quantity of money which the cash holders expect to use for transactions during the following period. So defined, M_T includes that part of the total quantity of money which is kept in order to be used as a medium of exchange during the period in question. Thus, M_T satisfies the transactions motive. As pointed out (see note 2) this definition does not exactly conform to the Keynesian transactions motive, since it includes only that part of the 'precautionary' balances which is expected to be used during the following period. That is to say, M_T includes that part of the 'precautionary' cash holdings which is expected to be used during the relevant period because of realized emergency. It also includes that part of total cash holdings, held to satisfy the speculative motive, which is expected to be used for transactions during the following period.

The basic reason for holding cash balances is simply that the streams of income and of expenditures do not coincide, either in respect to time or to their extent. The motives for holding active cash balances are mainly the following: (1) planned consumption expenditures, (2) planned investment expenditures, (3) planned financial transactions, (4) planned tax payments, (5) expenditures because of contingencies expected to emerge during the coming period, and (6) planned speculative transactions during the coming period. Briefly expressed: active balances are held in order to meet all those transactions which are expected to become realized during the coming period. Of these six motives, the first two are evidently the most important and constitute the main motives for keeping transactions balances during a 'normal'

[3] This definition of active cash holdings does not coincide with Angell's, which refers to »that part of the stock of money which is spent at an interval after its receipt not greater than what is for the holder — whether an individual or a business enterprise — one customary income-expenditure period» (*The Behavior of Money*, New York, 1936, p. 10). Our definition comes closer to that of D. Hammarskjöld, who designates the actually circulating money as the real cash holding and the noncirculating money as cash reserves; see *Konjunkturspridningen* (Statens offentliga utredningar 1933: 29), Stockholm, 1933, pp. 37—39.

period. They may also be characterized as primarily *objective* motives, as distinguished from the motives of keeping passive cash balances, which might be called *subjective*.[4]

It should be noticed that the active cash holdings do not necessarily perform *all* the different transactions mentioned above. Though they usually do in respect to consumption and investment expenditures (and tax payments), financial transactions may, to a certain extent, take place via cancelling of debts. And taxes, to a certain extent, may be paid by government bonds. The larger these kinds of transactions are, the smaller the importance of the motives for active cash holdings under (3)—(6). Under certain assumptions, they can be neglected in the analysis of the effects of changes in the quantity of money.[5]

The determinants of the active cash holdings, M_T, which are primarily used for consumption and investment expenditures, are (1) the stream of total income, Y, (2) the price level, (3) the rates of interest, r, and (4) the aggregate value of the cash holders' total assets, A. Since A is fairly constant in a short-run analysis, it can be neglected;[6] and since total income is expressed in monetary terms, the influence of the price level is indirectly accounted for. If, further, the stream of investment expenditures is relatively small in comparison to that of consumption expenditures, it can also be neglected. The demand for money as a medium of exchange, M_T, can thus be expressed as primarily a function of the stream of total income, $M_T = L_T (Y)$, which is an absolute demand for money, running in monetary terms. But since the exclusion of the demand for money for investment expenditures, which is mainly a function of the rates of interest, actually is unnecessary, the demand function for money as a medium of exchange should be written $M_T = L_T (Y, r)$.[7]

[4] These terms are used by E. Petersen in order to characterize the demand for money as a means of exchange and as a temporary investment, *i.e.*, as a store of value, respectively (*op. cit.*, p. 93).

[5] Angell estimates the total amount of annual financial transactions in the United States (from 1909 to 1930) to about ten or fifteen per cent of all transactions that required an actual exchange of currency and/or bank deposits (*op. cit.*, p. 134; also see p. 155). He is then referring to those financial transactions which were performed by an actual exchange of currency and/or deposits, not to the total volume of financial transactions performed.

[6] See A. Hansen, *op. cit.*, p. 57.

[7] Angell draws, from his study of the behavior of money in the United States, the conclusion that »the general path of movement of the national money income was very closely associated with that of the stock of the circulating money in 1909—1928» (*op. cit.*, p. 154; also see p. 162). Hansen, on the other hand, who studied the same ratio over

3. That part of total cash holdings which has not been used for any transactions during the relevant period constitutes the *passive* holdings and is denoted by M_S. It is sometimes called surplus cash. Here, money has been kept as a store of value. *Ex post,* M_S thus includes that part of the planned transactions cash holdings which has not been used during the past period (because of unrealized expectations).

The main reasons for holding passive cash balances are that the future is uncertain, and that there exists no dependable credit market to satisfy every desire to borrow money at the prevailing rates of interest (see note 6, p. 199). Therefore, people always want the highest liquidity. *Ex ante,* M_S includes primarily all cash holdings which are kept for satisfying the speculative motive; that is, people are waiting for a better way of keeping their wealth than in money — an alternative which is not expected to turn up during the relevant period.[8] A second motive for high liquidity is precaution which necessitates a cash reserve for future contingencies, not expected to occur during the next period. This definition does not cover the Keynesian one, for (1) it refers only to contingencies requiring sudden expenditures *after* the relevant period, and (2) it does not include »unforeseen opportunities of advantageous purchases» because those are already included under the speculative motive in so far as they are expected to become realized after the relevant period.[9] Nor does it refer to any kind of assets which are not labelled as money according to our definition. A third motive, though of minor importance, is that of keeping idle, or passive cash balances in order to satisfy pure avarice. If these cash balances were never to be used as media of exchange, they would not be included under our definition of money. But since misers also die, these idle reserves will, very likely, be used some day in the future. As a fourth

the period 1800—1950, demonstrates that the »money supply holds no dependable relation to the national income» (*op. cit.*, p. 3). The different conclusions are due solely to the fact that Angell's study is made over a period when »other things» remained fairly stable. Also, according to Hansen's figures, the ratio was almost constant from 1905—1920. But the longer the period studied is, the more likely is it that the ratio changes, as »other things» will change, *e.g.*, the banking and credit system, the length of the production processes, and payment and spending habits.

8 As R. A. Musgrave underlines, there is no sharp line of demarcation between money held as a store of wealth and other assets (»Money, Liquidity and the Valuation of Assets», in *Money, Trade, and Economic Growth,* pp. 216—217). This is no reason, however, for not splitting up the total quantity of money into active and passive cash holdings, although the passive cash holdings appear as only part of the total demand for liquid assets.

9 *General Theory,* p. 196.

motive, one might also mention the difficulty of exactly timing investment in so far as it extends over the relevant period.[10] These are the main motives for keeping money primarily as a store of value. Of these motives, the first and third ones may properly be described as subjectively determined, while the second motive largely depends upon objective factors.

The determinants of the passive cash holdings, M_S, are (1) the rates of interest, (2) the stream of total income, (3) the price level, and (4) the aggregate value of the cash holders' total assets. As mentioned in the previous section, the fourth determinant can be neglected. The main determinant is the rates of interest, which determine the proportion of the cash holders' liquid assets which they prefer to keep in money instead of earning assets. The demand for money as a store of value, M_S, can thus be expressed as a function of the rates of interest, $M_S = L_S(r)$. But this presumes a given level of income (as far as it is compatible with flexible rates of interest). Hence, a general formula for the demand for money as a store of value must consider also the level of income, and it will read $M_S = L_S (r, Y)$.

The total demand for money, M, is a function both of the income level and the interest rates, $M = L (Y, r)$. Since M_T is partly a function of the rates of interest and M_S partly a function of the level of income, it has been argued that it is often better to deal with the different cash holdings as a whole.[11] From the standpoint of our analysis, however, this would be meaningless, since our analysis is built on the distinct functions of money as a medium of exchange and as a store of value. Besides, these influences *are* considered in our formulation of the two demand functions, and, therefore, the total demand function for money does not contain more variables than the separate ones.

The direct influence of changes in the level of income upon passive cash balances will primarily be a question of the effect of unexpected income changes. Only in cases of significant and unexpected losses and profits will the influence be of any considerable degree.[12] When

---

[10] This factor is considered by E. Petersen (*op. cit.*, p. 69); also see Ohlin: »Some Notes on the Stockholm Theory of Savings and Investment», II, (*E. J.*, 1937), pp. 221—240), and Keynes' reply in the same journal: »Alternative Theories of the Rate of Interest», I, (pp. 241—252).

[11] See A. Hansen, *op. cit.*, p. 56.

[12] Keynes' term *windfall loss* is a typical example of how words receive an entirely different meaning in economics than in ordinary use. To speak of *windfall loss*, namely, is similar to speaking of gained losses, since the very word windfall actually means an unexpected *gain* of some kind.

businessmen anticipate a substantial decrease in the economic activity, that is, a decrease in the level of total income, they will build up a cash reserve. This merely means that passive cash balances are inversely related to changes in the level of income, and that has already been accounted for. The ratio M_T/M_S is greatest at the top of a business cycle, and smallest at the bottom, but then there are almost always corresponding changes in prices and in the total quantity of money. Even with a given quantity of money, however, one should get similar fluctuations.

4. The distribution of the total quantity of money in M_T- and M_S-balances, over a given period, is primarily determined by the level of prices, the rates of interest and the distribution of income. Weekly wage earners use almost all of their income for transactions purposes, primarily consumption expenditures, if the relevant period is defined as not less than their income period. The longer the period is in relation to their wage period, the more all their cash holdings approach the M_T-category. This is further accentuated by their high propensity to consume, and their, as a rule, limited liquid assets.

The higher the levels of individual incomes are, the higher are, generally, the total assets of the corresponding cash holders, and the less are their propensities to consume. To this group also belong cash holders who have a relatively small income, but whose income is primarily (if not exclusively) derived from earning assets. These income receivers are the main holders of the M_S-balances. In an analysis of the effects of changes in the total quantity of money, this distribution of the two types of cash holdings is of great importance.

5. The distinction between the quantity of money held as a medium of exchange, M_T, and as a store of value, M_S, is fundamentally determined by the length of the period chosen; indeed, has no meaning without reference to a certain period. In the long run all money will be used for some transactions, and thus $M_T = M$, and $M_S = 0$, when $t \rightarrow \infty$ (where t stands for time). Since one of the main purposes of economic theory is »to analyse changes in economic life with respect to time»,[13] a certain period must be chosen within which the analysis has to be carried out in still smaller periods in respect to the assumptions made. The distinction between fixed and variable costs, which has largely contributed to a realistic analysis of the price policy of an individual firm, is entirely dependent upon the period chosen. In the

[13] E. Lundberg, *Studies in the Theory of Economic Expansion,* London, 1937, p. 1.

long run, all costs become variable. The distinction between money as a medium of exchange and as a store of value is also well founded.

Another problem is to what length of period we refer when splitting up the total quantity of money, M, into M_T- and M_S-balances. Since we have maintained that the individual M_T-balances are primarily a function of the level of individual incomes, the period should not be less than the income period of the majority of income receivers, that is, a week. Otherwise, part of their cash holdings spent within the income period (*e.g.*, on consumption goods) would be classified as consituting passive cash holdings. On the other hand, it would not be appropriate to make it coincide with this income period, since part of the cash balances for consumption expenditures of income receivers with a longer income period would then be classified as passive cash holdings. Hence, the period chosen should not be less than the longest income period in the society. Since there is no such definite period, the line of distinction has to be drawn more or less arbitrarily. It can be said, however, that those income periods exceeding one year are very rare, whereas one year would correspond to the income period of all owners of earning assets paid out annually. But incomes paid out only once a year, even if they constitute the only source of income, will, as a rule, not be kept in the form of money during the following period of expenditure. Most of it will be turned into time deposits, that is, the annual income will be transformed into a monthly income-expenditure stream. From a realistic point of view, therefore, the monthly income-expenditure period should be chosen as the relevant period. The longer the period is, however, the more difficult it is, both from a theoretical and practical viewpoint, to distinguish between active and passive cash holdings. Since the purpose of our analysis is partly to provide a theoretical illustration of the difference between the function of money as a store of value and as a medium of exchange, in order to demonstrate the basic difference between the quantity-theory approach and the liquidity-preference approach, the relevant period will at first be assumed to be a day only. For the sake of consistency and simplification, the income period will also be assumed to be a day. Furthermore, it is presumed, in order to simplify the analysis as much as possible so as to bring out the main points of the discussion, that every medium of exchange to be used for transactions purposes, will be used only *once* during the period chosen. Without this presumption, the reasoning would become extremely complicated and could easily be lost in subtleties without relevance for the main purpose of the analysis.

6. An equilibrium situation requires that the M_T- and the M_S-balances of an individual cash holder are distributed in such a way that the anticipated marginal utility of the last unit expected to be used as a medium of exchange is equal to that of the last unit expected to be kept as a store of value. Speaking of total cash holdings, it means that »the proportion of the existing stock of money must be distributed so that the intensity of the two demands will be equal».[14] It is evident that the marginal utility of keeping money for transactions purposes must approach infinity as $M_T \rightarrow 0$; whilst it will probably reach zero as $M_T \rightarrow \infty$. It may also approach infinity, although it is less likely, when the M_S-balances $\rightarrow 0$, namely when it becomes a question of life and death if money is available for contingencies. Also, the marginal utility of keeping an increasing amount of passive balances may never become zero since future contingencies might require all the M_S-balances.

Since it is justifiable to assume that the price which the individual cash holder (indirectly) pays for the disposal of his cash balances is directly related to their marginal utilities, the demand for cash balances can be illustrated by drawing two demand curves as functions of the rates of interest, one illustrating the individual demand for money as a medium of exchange, and the other the individual demand for money as a store of value. The interest elasticity of the first-mentioned function is probably rather insignificant, whereas that of the other function must be more pronounced. Summarizing horizontally all these individual demand schedules for the M_T- and M_S-balances, we obtain the total demand schedule for money as a medium of exchange, L_T, and as a store of value, L_S, respectively. These two schedules are drawn in fig. 4. They are also summarized horizontally so that the total demand schedule, L, for money in a given society is obtained.

The price one has to pay (indirectly) for keeping cash balances is that price which a borrower is willing to pay and which is determined in the credit market. Since cash balances can be lent out under very different conditions, both in respect to time and security, there is a whole range of prices, that is, of interest rates. The LL-schedule indicates only that an increased quantity of money will be demanded if the rates of interest are lower. If the total supply of money is equal to M, then the intersection of the perpendicular to M with the LL-schedule, gives a point from which a line, parallel to the horizontal axis, can be drawn, and which will indicate how the quantity of money will

[14] E. Petersen, *op. cit.*, p. 93.

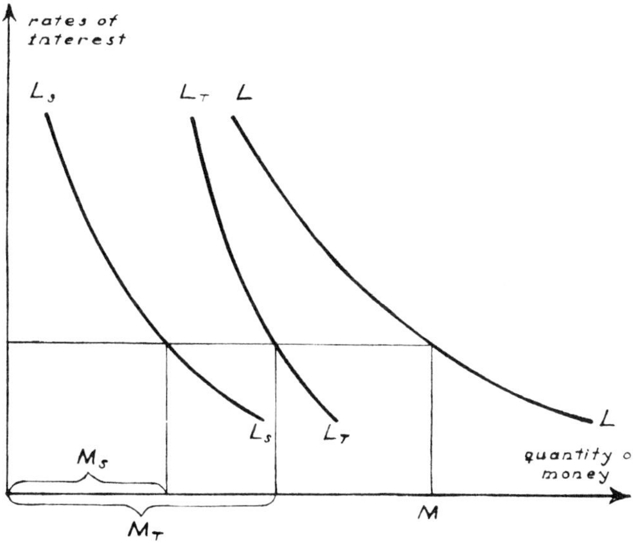

Fig. 4.

be *distributed* between M_T- and M_S-balances. A fundamental mistake in the simplified version of the Keynesian theory of interest lies in the conclusion that the rate of interest is *determined* by the intersection of the M-line and the LL-schedule. This cannot be correct for the intersection determines only those rates of interest which are compatible with a *given distribution of the total quantity of money in active and passive balances.* This is the same mistake which the classical theory of interest rate has been accused of making, namely, assuming one of the determinants constant. The classical theory assumed the level of income to be given; the simplified version of the Keynesian theory, the distribution of the quantity of money into different cash balances. The quantity of money does not determine the rates of interest, since different rates of interest are conceivable with the same quantity of money. This will be further demonstrated below.

The individual cash holder's distribution of a given amount of money kept as a medium of exchange and as a store of value in relation to various rates of interest is illustrated graphically in fig. 5. As the rates of interest increase, less money will be kept in passive balances, but the M_S/M_T-curve will very likely never intersect the vertical axis as the rates of interest become very high. As they decrease, on the other hand, the passive balances will increase, but they will not increase more than up to a certain point, determined by the minimum for transactions purposes. If the rates of interest become very low, the passive balances may even decrease at the expense of increased consumption expenditures, assuming that the cash holder is the owner of earning assets and, therefore, increases his consumption expenditures because of his relative increase in wealth.

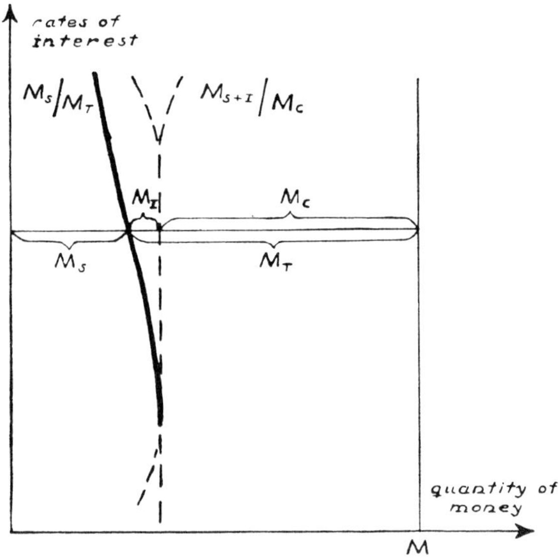

Fig. 5.

The dotted curve in the diagram denotes the relation between the cash balances for consumption expenditures and the remaining part. The horizontal distance between the dotted curve and the M_S/M_T-curve characterizes that part of the transactions cash holdings which constitute investment expenditures (= savings), which means that other transactions, *e.g.*, financial transactions, are assumed to be zero. Higher interest rates primarily mean that the passive cash balances are diminished, while those for consumption expenditures will remain almost the same. Only if there are more significant increases, may the consumption expenditures be influenced. As Cassel pointed out, one might just as well expect an increase in the cash balances for consumption expenditures if the cash holder's savings go to the purchase of life annuities. Accordingly, it is impossible to say what the total results will be. It can only be said that the passive cash balances will probably diminish, which might compensate for increasing M_C-balances, and thus leave the M_I-balances unchanged. This must be considered as a very extreme case, however.

As a rule, the amount of savings with a given quantity of money will increase at the expense of the passive cash balances.

Keynes was definitely correct in affirming that the rate of interest is the compensation for parting from liquidity (or the reward for not keeping passive cash balances). But this does not mean the quantity of money *determines* the rates of interest. It only means that it will *influence* the rates of interest by influencing the stream of savings, or loanable funds, coming into the credit market. The demand for loanable funds will be primarily determined by the marginal efficiency of capital. At a given level of income and quantity of money, the rates of interest will be determined by these demand and supply flows.

7. With a given quantity of money, M, the distribution of total cash holdings will be determined also by the price level. A rising price level will require more cash balances for transactions purposes. The (planned) transactions balances for both consumption and investment expenditures will increase, the latter because the increase in prices means a (relative) rise in the marginal efficiency of capital (assuming a wage lag), which will raise the interest rates in the credit market. At the same time the (planned) passive balances will diminish as it becomes less profitable to keep money as a store of value, both because of the higher price level and because of the higher rates of interest. A decreasing price level, on the other hand, will diminish the transactions balances and increase the passive balances as the value of money increases. This is further accentuated by the circumstance that the falling price level lowers the relative marginal efficiency of capital (assuming a wage lag) and thereby the demand for transactions balances for investment expenditures, which accentuates the fall in the rates of interest.

The relation between changes in the distribution of cash holdings with a given quantity of money, but with a varying price level and varying rates of interest, is illustrated in fig. 6. The upper half of the figure corresponds to fig. 5, whereas the lower part characterizes the distribution between the different cash holdings at a varying price level. The M_S/M_T-curve will obviously intersect the horizontal axis as $P \rightarrow 0$, but the vertical axis might be intersected as soon as every cash holder is convinced that a real inflation is under development. Then money loses its value as a dependable store of potential wealth and it becomes purposeless to keep passive cash balances except for contingencies. It is also to be expected that this curve will be fairly elastic, since changes in the price level mean changes in the value of money and, therefore, will have an immediate and direct effect upon passive balances, as well as upon the value of transactions balances. The influence of variations in the rates of interest will primarily influence transactions balances indirectly by first affecting the motives for keeping passive cash balances.

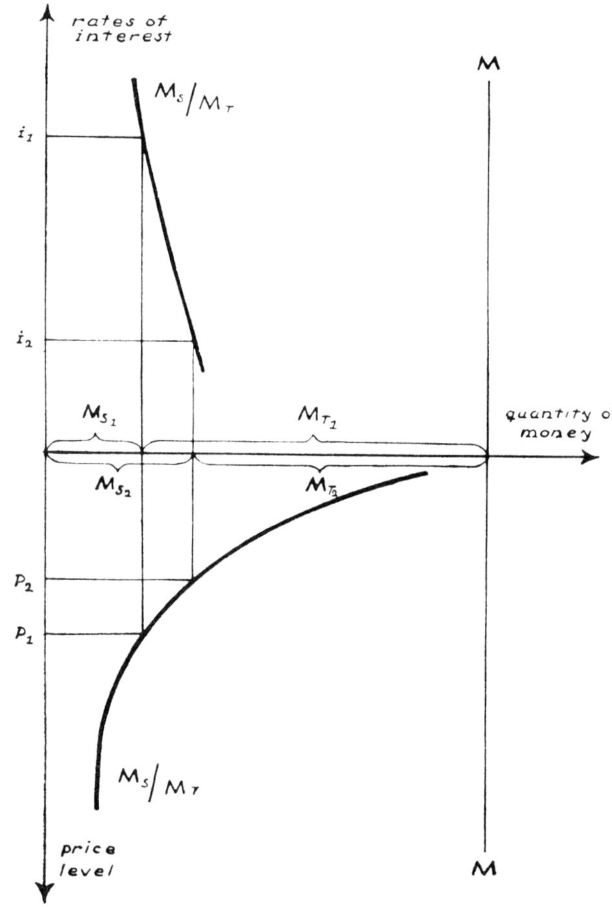

Fig. 6.

The figure illustrates that for every given set of interest rates, *ceteris paribus*, there also is a given price level, when the quantity of total money, M, is given. Since the two distribution curves refer to the same quantity of money, M, the price level, corresponding to a given set of interest rates, i_1, is easily obtained. It will thus be P_1, and the distribution of M into different cash holdings will be M_{S1} and M_{T1}. With a lower set of interest rates, i_2, the price level must also be lower, namely P_2, since M_S will increase to M_{S2}, and M_T decrease to M_{T2}. As is indicated by fig. 6, the rates of interest will be of consequence only within a limited range of price levels.[15]

It is easily seen that a change in the desire to keep passive (or active) cash holdings, that is, a shift in the M_S/M_T-curve at a given set of interest rates and a given level of income, must necessarily cause a change in the price level. If other things remain the same, the price change will be in a certain proportion to the change in the amount of transactions balances. To that extent the commonly accepted formulation of the quantity theory is correct. But this theory did not consider changes in the distribution of money into different cash holdings as quantitative changes. This will be discussed further in the next chapter, in which the concept of the 'velocity' of circulation of money will be scrutinized. The main purpose of this chapter has been to demonstrate the relation between changes in the distribution of a given quantity of money (in active and passive balances) and the rates of interest and the price level.

[15] Referring to fig. 6, a definition of so-called *neutral* money can be formulated. It would refer to that quantity of money which would offset the influence of changes in the desire to keep passive (or active) cash balances on the rates of interest and the price level. This would mean that there would be no movements along the M_S/M_T-curves; changes in the total quantity of money would shift the curves to the left or to the right, leaving the interest rates and the price level constant (presuming no changes in the relation between the two curves).

CHAPTER XIII

ON THE CONCEPT OF THE 'VELOCITY' OF CIRCULATION OF MONEY

Since the main purpose of the second part of this study is to provide an analysis of the effects of changes in the quantity of money on total income with particular reference to the fundamental idea of the quantity theory, a discussion of the concept of the 'velocity' of circulation of money is necessary. There has been extensive writing on this subject, which is still rather controversial. This controversy is to a large extent due to a confusion — once again — of arithmetic and causal relations, and to a lack of distinction between various cash holdings.

1. The definition of the 'velocity' of circulation of money depends upon the definition of money itself and the kind of payment transactions which are to be included. However it is defined, it must always refer to a given amount of transactions, performed during a given period, with a given amount of the medium of exchange. As soon as the medium of exchange is defined and the type of transactions has been decided upon, the choice of the relevant period determines the numerical value of the 'velocity' of circulation of money. This is best illustrated by using Fisher's equation $MV = PT$. It is quite obvious that this equation has no meaning until the factors mentioned above are properly defined. It also follows that the *only* thing the equation of exchange determines is the value of the 'velocity' of circulation of money. That the equation determines the price level, or the value of money, and thus provides the missing equation to Walras' or Cassel's system of equations, supposedly determining prices close to a multiple factor, is an untenable proposition (see note 43, p. 93, and note 18, p. 185).

The equation of exchange is based upon the very fact that a certain amount of transactions *has taken place* with a given quantity of the medium of exchange. Consequently, the prices of the individual transactions are settled also. As soon as the relevant period is defined, the amount of money used for these transactions is given. When the relevant period is chosen so that the monetary value of the transactions exceeds the quantity of money, then the *arithmetic* relation between these two factors evidently becomes greater than unity. This arithmetic relation has been called the 'velocity' (of circulation) of money.[1] Accordingly, the equation of exchange should be written $\frac{PT}{M} = V$, since V is the only factor determined by the equation, and since there is no longer any need to illustrate the once so highly discussed, but always so obvious fact, that the amount of money paid for a given amount of transactions equals the monetary value of these transactions. Thus the numerical value of the 'velocity' of circulation of money is primarily a function of the period chosen, namely of choosing the period so that $M < PT$.[2] It does not matter in how complicated a way the 'velocity' of circulation of money is defined; it will always remain the name for a simple arithmetic relation. And it can only be determined at the end of the relevant period.

2. The affirmation that the 'velocity' of money can act as an independent cause is frequently based upon a confusion of arithmetic and causal relations or upon a lack of distinction between active and passive cash holdings.[3] The former mistake is easily illustrated by using the equation $\frac{PT}{M} = V$. How absurd it is to say that if V changes, while T and M remain constant, P must change in the same proportion and to characterize this as an extended form of the quantity theory, must then be immediately recognized. But in order to disperse all doubts, let us substitute figures for the letters in the formula and write $\frac{2 \times 100}{50} = 4$. To assume now, for example, that 4 (V) is doubled, while 100 (T) and 50 (M) remain constant, asserting that 2 (P) also must be doubled, is, of course, wholly illegitimate. Such assumptions »assume nonsense problems and lead to nonsense solutions», to use a

---

[1] See, for example, Holtrop's definition in *Die Umlaufsgeschwindigkeit des Geldes* (in *Beiträge zur Geldtheorie,* ed. by F. von Hayek), Wien, 1933, p. 128, and Ellis, »Some Fundamentals in the Theory of Velocity», *Q. J. E.*, 1938, especially pp. 441, and 452, note 7.

[2] For a discussion of Stuart Mill's famous remark that time has nothing to do with the concept of the velocity of money, see pp. 68—69.

[3] The latter inaccuracy is pointed out by Hammarskjöld in his dissertation of 1933 (*op. cit.*, p. 38).

phrase by Davenport.[4] For it is obvious that every change in the relation depends upon a change in the *determinants* of this arithmetic relation. Every change in the 'velocity' of circulation of money, *presumes* a change in one or several of its determinants.

3. The lack of a clear definition of active and passive cash holdings is the other reason for the confused discussion of changes in the 'velocity' of circulation of money.[5] This confusion goes back to the so-called extended formulation of the quantity theory, especially to Cantillon's statement that changes in the 'velocity' of circulation of money must have the same effects as changes in the quantity of money (see p. 40). Since the quantity theory did not distinguish between various cash holdings, changes in the 'velocity' of circulation of money actually meant changes in the *distribution* of active and passive cash holdings.[6] For the quantity theory included both active and passive balances in the total quantity of money 'in circulation', but it tacitly assumed that every *change* in the quantity of money meant only a change in the *active* cash holdings. Tooke's criticism was directed against just this implicit assumption, and he proved that changes in the total stock of money might well occur without any corresponding changes in the *active* cash balances (see p. 61). The total quantity of money *in circulation* did not mean that the whole quantity had circulated during the *relevant* period. The only way the quantity theory could allow for changes in the *distribution* of the two cash holdings was to speak about changes in the *'velocity' of circulation of money.* Since the whole quantity of money ($M_T + M_S$) was conceived of as 'circulating' and as *given* during the relevant period, changes in the relation M_T / M_S were spoken of as changes in the 'velocity' of circulation of money. Indeed, this is the foundation of the general idea of changes in the 'velocity' of circulation of money.[7]

[4] »Velocities, Turnovers and Prices», *A. E. R.*, 1930, p. 9.

[5] Harrod speaks very appropriately about »the failure of monetary theory to explain how the total stock of money is divided between liquid reserves and active circulation, or in other words, the unsatisfactory character of the theory of velocity of circulation» (*op. cit.*, p. 85).

[6] Ellis' assertion that »Mr. Harrod errs when he states that the quantity theory provides no determinate division of the money stock between working and idle balances», (*op. cit.*, p. 464) is hard to understand. Harrod is, indeed, correct in his statement, for the 'quantity theorists' simply assumed a change in the total quantity money, without distinguishing between any cash holdings (*op. cit.*, p. 83).

[7] *Cf.*, for example, the following statements by two experts on the 'velocity' of money: »If money does not rest in idle balances, it circulates at a predetermined rate; and

4. A meaningful definition of the 'velocity' of circulation of money must refer to the relation betwen the relevant amount of transactions and the quantity of money *actually used* for the turnover of these transactions.[8] There is no reason for including the *total* quantity of money just because it was done by the so-called extended quantity theory. The inconsistency of this theory is quite obvious: when it dealt with changes in the quantity of money, then it tacitly referred to *active* money only; but when it spoke of changes in the velocity of circulation of money, then it referred to *both active and passive* money, that is, to the total quantity of money. Only by first separating the total quantity of money into active and passive cash holdings, can a fruitful discussion of the 'velocity' of circulation of money be carried through.

According to our definitions, the 'velocity' of circulation of the passive cash balances, V_S, is equal to zero during the relevant period, whereas that of the active balances, V_T, is equal to unity. Every change in the distribution of the various cash balances, consequently, means a change in M_T and M_S, and has nothing to do with the rate of circulation, as such, of these cash holdings. A realistic discussion, however, of the determinants of V_T necessitates the abandonment of the assumption that every medium of exchange performs only one purchase. In the following analysis, therefore, the reasoning is built upon the assumption that the same medium of exchange performs several transactions during the relevant period.

5. A clear analysis of the determinants of the rate of circulation of money and their interdependence requires a further splitting up of the M_T-balances into balances used for consumption expenditures, M_C, for investment expenditures, M_I, and for financial transactions, M_F. Corresponding price levels are denoted as P_C, P_I, P_F, the

whether velocity rises or falls depends upon whether less or more finds its way into idle balances» (Ellis, *op. cit.*, p. 463).

»Diese Veränderungen im Umfange des Geldstromes [*i.e.*, between active and passive cash holdings], die nicht mit einer Veränderung der Geldmenge Hand in Hand gehen, sind es, die allgemein als Veränderungen in der Umlaufsgeschwindigkeit des Geldes bezeichnet werden, da bei ihrem Eintreten die Bewegung des Geldes beschleunigt wird» (Holtrop, *op. cit.*, p. 127).

Halm is a little more careful and mentions »that the velocity of circulation of money depends partly on the degree to which cash balances may be economized» (*op. cit.*, p. 76). But since he does not split up M into M_T and M_S, he has to consider, as he points out, changes in the relation between M_T and M_S as changes in the 'velocity' of circulation of money (see especially p. 69).

[8] This is the same conclusion as Hammarskjöld's (*op. cit.*, pp. 38—39 and 47 ff.).

corresponding transactions T_C, T_I, and T_F, and the respective 'velocities' of circulation of these various cash balances, V_C, V_I, and V_F. Thus we can write:

$$\frac{P_C T_C + P_I T_I + P_F T_F}{M_C + M_I + M_F} = \frac{PT}{M_T} = V_T$$

It is quite evident how meaningless it is to speak of *the* (transactions) 'velocity' of circulation of money, since it is merely a weighted average of various 'velocities' of circulation of money employed in different transactions. The numerical value of V_T can only be a curiosity. Of real interest is the effects of changes, both relative and absolute, in the distribution of the various cash holdings on the rate of circulation of the medium of exchange. The most fluctuating factor is obviously V_F, as its determinants are chiefly subjectively conditioned. A close analysis of its determinants is not only extremely difficult from a purely theoretical point of view but brings also up the whole problem of business cycles. For the sake of simplification, therefore, M_F is assumed to be zero (as is also done in ch. XII). The greatest stability is to be expected in V_C, since the income-consumption expenditure period is fairly stable under 'normal' conditions. Another factor working for stability both in V_C and in V_I is the almost fixed number of production stages in a limited interval of time.

The average — if it is possible to speak of an average with any meaning — number of production stages, Angell has detoned by n, whereas Holtrop merely speaks of the »Differenzierungskoeffizienten».[9] And instead of Angell's concept of the circular 'velocity' of money, C, Holtrop speaks of the efficiency of money, a concept originated by Schumpeter.[10] In Holtrop's terms the 'velocity' of circulation

[9] See Angell: »Money, Prices and Production: Some Fundamental Concepts of Money», *Q. J. E.*, 1933, pp. 44—45, and »The General Dynamics of Money», *J. P. E.*, 1937, pp. 296—297; Ellis, *op. cit.*, pp. 435—436; and Holtrop, *op. cit.*, p. 129; also see Marget: »A Further Note on Holtrop's Formula for the 'Coefficient of Differentiation and Related Concepts», *J. P. E.*, 1933, pp. 237—241.

[10] See Angell, *loc. cit.*, and *The Behavior of Money*, pp. 130—131 and 148—149; Angell's definition of the circular velocity of money is not quite clear, for it is said to be equal to those »consumer-producer-consumer circles, which the *average* unit of money completes per unit time period» (p. 131). This actually means that the 'saver-producer-saver' circles, that is, the investment industries, are excluded; hence M (the stock of money) times C cannot equal total national income, NI; only the total income earned in the consumption industries. The simplest definition of C is that number of times the active quantity of money has circulated in order to generate a certain national income during a given period. See also Holtrop, *loc. cit*; and Schumpeter: »Das Sozialprodukt und die Rechenpfennige», p. 650.

of money is equal to the differential coefficient plus 1, times the efficiency of money; and in Angell's terms, it is equal to the number of stages the money unit passes in traversing one average payment circle (L) times the circular velocity of money (C). Consequently, the differential coefficient plus 1, times the efficiency of money is equal to L times C. Since Holtrop's efficiency of money and Angell's circular velocity of money are identical, when the circular 'velocity' of money is correctly defined (see note 11), the differential coefficient plus 1 must coincide with Angell's L. It also follows from the fact that $L = n + 1$. Consequently, Holtrop's »Differenzierungskoeffizienten» and Angell's n — the number of vertical steps into which the production process is divided — are also identical.[11]

In a limited period, the number of production stages, both within the consumption and the investment sector, can be considered as given. Hence changes in the rate of circulation of money are determined primarily by changes in the income-expenditure period. But also this period can be regarded as given. Though the individual cash holder determines the average period he wants to keep active cash balances, he cannot, as a rule, determine the income period. If he diminishes the average period he keeps active cash balances, this will, very likely, have no direct influence. It merely means that someone else will keep his cash balances over a longer average period than usual. From a total point of view, V_T will remain fairly unchanged. Only if the individual cash holder continues to keep his balances over a diminished period of time, will there be any lasting effects. But since his stream of expenditures is largely determined by his stream of income, and since the latter stream is mainly determined institutionally, the possibility for the individual cash holder to influence the rate of circulation of money can be neglected. Accordingly, V_C and V_I can be considered as given in a short-run analysis.

6. In an analysis of the effects of changes in the quantity of money upon total income, the concept of a *transactions* velocity of money is rather inadequate, since the total amount of transactions bears no direct

[11] Both Angell's and Holtrop's definition of the circular 'velocity' of money is a »hybrid concept» for they both define it in relation to the *total* quantity of money, instead of in relation to the quantity of money actually used. Though Keynes used the appelation in referring primarily to the definition of the 'velocity' of money as the relation between various, entirely different, transactions in relation to the total quantity of money, the appelation can appropriately refer also to the latter inconsistency (*A Treatise on Money*, vol. II, p. 24).

relation to total income. For the following discussion, therefore, we will use the basic idea of Angell's concept of a circular 'velocity' of money, though first it has to be redefined as follows: the income circulation of money, C_T, is characterized by the number of times the *active* quantity of money, M_T, has circulated during a given period for the generation of a given income, Y. Thus $C_T = \frac{Y}{M_T}$. This definition differs from Angell's by not relating the *total* quantity of money, $M = M_T + M_S$, to the total income. It comes closer to Keynes' definition, but differs also from the latter, since, as a rule, M_T, will not be equal to M_1.[12] It also differs in the usage of the term *circulation* instead of velocity, which really is a very inappropriate term. *There is no velocity of money* in the sense in which physics uses the concept. Velocity denotes the distance an object covers per unit of time. Monetary theory uses the concept quite differently from physics. What takes place during a given period and has economic relevance is that the quantity of active money changes hands a certain number of times. Hence the term *the rate of circulation*, or *frequency of turnover, of money* seems much more appropriate. These terms will be used, therefore, in spite of the commonly accepted term, 'velocity' of money, simply because the latter implies an incorrect usuage of the word. That the inverted value of C_T signifies the average time the quantity of active money, M_T, remains passive in relation to the relevant period, requires no comment.

If M_T changes, it can mean two different things: either that people change the amount of their given, active cash holdings, which can be characterized as subjective changes in M_T, or that the *number* of active cash holdings has changed, which can be characterized as objective changes in M_T. In the first case, the effect of increased (or decreased) purchases can be either a price increase (or decrease) with the same number of total transactions, or an increased (decreased) number of

---

[12] Keynes' definition of M_1 reads: »Let the amount of cash held to satisfy the transactions- and precautionary-motives be M_1.... Thus if V is the income-velocity of money, $L_1(Y) = \frac{Y}{V} = M_1$», (*General Theory*, pp. 199 and 201).

Angell's unwillingness to accept the definition of his circular 'velocity' of money as the income 'velocity' of money, is understandable, when the discussion primarily centers around the behavior of money as such (see *The Behavior of Money*, p. 131, note 1). But when emphasis is laid upon the arithmetic relation between total income and active cash holdings, the term income circulation of money seems acceptable.

transactions, that is, output, at constant prices. The most probable result is a combination of these two, principal effects.[13]

An increasing number of active cash holdings can depend upon either an increase in individual cash holdings, for example, because of an increasing population, or by merely increasing the number of employees, or it can depend upon an increase of the number of productive stages. During a period of constant employment, the number of income receivers can be regarded as constant. Then changes in M_T can be referred primarily to variations in the amount of money of the given number of cash holdings. These latter variations must be due to either a shift in total demand or to price changes. The final result, therefore, must be a change of total income (in monetary terms).

Since total income can be written $Y = C_T \cdot M_T$, a change in total income, ΔY, caused by a change in the quantity of active cash balances ΔM_T, can be written $\Delta Y = c \cdot \Delta M_T$, where $c = \dfrac{\Delta Y}{\Delta M_T}$. Now there appears a very pertinent question: What is the relation between C_T and c? Is $c \gtreqqless C_T$? Since C_T must be more stable than V_T, the conclusion, based upon the foregoing reasoning, must be that 'normally' c is equal to C_T. This means a great simplification for the discussion in the next chapter of the effects of changes in the quantity of money.

An increase in total income can also be written $\Delta Y = k \cdot \Delta I$, where k stands for the Keynesian multiplier. The fundamental difference between the two formulations, however, is that $\Delta Y = c \cdot \Delta M_T$ refers to *one* given period, whereas $\Delta Y = k \cdot \Delta I$ includes an *infinite* number of (the same) periods. Consequently, the Keynesian multiplier concept, from a purely logical point of view, cannot be used for a period analysis. It might then be argued that the value of the Keynesian multiplier approaches its limiting value very soon; after five periods, the difference is not of too great importance, and after ten periods, it is entirely insignificant from a practical point of view. But it should then also be mentioned, from a practical point of view, that this approximate value of the Keynesian multiplier, for a short run analysis, is based upon the

[13] Davenport's main argument is that to »interpret changes in prices as themselves changes in the velocity of media is to confuse ratios of exchange with frequencies of transfers» (*op. cit.*, p. 9). In his opinion the rate of circulation of money means the number of times a *given* quantity of money is turned over with *given* prices. Changes in prices, *ceteris paribus*, requires changes in the quantity of money; or it must lead to changes in the frequencies of transfers.

very unrealistic assumption of no time lags. The actual value of the multiplier for a limited number of periods can obviously differ greatly from its limiting value.

An important relation is now apparent. If the Keynesian multiplier is approximated for a given number of periods, the total length of which corresponds to the same period to which ΔM_T refers, then the two arithmetic relations must be identical, that is $\frac{\Delta Y}{\Delta M_T} = \frac{\Delta Y}{\Delta I}$ or $c = k$. For ΔM_T must be the same as the increase in the stream of 'investment' expenditures, ΔI, or for whatever purpose the stream of total income is increased. Consequently, there is no need for the Keynesian multiplier in our analysis, even from a practical point of view, since the relation $\frac{\Delta Y}{\Delta M_T}$ is already considered. Since the multiplier concept is inconsistent with short run analysis and, theoretically, can never be used in a short run analysis, which must be based upon a *limited* number of periods, we suggest the exclusion of the whole concept from monetary theory and the use of the relevant value of the income circulation of money instead.[14] This reasoning is illustrated in the fourth quadrant in fig. 7 (p. 230).

7. When the concept of hoarding is treated as a reciprocal to the rate of turnover of money, then there is the lack of distinction between active and passive cash holdings. As pointed out, the idea of relating the *total* quantity of money $(M_T + M_S)$ to a given amount of transactions or incomes necessitated the introduction of a term for changes in the distribution between active and passive cash holdings with a given quantity of money. Changes in the circulation of a given quantity of money then meant either (1) a change in the rate of turnover of a given quantity of money (M_T) for transactions, or (2) a change in the *distribution* of active and passive cash holdings. The latter case has generally been described as changes in the quantity of money hoarded.

When hoarding means the actual holding of cash, that is, of both active and passive cash balances,[15] then changes in the amount of hoarded money obviously mean changes in the *total* quantity of money. Such a definition of hoarding, though, seems very peculiar, and has certainly no relation to the original meaning of the word hoarding.

---

[14] The Keynesian multiplier approach is simply »an analytical fifth wheel», as A. G. Hart pointingly expressed it (*Money, Debt and Economic Activity,* New York, 1948, p. 190).

[15] Keynes mentions this as a possible concept of hoarding (*General Theory,* p. 174).

A third concept of hoarding refers to the idea of treasuring coins only for the sake of amassing a store of liquid wealth. This comes closest to the real meaning of the word. Collections of this kind were not achieved, as a rule, at the expense of a decrease in the amount of active cash holdings, M_T, but originated from export surplus or directly from the production of precious metals. In so far as these hoards did not enter the monetary circulation during the relevant period, they had no direct influence on either active and passive balances, or hence, on the level of prices or the rates of interest. In modern times, individual hoarding of this kind is rather insignificant and is disappearing. True, the collection of gold at Fort Knox is the most outstanding example of hoarding gold, but this kind of hoarding has a different economic significance.

Since hoarding, implying the accumulation of money as a store of wealth never to be used as a medium of exchange, has no relevance for monetary theory, and since other definitions of hoarding have caused more confusion than clarification, we suggest the exclusion of the entire concept, and propose the distinction between active and passive cash holdings instead.

8. The chief conclusion from the discussion in this chapter is that the rate of income circulation of money can be regarded as fairly stable in the short run, as it depends primarily upon institutional conditions. Consequently, changes in the total amount of active cash holdings will not affect the rate of income circulation of money. The main proposition based upon the essence of the original quantity theory, namely that changes in the quantity of money used as a medium of exchange will not influence the rate of circulation of money, also appears as basically correct. Our conclusion is very much due to the separation of the total quantity of cash balances into active and passive balances, so that the income circulation refers to that quantity of the medium of exchange which has actually circulated during the relevant period. Hence changes in the distribution of these two groups of cash holdings are distinguished from changes in the rate of turnover of the same cash holdings. A discussion of the effects of changes in the total quantity of money must therefore start with a discussion of how the quantity of money is changed and its immediate effect upon the distribution of total cash holdings into active and passive balances.

CHAPTER XIV

THE EFFECTS OF CHANGES IN THE QUANTITY OF MONEY

1. The purpose of this final chapter is to discuss the effects of changes in the *total* quantity of money in respect to the basic idea of the quantity theory and of the Keynesian monetary theory, *i.e.*, of the theory of liquidity preference. The former approach is an exclusive emphasis upon the function of money as a medium of exchange, whereas the latter primarily emphasizes the function of money as a store of value. Presuming that *every* change in the total quantity of money means a corresponding change in the amount of money outlays, the essence of the quantity theory is that the rate of turnover of money has an autonomous meaning, and will not be influenced. If other things remain equal, the price level must vary in the same proportion as the quantity of money. This is a special case and should be interpreted merely as an *illustration* of a specific peculiarity of the medium of exchange, not as the essence of the quantity theory.[1]

The fundamental fallacy in the quantity theory lies in the assumption, which is based upon the false idea that money is a medium of exchange only, that *every* change in the total quantity of money means a corresponding change in the quantity of money outlays. The effects of a change in the total quantity of money is determined by *how* the change takes place and by the actual economic situation. Thus, the total quantity of money may be changed by a budget deficit or surplus, by open market operations, and, under certain assumptions, by changes in the supply of precious metals. The last alternative will not be dealt with, since these changes will be rather insignificant under modern monetary conditions. Variations in the total quantity of money can also take place because of changes in the reserve requirements of the banks.

[1] According to H. Villard, however, and many others, this is the essence of the quantity theory (»Monetary Theory» in *A Survey of Contemporary Economics*, ed. by H. S. Ellis, Philadelphia, 1948, pp. 320—321).

These changes, however, operate only indirectly since they require, in an equilibrium situation, other changes, *e.g.*, in the rates of interest, in the demand for capital funds, *etc.*, in order to become effectuated. Moreover, their effects will be a mixture of the two cases discussed. Therefore, they will not be considered as separate cases. The total quantity of money can also vary because of changes in the amount of outstanding bank loans. Since we will assume an equilibrium situation in the credit market, these changes will appear only as secondary effects; therefore, they will not be considered. Changes in the quantity of money can also originate in the selling or buying of foreign currencies. This case will also be neglected by assuming a closed economy. Furthermore, changes in the distribution of the total quantity of money between active and passive cash holdings can cause changes in the total quantity of money; namely, if active cash holdings are transformed into time deposits that will enable the banks to increase their loans more than the corresponding increase in their time deposits. Therefore, it is assumed that changes in the distribution of the total quantity of money in active and passive cash holdings will not change the total quantity of money.

The analysis will run in terms of comparative equilibria. No period analysis will be undertaken, partly because it limits the generality of the conclusions reached, and partly because a detailed analysis of all the effects that changes in the total quantity of money will have on economic relations seems to be out of place when the issue is a discussion of rather basic relations. Instead, a more general solution, aiming at a synthesis of the basic ideas in the quantity theory and in the Keynesian monetary theory, will be suggested.

2. In order to demonstrate the main effects of a change in the total quantity of money, caused by budget deficit spending, fig. 7 has been drawn. It illustrates the relation between the quantity of active cash holdings, total income, savings and investment (in real terms), and the rates of interest in a given equilibrium situation.[2] The period of time to which the various functions refer is a year, and not, as in our previous analysis, a day. The reason for this change in our assumptions is simply because most of our income statistics and our estimates of the rate

[2] The idea of using four quadrants for illustrating the relation between more than two variables was employed by Palander in his discussion of Keynes' *General Theory* (*op. cit.*, pp. 239 and 241). No other treatment demonstrates so clearly and in such an elegant way how extremely special Keynes' »general» theory actually is. Unfortunately, the analysis is only available in the Swedish language.

of income circulation of money refer to this period. Hence we speak of *average* active and passive cash balances over a year. In point of principle, this does not change anything of the previous analysis as long as we assume that changes in the distribution of active and passive cash holdings have no influence on the total quantity of money. The difficulty lies obviously in the statistical measurement of the relation between active and passive cash holdings when the period of time is a year. Since this is a theoretical discussion of the effects of changes in the quantity of money with respect to the various functions of money, we can neglect this practical difficulty.

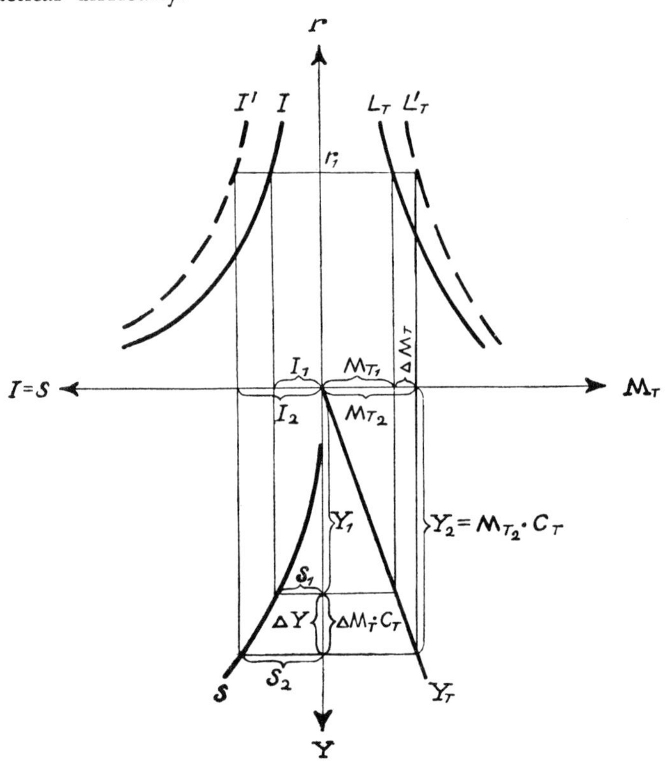

Fig. 7.

The vertical axis in the first quadrant in fig. 7 signifies the rates of interest, and the horizontal axis the average quantity of active cash balances during a year. The quantity of active cash balances is both a function of the rates of interest, although to a minor degree, as the rates of interest are the prices for keeping cash balances, and an indirect function, since changes in M_S generally imply the opposite changes in M_T; and always if the total quantity of money is considered to be given. Hence the L_T-curve will have a negative slope.

Because of our assumptions, changes in the quantity of active cash balances will cause corresponding changes in total income. Accordingly, the relation between total income, Y, and various amounts of active cash balances, M_T, appears as a straight line, Y_T, in the fourth quadrant, since the income velocity of money, C_T, is considered to be constant (in the short run). The equation of the Y_T-curve thus reads $Y = M_T \cdot C_T$. In the third quadrant the relation between total income and saving has been indicated by the S-curve, characterizing that saving is an increasing function as total income increases. It is assumed to be zero at low values of Y. It now appears quite clearly that the multiplier is »an analytical fifth wheel». For there is no need for expressing the relation between total income and saving (or investment) as $Y = k \cdot S$, where k stands for the Keynesian multiplier, when we use the concept of the income circulation of money.

Finally, in the second quadrant, the investment schedule has been depicted as a function of the rates of interest. It illustrates the amount of investment that would take place annually at various interest rates. Since investment and savings refer to the Keynesian definitions, they must coincide in every given situation, as is illustrated by their both being plotted on the left part of the horizontal axis. The propensity to save is also a function of the interest rates. Changes in the rates of interest will, therefore, cause a shift in the S-function with a given level of income. The investment schedule is a function of the level of total income, also. Accordingly, changes in total income, *ceteris paribus*, will cause parallel shifts in the horizontal direction of the investment schedule, so that the new level of savings will coincide with a new level of investment without any changes in the rates of interest. In an equilibrium situation with a given set of interest rates, r_1, the amount of active cash holdings must correspond to M_{T1}, the amount of investment to I_1, the amount of saving to S_1, where $I_1 = S_1$, and the amount of total income to Y_1.

Suppose that the total quantity of money is increased by budget deficit spending, ΔM, and that ΔM remains in active cash holdings over the relevant period, *i.e.*, $\Delta M = \Delta M_T$. There will be a shift in the M_T-function to the right, indicated by the dotted curve, L'_T. As a result, total national income will increase in proportion to ΔM_T, namely with $\Delta Y = \Delta M_T \cdot C_T$. If we accept, as an approximate assumption, that the expansion of the quantity of money takes place in a depression situation with a considerable amount of unused resources of land, labor and capital equipment, and that there is a perfect elasticity of supply, then the increase in total income means a corresponding increase in real terms. There will be an increase in savings, along the S-function, but an increase in investment because of a shift in the investment schedule to the left, $I \rightarrow I'$. For the rates of interest must remain constant because the amount of passive cash holdings, which are largely a function of the rates of interest, remains constant since no other change is assumed in the liquidity preference function. The new equilibrium situation is indicated by the straight lines connecting the relevant points of the various functions in the four quadrants, M_{T2}, Y_2, S_2, and I_2.[3] In the long run, however, the rates of interest will be affected as the output of capital equipment is steadily increasing as long as there is any net investment. But we are concerned with short-run equilibria only and can, therefore, neglect this factor.[4]

3. As a second extreme case of an increased quantity of money, we will assume an increase in the amount of passive cash holdings only. Suppose that the monetary authorities increase the quantity of money by open market operations, and that this increment remains in passive cash holdings over the relevant period, *i.e.*, $\Delta M = \Delta M_S$. If the liquidity preference function L_S, is interest elastic, as indicated by the first quadrant in fig. 8., then the rates of interest will decrease, say from r_1 to r_2. Since we have assumed that the total increment in money will remain in passive cash holdings, and that the circulation of the active cash holdings is constant, no increase can take place in investment (or consumption) outlays. Hence it must also be assumed that the investment schedule is interest inelastic within the relevant range of interest rates, as is illustrated by the second quadrant, fig. 8. If, on the other hand, we had assumed that the liquidity preference function was perfectly interest inelastic over the relevant range of interest rates, then the investment schedule could just as well have been as interest elastic as in fig. 7. These are merely two ways of explaining why open market operations will not influence the level of income. And they both formed an

[3] Since such a development, *i.e.*, that $\Delta M = \Delta M_T$, is conceivable, Keynes' following statement has no general validity, but depends wholly on *how* the quantity of money is changed: »The primary effect of a change in the quantity of money on the quantity of effective demand is through its influence on the rate of interest» (*General Theory*, p. 298).

[4] The effects of changes in the distribution of active and passive cash holdings with a given quantity of money can easily be demonstrated by substituting fig. 5 (chapter XII) for the first quadrant in fig. 7, *mutatis mutandis*.

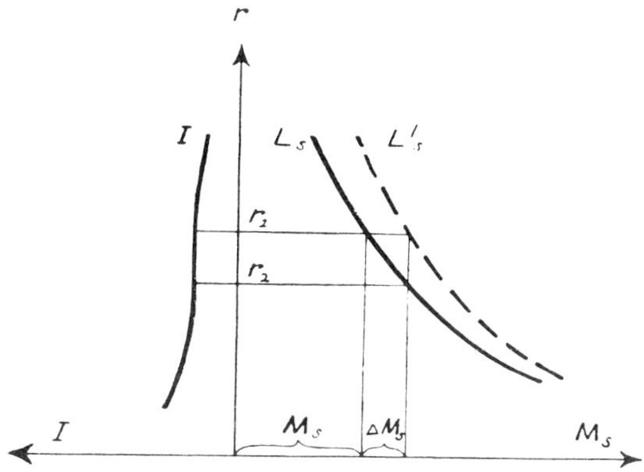

Fig. 8.

argument for Keynes' explanation that open market operations were ineffective. Consequently, he recommended increases in the amount of active cash balances, namely by an increase in investment outlays.

But let us drop these two assumptions, the validity of which has not been proved so far. The effect of the open market operations will then be lower rates of interest, say r_3 (fig. 9), which will induce an increased demand for capital funds for investment outlays. We have here, of course, a contrasting effect. For whereas the liquidity preference increases at gradually lower interest rates, the demand for liquid funds for investment outlays increases. If we do not assume any simultaneous increase in active cash holdings which will satisfy the demand for cash for new investment outlays at the low interest rates, then some borrowers will raise the price they are willing to pay for commanding liquid funds. The rates of interest will rise and this will continue until a new set of interest rates, say r_2, is reached, at which the supply of liquid funds from the passive cash balances matches the increased quantity demanded for active cash balances, because of the original decrease of the interest rates. The original increment in the quantity of money, ΔM, which was at first all turned into passive cash holdings, is then divided into active and passive cash balances, namely, $\Delta M = \Delta M_S + \Delta M_T$. The new investment outlays will then generate an increase in total income, ΔY, as indicated by fig. 9, and the new equilibrium situation is indicated by the straight lines connecting the relevant points of the various functions, namely, r_2, M_{S2}, Y_2, S_2 and I_2.

It should be mentioned that we have not considered the effect of a change in the interest rates on savings. On account of the lower interest rates, the S-function may be shifted to the right, which means that the subsequent income effects of the original increase in investment outlays will be greater, *ceteris paribus*. This neglect is motivated by a desire to make the graphical illustration easy to understand.

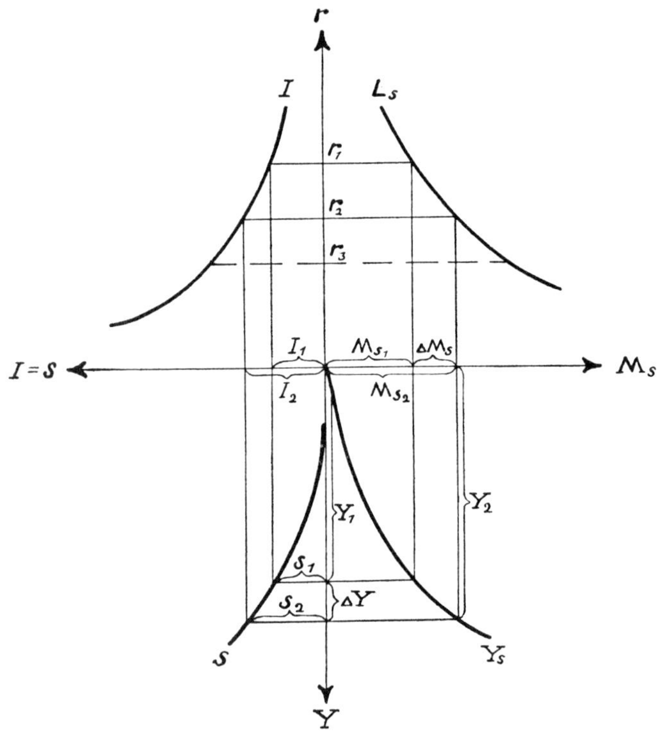

Fig. 9.

Let us briefly explore the effects of a decrease in the propensity to save, which means a shift of the S-function to the right, and a corresponding increase in the propensity to consume. Suppose that we can neglect all kinds of important frictions and time-lags, so that total income still remains at the same level. The rates of interest will increase and the amount of investment outlays decrease. If the liquidity preference function is interest elastic, then the higher rates of interest will induce a decrease in the amount of passive cash holdings. Since these cash holdings are held largely for speculative purposes, the effect will be an increased demand for various kinds of securities, resulting in a decrease in interest rates again, and some decrease of the supply of funds. As in our previous case (see fig. 9) a new equilibrium will be reached, with a given set of interest rates, at which the decrease in passive cash balances is matched by a corresponding increase in the demand for active cash balances (for investment outlays). The new investment outlays will generate a higher level of total income until a corresponding amount of (annual) planned savings is forthcoming. In this case, therefore, a decrease in savings will lead to a higher level of income because of the assumption of an interest elastic liquidity function. Whether this increment in total income means more employment and a higher level of output, or merely a monetary increase, depends upon the amount and kind of unused resources. (It is assumed, in fig. 9, that the amount of passive cash holdings is an increasing function as total income increases, indicated by the Y_S-curve.)

The functional and algebraical relations between the various variables illustrated in figures 7—9 can be summarized as follows:

$$
\begin{aligned}
C &= C\,(Y) & \qquad r &= r\,(S, I, M_S) \\
S &= S\,(Y, r) & \qquad M_T &= L_T\,(Y, r) \\
I &= I\,(r, Y) & \qquad M_S &= L_S\,(r, Y) \\
S &= I & \qquad M &= M_T + M_S
\end{aligned}
$$

In this system of equations, no function can be selected and described as *the* determinant of total income. It is incorrect, in point of principle, to say, for example, that the amount of investment in a given period of time, is *the* determinant of total income. All the various functions determine mutually the level of total income, since they are all interdependent. But to analyze the different effects of changes in the various variables upon the others would require too much space. We are primarily concerned here with the effects of changes in the total quantity of money.

4. In order to illustrate the combined effects of simultaneous changes in active and passive cash holdings resulting from a change in the total quantity of money, fig. 10 has been drawn. The horizontal axis shows the amount of active cash holdings, M_T, and the vertical axis shows the amount of passive cash holdings, M_S. The 45°-lines (*i.e.*, the M-lines) are the locus of a given total quantity of money, so that every point on each 45°-line signifies a certain distribution of a given quantity of money into active and passive cash holdings. Thus we have $M_1 = M_{T1} + M_{S1}$, $M_2 = M_{T2} + M_{S2}$, *etc.* With every given quantity of money, there is a certain distribution of active and passive

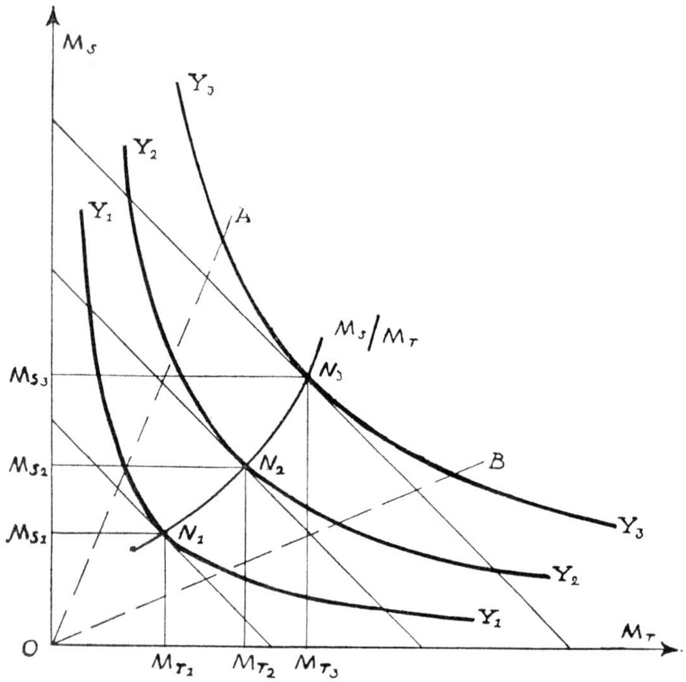

Fig. 10.

cash holdings, which gives a maximum real income, Y.[5] In order to obtain this distribution, various indifference' curves have been drawn, which signify the same total real income, *e.g.*, Y_1, Y_2, or Y_3, with various combinations of active and passive cash holdings. That distribution of a given quantity of money into active and passive cash holdings which gives a maximum real income is obviously indicated by that point at which a Y-curve touches a given 45°-line. Take, for example, the tangential point between the Y_3-curve and the M_3-line, *i.e.*, N_3. Every point on the M_3-line to the left of N_3 will give a lower real income than Y_3, because of smaller active cash holdings (implying an insufficient demand), whereas every point to the right of N_3 will give a lower real income because the small amount of passive cash holdings is conditioned by a too high set of interest rates.

The curve connecting the various maximum points, N_1, N_2, *etc.*, can be called the optimum way of real income expansion as the quantity

[5] *Cf.* H. Villard, *op. cit.*, p. 320. See also E. Petersen's discussion (*op. cit.*, pp. 66—67), which originally suggested this illustration.

of money increases. Every point on a given Y-curve, to the left of this optimum line, can be said to indicate a (relative) deflation, whereas every point to the right of this optimum curve can be said to indicate a (relative) inflation. The optimum curve thus characterizes that income expansion (in real terms) which takes place without any changes in the price level. A *neutral* combination can be defined as that combination of active and passive cash holdings, when the quantity of money changes, which leaves the price level stable. This definition is similar to the definition of neutral money provided earlier (note 15, p. 217).

The range of this optimum curve, as well as of the various indifference curves, must be rather narrow. Its slope is determined both by the given institutions, and by psychological preferences. Very little can be said about it. The slope gradually increases as the quantity of money increases because an increasing amount of money will probably be turned into passive cash holdings, at least up to a certain point. Thereafter, the slope will probably decline, illustrating a relative increase of active cash holdings. But as long as a considerable number of wage earners are unemployed, then $\Delta M_S / \Delta M_T < M_S / M_T$.[6] There is little use in theorizing over the probable appearance of the optimum curve in the long run, since monetary (and other) institutions, and various preferences, will change. The area between the dotted lines $O-A$ and $O-B$ indicates the range within which the various indifference curves can be expected to have any relevance. This figure clearly illustrates that every discussion of the effects of changes in the distribution and in the total quantity of money must consider the effects on the amount of both active and passive cash holdings, since they *together* influence the development of total income. The one-sidedness of the quantity-theory approach is thus very obvious, but also that of the liquidity-preference approach. Fig. 9 may be viewed as a shorthand illustration of the final synthesis of these two different approaches.

5. Let us write P_C and P_I for the price levels and O_C and O_I for the output of consumption and investment goods respectively, M_C and M_I for the quantity of active cash holdings used in the respective production of these goods, and C_C and C_I for the income circulation of M_C and M_I during the relevant period. Thus $M_T = M_C + M_I$. The following identities, — assuming an increase in the various variables,

[6] This is pointed out also by Pigou, who speaks, however, in terms of changes in the income velocity of money since he does not draw the same distinction between active and passive cash holdings (*The Veil of Money*, London, 1949, p. 82).

and neglecting all other kinds of transactions, *eg.*, financial transactions, *etc.*, — may then be formulated:

$$\Delta Y = \Delta O_C \cdot P_C + O_C \cdot \Delta P_C + \Delta O_I \cdot P_I + O_I \cdot \Delta P_I \quad (1)$$

$$\Delta M = (\Delta M_C + \Delta M_I) + \Delta M_S \quad (2)$$

$$\Delta Y = \Delta M_C \cdot C_C + \Delta M_I \cdot C_I \quad (3)$$

The relevant questions from the viewpoint of the quantity theory are: (1) How will an increase in the total quantity of money be distributed between active and passive cash holdings, and (2) how will the income circulation of money be affected? When these questions have been answered, the following questions may be raised: (3) How will total output, and (4) how will prices be affected?

As indicated by our first example of an increased quantity of money (section 2), the effect may conceivably be an increase in active cash holdings only. It is very likely that the rate of turnover of the income circulation in the consumption sphere can be regarded as almost constant over a limited number of periods because of the constancy of the number of production stages and the fairly regular habits of consumption expenditures. But in respect to the increment of investment expenditures, such a constancy cannot be expected, except for those cases where new investment outlays imply a »widening» of the capital equipment only. Hence, the income circulation of money within this industry may probably undergo some change. This means that it will be somewhat more difficult to predict the subsequent income effects of an original increment in investment outlays.[7] But such a change in the rate of the income circulation of money is not related to changes in spending habits of the various cash holders. It is connected with structural changes of the economy; hence it does not invalidate the basic idea of the quantity theory.

If the quantity of money is increased by open market operations, then there will be an increase in both passive and active cash holdings if the liquidity preference function *and* the investment function are interest elastic. The preceding conclusions will then be applicable. Even if the liquidity preference function, and not the investment function,

[7] As is clearly emphasized by Joseph J. Spengler, the various cash holders fall into distinct classes with different habits of spending, which makes it impossible to infer the effect of a change in the quantity of money from the behavior of only one class (»The Future of Prices», *S. E. J.*, 1946, p. 27). This circumstance evidently refers to the cash holdings both within the consumption sector and within the investment sector of the economy.

should be interest elastic, the special case of the quantity theory will, very likely, not be realized; namely, the increase in prices of government bonds is directly proportionate to the increased demand, *i.e.*, to ΔM_S $(= \Delta M)$. For the price increase will cause some increase in supply. Only if the liquidity preference function is perfectly interest inelastic will the prices of bonds and securities increase in the same proportion.

These cases can be considered as special cases of the distribution of an increment in the total quantity of money. As a rule, both active and passive cash holdings will increase somewhat. Hence, any proportionate changes in the price level, *ceteris paribus*, are excluded, since $\Delta M \neq \Delta M_T$. And only if $\Delta M_T = \Delta M_C$, can the rate of turnover of the income circulation of money be expected to remain constant, provided that the income-expenditure habits of the various cash holders are unaffected. The greatest difficulty lies in predicting the effect of a change in the quantity of money upon those consumption expenditures which are not directly related to a given income period. Here, one may very well expect some fluctuations in the income circulation of money because of changes in the average time of keeping active cash balances. At any rate, this sector of the economy is the only one where the rate of income circulation is fairly constant in the short run. In the longer run, statistics show a steady decline (in the United States), except for certain periods which show a remarkable constancy, of the income circulation of money.[8] This is to be expected, since the steady increase in total national income (in real terms) makes the consumption expenditures less dependent upon the income period. Thus, only in the short run will the income circulation of money remain constant as the total quantity of money changes. But this proposition, which is built upon the essence of the original quantity theory, is nevertheless basically true.

Of more general interest is the question: How will the increase in total income be divided between an increment in real income (and employment) and price increases? As is clearly displayed by the first identity on page 238, there are two extreme cases, between which the probable development will take place: Either ΔP_C and ΔP_I can be zero, *i.e.*, output is perfectly elastic, or ΔO_C and ΔO_I can be zero,

[8] See Angell: *Investment and Business Cycles*, New York and London, 1941, pp. 337—338, and A. Hansen, *op. cit.*, pp. 3—5. Their definition, however, of the income circulation of money is not exactly the same as ours, but the tendency must also apply to that definition of the income circulation of money which we have put forward.

i.e., output is perfectly inelastic. In the latter case, a proportionate price increase will occur only if $\Delta M_S = 0$, and if C_C and C_I remain constant. This is conceivable in a situation of full utilization of all resources and with perfect foresight which makes passive cash holdings unnecessary. Classical economics presumed the first condition and neglected the second, and maintained that changes in the quantity of money will cause proportionate price changes. But this must be regarded as a special case, the realization of which seems extremely doubtful. For even in a situation of full employment, there is no reason to expect the relation between active and passive cash holdings to remain unaffected as the total quantity of money changes. And a decrease in the quantity of money may lead to a decrease in employment, which means that one of the basic assumptions of the classical school actually excludes all possibilities of the effects of changes in the total quantity of money except one, namely a price increase.

As has been demonstrated, the effects of changes in the total quantity of money are chiefly determined by how the changes take place, which largely determines the distribution of the new money in active and passive cash holdings, and by the actual economic situation, which determines the various elasticities of supply. To answer the question: What are the effects of a change in the total quantity of money? thus requires a careful study of the actual economic situation in which the change is assumed to take place. Such an analysis, however, seems to be much more fruitful if it is based upon a clear distinction between the role of money as a medium of exchange and as a store of value. The synthesis of these two functions of money, in a general analysis, could be pursued in much greater detail, but it has been necessary to limit this discussion to the basic idea of the quantity theory. The recognition of the basic truth in this idea is one of the fundamental requisites of an adequate monetary theory.

CONCLUSIONS

The main purpose of this study has been to scrutinize the historical development and interpretation of the quantity theory. This task was undertaken without any preconceived opinions of the 'correct' interpretation of this much debated theory. But it was, and still is, our belief that only a close examination of how and why the quantity theory was originally formulated can provide a satisfactory answer. Only a lack of knowledge of the historical emergence of the quantity theory can explain the multitude of its misinterpretations and all the ineffectual criticism of its content. It can be easily demonstrated that most modern textbooks on money and banking' still give an inadequate representation of the essence of the quantity theory. While the space devoted to the discussion of the quantity theory in modern works on money and monetary theory has gradually declined, it has always been enough to state the theory in the following way, which also is its commonly accepted version: If other things remain equal, prices will vary in proportion to changes in the quantity of money. The criticism of this statement amounts only to saying that since other things will not remain equal, the proposition is of no significance for an analysis of real monetary problems. The main conclusion of this study is that the representation of the quantity theory in this or similar ways is simply based upon a misinterpretation, mainly due to a confusion of arithmetic and causal relations. This conclusion is founded on a close analysis of the purpose of Locke's and Hume's formulations of the relation between the quantity of money and prices. Since Locke's proposition that, if other things remain equal, prices are always in proportion to the quantity of money obviously is a truism, his purpose must have been something else than to state mere truisms. The main argument in this study has been that the purpose of his formulation was to illustrate a specific peculiarity of money, namely that money as such is of no value and does not add to the output of real wealth, thereby emphasizing the function of money as being fundamentally a medium of exchange. His proposition was directed primarily toward the mercantile view that money *per se* constituted (the most important) part of the wealth of a nation. But partly because of Hume's less careful formulation of the same idea and partly because of a lack of distinction between his and Locke's proposition from Bodin's explanation of the great price increase on the continent in the sixteenth century, a causal proposition was ascribed to Locke's original statement. How easy it was to make this confusion is demonstrated by the multitude of confusions of the equation of exchange with the quantity theory, which actually is the same kind of confusion since the equation of exchange can be used as an algebraic illustration of Locke's fundamental idea. Locke's formulation of the original quantity theory amounted only to an *illustration* of money as essentially a medium of exchange. Hence it was no real theory. But a simple theory based upon this idea can easily be formulated, namely that changes in the quantity of money (used as a medium of exchange) will not influence the spending habits of the individual cash-holder, *i.e.*, the rate of circulation of money. In other words: since money is fundamentally a medium of exchange, changes in the quantity of money (used as a medium of exchange) will not influence the basic relations of an economy. This view was generally accepted by the classical economists, and since they presumed full utilization of the total resources of society, changes in the quantity of money, *ceteris paribus*, were said to cause corresponding changes in prices. Then they either neglected the available stocks or they were speaking of long-run effects. This *special* case of the quantity theory then seemingly coincided with Locke's original proposition of proportionality and accounts partly for the confusion of these two separate statements. For it was overlooked that Locke's original proposition did not contain any proposition of causality. But if by 'changes in the quantity of money' is meant changes in the amount of monetary purchases, then the commonly accepted formulation of the quantity theory — when the *ceteris-paribus* premise is kept — appears as a truism of the same kind as Locke's original proposition. To make it worthy the name of a theory, therefore, requires the abandonment of the *ceteris-paribus* premise. This was clearly realized by Fisher, who also was the first to carry out this line of thought. But the influence of the essence of the original quantity theory was quite evident as his whole discussion of money was a discussion of money as a pure medium of *exchange*, which is also indicated by the characterization of his famous equation as the equation of exchange.

As a reaction against this one-sided approach the Cambridge School emphasized the function of money as a store of value from the viewpoint of the individual cash holder. The fundamental difference between these two approaches lies just in their emphasis on the function of money as a medium of exchange and as a store of value, respectively. The Cambridge School discussed changes in the desire to keep cash balances over a given period of time, presuming a given quantity of money, whereas the quantity theory assumed changes in the quantity of money, maintaining that the rate of circulation of money will not be influenced. But since the Cambridge School discussed changes in the rate of circulation of money in relation to the total quantity of money, it actually dealt with changes in the distribution of the total quantity of money in active and passive cash balances. And when the 'quantity theorists' spoke of changes in the rate of circulation of money they also dealt with the effects of changes in the distribution of money in active and passive cash balances.

Because of the 'hybrid' concept of the rate of circulation of money Keynes avoided the use of it as much as possible. Instead of discussing the effects of changes in the amount of total cash holdings on the price level, he traced their influence on the rate of interest and on the whole economic activity, thereby continuing the line of thought originated by Wicksell. Keynes aimed at the integration of his monetary theory with a general theory of employment. But because of his, naturally enough, great emphasis on the role of money as a store of value in order to bring out his main ideas, he minimized the importance of the role of money as a medium of exchange.

The purpose of the second part of this study, therefore, has been to integrate *both* these functions of money with an analysis of the effects of changes in the total quantity of money and in the distribution of a given quantity of money. For these two separate views can properly be described as half-truths. The first chapter of the second part of this study is therefore a discussion of the various functions money, and it is maintained that the basic function of money is that of being a medium of exchange, not a store of value, though the second function is a necessary attribute because of market imperfections and of the uncertainty of the future. By splitting up the total quantity of money into active and passive cash holdings which represent money kept as a medium of exchange and as a store of value, respectively, the effects of changes in the distribution of a given quantity of money on the rates of interest and on the price level was discussed in chapter XII.

Since the fundamental proposition that can be derived from the original formulation of the quantity theory is that changes in the quantity of money (used as a medium of exchange) will not influence the spending habits of the individual cash holders, the concept of the so-called 'velocity' of circulation of money was scrutinized in the following chapter. The first conclusion was that the rate of circulation of money must be related to a quantity of money that has actually circulated during the relevant period. Otherwise changes in the distribution of the quantity of money in active and passive cash holdings are treated as changes in the rate of circulation of money. This also makes it impossible to discuss the effects of changes in the quantity of money with respect to the basic functions of money. The second and main conclusion was that the rate of circulation of money is essentially determined by the prevailing institutions and that therefore changes in the quantity of money, as a rule, do not influence this factor. The quantity theory, therefore, is basically correct in so far as it maintains that changes in the quantity of money do not cause any changes in the spending habits of the cash holders. It was also maintained that the use of the word 'velocity' is extremely inadequate, since there is no 'velocity' of money.

In the final chapter the effects of changes in the total quantity of money were analyzed, in point of principle, with due regard to the function of money as both a medium of exchange and as a store of value. The analysis showed that these two functions must both be considered in a satisfactory analysis of the effects of changes in the quantity of money upon total income, and that both functions, as well as the corresponding cash holdings, were equally important, *ceteris paribus*, for obtaining a given level of income. It was clearly demonstrated that only if the change of the passive cash holdings were zero when the total quantity of money changed, would the special case of the quantity theory, *ceteris paribus*, be correct; and only if the change of the active cash holdings were zero, would the liquidity preference theory be sufficient for the analysis of the effects of changes in the total quantity of money. Although both cases are conceivable, there is but a remote probability of their realization. The real difficulty in an analysis of this kind lies in the determination of how a change in the total quantity of money will be distributed between active and passive cash holdings. The analysis aimed both at the illustration of the fundamental difference between the quantity-theory and the liquidity-preference approach, which is based upon a difference in the emphasis of the two main functions of money, and at a synthesis of these different views in an analysis of the effects of changes in the total quantity of money. The merit of the quantity theory is its clear illustration of the basic function of money as being a medium of exchange; a merit, however, which was achieved at the expense of neglecting the role of money as a store of value and which led to an isolated existence of monetary theory almost up to the beginning of this century.

SELECTED BIBLIOGRAPHY

I. BOOKS

AFTALION, A.: *Monnaie, prix et change*, Paris, 1927. (3 ed., 2 vols. Paris, 1948—50.)

— —: *L'or et sa distribution mondiale*. Paris, 1932.

ÅKERMAN, G.: *De penningpolitiska normernas utveckling*. Lund, 1926.

ÅKERMAN, J.: *Ekonomisk teori*. 2 vols. Lund, 1939—1944.

ALTMANN, S. P.: *Zur deutschen Geldlehre des 19. Jahrhunderts*. (In G. SCHMOLLER: *Die Entwicklung der Volkswirtschaftlehre*, vol. I, Leipzig, 1908.)

American Economic Association: *A Survey of Contemporary Economics*. Ed. by H. S. ELLIS. Philadelphia, 1948.

— —: *Readings in Monetary Theory*. Selected by a committee of the American Economic Association. Philadelphia, 1951.

ANDERSON, B. M.: *The Value of Money*. New York, 1917.

ANGELL, J. W.: *The Theory of International Prices*. Cambridge, Mass., 1926. (Harvard Economic Studies, vol. XXVIII.)

— —: *The Behavior of Money*. New York, 1936.

— —: *Investment and Business Cycles*. New York, 1941.

BAUDIN, L.: *La Monnaie et la formation des prix*. Part 1: *Les éléments* (part VI of *Traité d'économie politique*, publ. under the direction of HENRI TRUCHY, 2 ed., Paris, 1947).

BENDIXEN, F.: *Das Wesen des Geldes*. Leipzig, 1908.

BERKELEY, G.: *The Works of George Berkeley*. Ed. by A. C. FRASER. 4 vols. Oxford, 1901.

BIEL OF SPEYER, G.: *Treatise on the Power and Utility of Moneys*. Reprinted, London, 1930.

BLOCK, M.: *Le progrès de la science économiques depuis Adam Smith*. 2 vols. Paris, 1897.

BODIN, JEAN: *Réponse au paradoxe de M. de Malestroit*. (Publ. by HENRI HAUSER under the title: *La vie chère au XVIe siècle, la response de Jean Bodin à M. de Malestroit*, 1568.) Paris, 1932.

BODIN DE SAINT-LAURENT, JEAN DE: *Les idées monétaires et commerciales de Jean Bodin*. (Diss.) Bordeaux, 1907.

BONN, M. J.: *Spaniens Niedergang während der Preisrevolution des 16. Jahrhunderts*. Stuttgart, 1896.

BOSANQUET, C.: *Practical Observations on the Report of the Bullion Committee*. London, 1810.

BRESCIANI-TURRONI, C.: *The Economics of Inflation*. Transl. by M. SAYERS. London, 1937.

BRIDREY, E.: *La théorie de la monnaie au XIVe siècle. Nicole Oresme; étude d'histoire des doctrines et des faits économiques*. Paris, 1906.

BURNS, A. R.: *Money and Monetary Policy in Early Times.* London, 1927.
BUSSCHAU, W. J.: *The Theory of Gold Supply.* Oxford, 1936.
CANNAN, E.: *Modern Currency and the Regulation of Its Value.* London, 1931.
— —: *Money, Its Connection with Rising and Falling Prices.* London, 1935.
CANTILLON, R.: *Essai sur la nature du commerce en général.* 1755.
CARLILE, W.: *The Evolution of Modern Money.* London, 1901.
CASSEL, G.: *Dyrtid och sedelöverflöd.* Stockholm, 1917.
— —: *Penningväsendet efter 1914.* Stockholm, 1922. (German ed.: *Das Geldwesen nach 1914.* Leipzig, 1925.)
— —: *The Theory of Social Economy.* Transl. by B. L. BARRON. 2 vols. London, 1932. (Swedish ed., Stockholm, 1938.)
— —: *On Quantitative Thinking in Economics.* Oxford, 1935.
— —: *The Downfall of the Gold Standard.* Oxford, 1936.
CHANDLER, L.: *An Introduction to Monetary Theory.* New York, 1940.
CHEN HUAN-CHANG: *The Economic Principles of Confucius and His School.* New York, 1911. (*Studies in History, Economics and Public Law*, ed. by the Faculty of Pol. Science of Columbia Univ., vol. XLIV—XLV, no. 112—113.)
Corpus Juris Civilis. Impressio nona. Lipsiae, 1861.
CROWTHER, G.: *An Outline of Money.* London, 1940.
CURRIE, L.: *The Supply and Control of Money in the United States.* Cambridge, Mass., 1935. (Harvard Economic Studies, vol. XLVII.)
DAVANZATI, B.: *Lezione delle Monete.* (Scrittori Classici Italiani di Economia Politica, vol. 2, Milano, 1804.)
DENIS, H.: *Les récentes théories monétaires en France. Idée quantitative et conflit des méthodes.* (Diss.) Paris, 1938.
DESPAUX, A.: *Les dévaluations monétaires dans l'histoire.* Paris, 1936.
DIEHL, K.: *Die Entwicklung der Wert- und Preistheorie im 19. Jahrhundert.* (In G. SCHMOLLER: *Die Entwicklung der Volkswirtschaftslehre*, vol. I. Leipzig, 1908.)
DILLARD, D.: *The Economics of John Maynard Keynes. The Theory of Monetary Economy.* New York, 1948.
DIVISIA, F.: *Economique rationelle.* Paris, 1928.
DOLLEANS, E.: *La Monnaie et les prix.* Paris, 1905.
DÖRING, H.: *Die Geldtheorien seit Knapp.* 2 ed., Greifswald, 1922.
DUBOIS, A.: *Précis de l'histoire des doctrines économiques.* Paris, 1903.
DUPRIEZ, L.: *Des mouvements économiques généraux.* Louvain, 1947.
DURBIN, E.: *The Problem of Credit Policy.* London, 1935.
EINZIG, P.: *Primitive Money in Its Ethnological, Historical and Economic Aspects.* London, 1949.
ELLIS, H.: *German Monetary Theory 1905—1933.* Cambridge, Mass., 1934. (Harvard Economic Studies, vol. XLIV.)
EMRICH, I.: *Die Geldtheoretischen und Geldpolitischen Anschauungen John Lockes.* Leipzig, 1927.
ENDEMANN, W.: *Studien in der Romanischkanonistischen Wirtschafts- und Rechtslehre.* Berlin, 1883.
FANNO, M.: *La Moneta.* Torino, 1908.
FELLNER, W.: *Monetary Policies and Full Employment.* Los Angeles, 1946.
FISHER, I.: *The Purchasing Power of Money.* New York, 1911.

FISHER, I.: *Stabilizing the Dollar.* New York, 1920.

— —: *The Money Illusion.* New York, 1928.

— —: *100 % Money.* New York, 1935.

— —: *Stable Money, a History of the Movement* (with the assistance of H. R. L. COHRSSEN). New York, 1935.

FÖHL, C.: *Geldschöpfung und Wirtschaftskreislauf.* München, 1937.

FOSTER, W. and CATCHINGS, W.: *Money.* New York, 1927.

FOVILLE, A. DE: *La Monnaie.* Paris, 1907.

FULLARTON, J.: *On the Regulation of the Currencies.* 2 ed., London, 1845.

GIDE, C. and RIST, C.: *Histoire des doctrines économiques.* Paris, 1909.

GONNARD, R.: *Histoire des doctrines monétaires.* 2 vols. Paris, 1935—36.

GREIDANUS, T.: *The Value of Money.* London, 1932.

HALES, J.: *A Discourse of the Common Weal of this Realm of England.* Ed. by ELIZABETH LAMOND, Cambridge, 1893.

HALM, G.: *Monetary Theory.* 2 ed., Philadelphia, 1948.

HAMILTON, E. J.: *American Treasure and the Price Revolution in Spain, 1501—1650.* Cambridge, Mass., 1934. (Harvard Economic Studies, vol. XLII.)

— —: *War and Prices in Spain, 1651—1800.* Cambridge, Mass., 1947. (Harvard Economic Studies, vol. LXXXI.)

HAMMARSKJÖLD, D.: *Konjunkturspridningen. En teoretisk och historisk undersökning.* Stockholm, 1933. (Statens offentliga utredningar, 1933: 29.)

HANEY, L. H.: *History of Economic Thought.* New York, 1949.

HANSEN, A.: *Monetary Theory and Fiscal Policy.* New York, 1949.

HANSEN, B.: *A Study in the Theory of Inflation.* London, 1951. (The Library of Economics, section 2; New Works, 4.)

HARRIS, J.: *An Essay upon Money and Coins.* (In *Old and Scarce Tracts on Money,* London, 1933.)

HARRIS, S. E.: *Inflation and the American Economy.* New York, 1945.

HARSIN, P.: *Les doctrines monétaires et financières en France du XVIe siècle.* Paris, 1928.

HART, A. G.: *Money, Debt and Economic Activity.* New York, 1948.

HAWTREY, R. G.: *Currency and Credit.* London, 1919. (4 ed., London, 1950.)

— —: *Trade and Credit.* London, 1928.

HAYEK, F. VON: *Geldtheorie und Konjunkturtheorie.* Wien, 1929.

— —: *Prices and Production.* New York, 1932.

HECKSCHER, E. F.: *Mercantilism.* Transl. by M. SHAPIRO. 2 vols. London, 1935.

HEIMANN, E.: *History of Economic Doctrines.* 2 ed., London and New York, 1947.

HELFFERICH, K.: *Das Geld.* 6 ed., Leipzig, 1923.

HERTZKA, T.: *Das Wesen des Geldes.* Leipzig, 1887.

HILDEBRAND, R.: *Die Theorie des Geldes.* Jena, 1883.

HODGES, J.: *The Present State of England as to Coin and Publick Charges.* London, 1697.

HOFFMAN, F.: *Kritische Dogmengeschichte der Geldwerttheorien.* Leipzig, 1907.

HOLTROP, M.: *De omloopssnellheid van het geld.* Amsterdam, 1928.

— —: (German ed.: *Die Umlaufsgeschwindigkeit des Geldes* in *Beiträge zur Konjunkturforschung,* ed. by F. VON HAYEK, Wien, 1933.)

HORNBOSTEL, H.: *La Vitesse de la circulation de la monnaie et les variations de pouvoir d'achat.* Paris, 1930.

Hume, David: *Essays and Treatises.* A New Edition. 2 vols. London, 1825.
Jevons, W. Stanley: *Money and the Mechanism of Exchange.* London, 1875.
— —: *Investigations in Currency and Finance.* London, 1884.
— —: *The Principles of Economics.* New York and London, 1905.
Juglar, C.: *Du Change et de la liberté d'émission.* Paris, 1868.
Kaulla, R.: *Die geschichtlische Entwicklung der modernen Werttheorien.* Tübingen, 1906.
Kellenberger, E.: *Geldumlauf und Thesaurierung.* Zürich, 1920.
Kemmerer, E. W.: *Money and Credit Instruments in Their Relation to General Prices.* New York, 1907.
— —: *Money.* New York, 1935.
Keynes, J. M.: *A Tract on Monetary Reform.* New York, 1924.
— —: *A Treatise on Money.* 2 vols. London, 1930.
— —: *The General Theory of Employment, Interest and Money.* London, 1936.
Kinley, D.: *Money, a Study of the Theory of the Medium of Exchange.* New York, 1904.
Kirmaier, K.: *Die Quantitätstheorie.* Jena, 1922.
Knapp, G. F.: *Staatliche Theorie des Geldes.* Leipzig, 1905.
Knies, C.: *Geld und Credit.* Berlin, 1873.
Lambert, P.: *La Théorie quantitative de la monnaie.* Paris, 1938.
Lange, O.: *Price Flexibility and Employment.* Bloomington, Indiana, 1944.
Laughlin, J. L.: *The History of Bimetallism in the United States.* 4 ed., New York, 1897.
— —: *Money and Prices.* New York, 1924.
— —: *The Principles of Money.* New York, 1926.
— —: *A New Exposition of Money, Credit and Prices.* 2 vols. Chicago, 1931.
Law, John: *Money and Trade Considered.* Glasgow, 1750.
Le Branchu, J. Y.: *Ecrits notables sur la monnaie. De Copernic à Davanzati.* 2 vols. Paris, 1934.
Leroy-Beaulieu, P.: *Traité théoretique et practique d'économie politique.* 4 vols. 3 ed., Paris, 1900.
The Lessons of Monetary Experience. Essays in Honor of Irving Fisher. Ed. by A. D. Gayer. New York, 1937.
Liautey, A.: *La hausse des prix et la lutte contre la cherté en France au XVIe siècle.* (Diss.) Paris, 1921.
Lindahl, E.: *Studies in the Theory of Money and Capital.* London, 1939.
Locke, John: *The Works of John Locke.* Publ. by Ward, Lock and Co., London and New York, [1883?].
Loria, A.: *Studi sul valore della moneta.* 2 ed., Torino, 1901.
— —: *Il valore della moneta.* Torino, 1905.
Lotz, W.: *Die drei Flugschriften über den Münzstreit der sächsischen Albertiner und Ernestiner um 1530.* Leipzig, 1893.
Lundberg, E.: *Studies in the Theory of Economic Expansion.* London, 1937.
Lütge, F.: *Einführung in die Lehre vom Gelde.* München, 1948.
Luzzati, G.: *Prezzi ideali e prezzi effettive.* Milano, 1892.
Malynes, G.: *A Treatise of the Canker of England's Common Wealth* (1601). (In Tawney and Power: *Tudor Economic Documents*, III, 1924.)

MARGET, A. W.: *The Theory of Prices.* 2 vols. New York, 1938—1942.

MARSHALL, A.: *Money, Credit and Commerce.* London, 1923.

— —: *Official Papers by Alfred Marshall.* Ed. by J. M. KEYNES, London, 1926.

MARX, K.: *Till kritiken av den politiska ekonomien.* (Swedish transl. by R. WAGNER, Stockholm, 1943.)

MICHAELIS, A.: *Die Quantitätstheorie als Grundlage der Konjunkturforschung.* Jena, 1929.

MILL, JAMES: *Elements of Political Economy.* London, 1821.

MILL, J. STUART: *Principles of Political Economy.* Ed. by W. J. ASHLEY, London, 1923.

MINTS, L.: *Monetary Policy for a Competitive Society.* New York, 1950.

MISES, L. VON: *Theorie des Geldes und der Umlaufsmittel.* 2 ed., München, 1924. (English ed. 1934.)

MITCHELL, W. C.: *The Backward Art of Spending Money and Other Essays.* London and New York, 1937.

MONROE, A. E.: *Monetary Theory before Adam Smith.* Cambridge, Mass., 1923. (Harvard Economic Studies, vol. XXV.)

MONTANARI, G.: *Della Moneta.* (Scrittori Classici Italiani di Economia Politica, vol. 3, Milano, 1804.)

MONTCHRÉTIEN, A. DE: *Traicté de l'œconomie politique. 1615.* (Ed. by FUNCK-BRENTANO, Paris, 1889.)

MONTESQUIEU, C.: *The Spirit of Laws.* Transl. by THOMAS NUGENT. 2 vols. London, 1823.

MOSAK, J.: *General-Equilibrium Theory in International Trade.* Bloomington, Indiana, 1944.

MUN, THOMAS: *England's Treasure by Foreign Trade.* (In McCULLOCH's *Early English Tracts on Commerce*, London, 1856.)

MYRDAL, G.: *Monetary Equilibrium.* London, 1939.

NEWCOMB, S.: *Principles of Political Economy.* New York, 1886.

NEWMARCH, W.: See T. TOOKE.

NICHOLSON, J. S.: *Principles of Political Economy.* 3 vols. New York and London, 1893—1901.

— —: *A Treatise on Money and Essays on Monetary Problems.* 5 ed., London, 1901.

NIEBYL, K. H.: *Studies in the Classical Theories of Money.* New York, 1946.

NOGARO, B.: *Le rôle de la monnaie dans le commerce international et la théorie quantitative.* (Diss.) Paris, 1904.

— —: *La monnaie et les phénomènes monétaires contemporains.* Paris, 1935.

NORMAN, G. W.: *Remarks upon Some Prevalent Errors with Respect to Currency and Banking.* London, 1838.

OERTMANN, P.: *Die Volkswirtschaftslehre des Corpus Juris Civilis.* Berlin, 1891.

OHLIN, B.: *Bidrag till expansionens teori.* Stockholm, 1934. (Statens offentliga utredningar, 1934: 12.)

ONCKEN, A.: *Geschichte der Nationaloekonomie.* Band I: *Die Zeit vor Adam Smith.* Leipzig, 1902.

ORESME, NICOLE: *Traictie de la première invention des monnaies de Nicole Oresme et Traité de la monnaie de Copernic.* (Publ. by M. L. WOLOWSKI, Paris, 1864.)

ÖSTLIND, A.: *Svensk samhällsekonomi 1914—1922.* Stockholm, 1945.

OVERSTONE, LORD: *Tracts and Other Publications on Metallic and Paper Currency.* London, 1858.

PANTALEONI, M.: *Pure Economics.* Transl. by T. B. BRUCE. 2 vols. London, 1898.

PEARSON, F. A.: See G. F. Warren.

PEDERSEN, J.: *Pengeteori og Pengepolitik.* København, 1944. (2 ed., 1948.)

PETERSEN, E.: *Den moderne kvantitetsteoris gyldighet for pengeverdiens bestemmelse.* Oslo, 1933.

— —: *Macro-Dynamic Aspects of the Equation of Exchange.* Oslo, 1938. (Skrifter utgitt av Det Norske Videnskapsakademi i Oslo, II. Hist.-Filos. Klasse. No. 6.)

PETTY, W.: *The Economic Writings of Sir William Petty.* Ed. by C. H. HULL. 2 vols. Cambridge, 1899.

— —: *Quantulumqunque Concerning Money.* 1682. (In *Old and Scarce Tracts on Money*, London, 1933.)

PIGOU, A. C.: *Industrial Fluctuations.* 2 ed., London, 1929.

— —: *The Veil of Money.* London, 1949.

— —: *Keynes' General Theory. A Retrospect.* London, 1950.

POSE, A.: *De la théorie monétaire à la théorie économique.* Paris, 1930.

POTTER, W.: *The Key of Wealth.* 1650.

PRICE, BONAMY: *The Principles of Currency.* Oxford and London, 1869.

— —: *Currency and Banking.* New York, 1876.

RAU, K. H.: *Lehrbuch der politischen Ökonomie.* Heidelberg, 1826.

Readings in Money & Banking. Ed. by E. M. ROSENGREN, Toronto, 1948.

RICARDO, D.: *The Works of David Ricardo.* Ed. by J. R. MCCULLOCH, London, 1846.

RIST, C.: *Essais sur quelques problèmes économiques et monétaires.* Paris, 1933.

— —: *Histoire des doctrines relatives au crédit et à la monnaie, depuis John Law jusqu'à nos jours.* Paris, 1938.

GIDE and RIST: See GIDE.

ROBERTSON, D. H.: *Money.* London, 1922. (6 ed., London, 1948.)

— —: *Banking Policy and the Price Level.* London, 1926. (3 ed., London, 1932.)

— —: *Essays in Monetary Theory.* London, 1940.

ROBINSON, H.: *England's Safety; in Trade Encrease.* 1641.

ROLL, E.: *A History of Economic Thought.* London, 1938.

ROSCHER, W.: *System der Volkswirtschaft.* 5 vols. 11 ed., Stuttgart, 1874.

— —: *Geschichte der National-Oekonomik in Deutschland.* München, 1874.

ROST, BERNHARD, *i. e.*, FRIEDRICH BERNHARD: *Die Wert- und Preistheorie, mit Berücksichtigung ihrer dogmengeschichtlichen Entwickelung.* Leipzig, 1908.

RUEFF, J.: *Sur une théorie de l'inflation.* Paris, 1925.

— —: *Théorie des phénomènes monétaires.* Paris, 1927.

SAULNIER, R. J.: *Contemporary Monetary Theory.* New York, 1938.

SAY, J. B.: *Traité d'économie politique.* Publ. by HORACE SAY, 6 ed., Paris, 1841.

SCHÄFFLE, A. E. F.: *Das gesellschaftliche System der menschlichen Wirtschaft.* Tübingen, 1873.

SCHREIBER, E.: *Die volkswirtschaftlichen Anschauungen der Scholastik seit Thomas v. Aquin.* Jena, 1913.

SCHUMPETER, J.: *Epochen der Dogmen- und Methodengeschichte.* (In *Grundriss des Sozialökonomi*, vol. I, Tübingen, 1914.)

— —: *Business Cycles.* 2 vols. New York and London, 1939.

SENIOR, W. N.: *Three Lectures on the Transmission of the Precious Metals from Country to Country and the Mercantile Theory of Wealth.* (No. 3 in *Series of Reprints of Scarce Tracts in Economic and Political Science*, London, 1931.)

— —: *Three Lectures on the Value of Money.* (No. 4 in *Series of Reprints etc.*)

— —: *Three Lectures on the Cost of Obtaining Money.* (No. 5 in *Series of Reprints etc.*)

SEWALL, H. R.: *The Theory of Value before Adam Smith.* New York, 1901.

SIMONS, H. C.: *Economic Policy for a Free Society.* Chicago, 1947.

SMITH, ADAM: *The Wealth of Nations.* Publ. by G. BELL & SONS, 1901.

— —: *Lectures on Justice, Police, Revenue and Arms.* Reported by a Student in 1763 and edited with an introduction and notes by E. CANNAN. Oxford, 1896.

STEUART, J.: *An Inquiry into the Principles of Political Economy.* 5 vols. 1796.

STUCKEN, R.: *Geld und Kredit.* Tübingen, 1949.

SUBERCASEAUX, G.: *Essai sur la nature du papier monnaie.* Paris, 1909.

— —: *Le papier monnaie.* Paris, 1920.

TAUSSIG, F. W.: *Principles of Economics.* 2 vols. 3 ed., New York, 1933.

THOMAS, P.: *Essai sur quelques théories éonomiques dans le Corpus juris civilis.* (Diss.) Paris, 1899.

THORNTON, H.: *An Inquiry into the Nature and Effects of the Paper Credit of Great Britain.* (Repr. 1939.)

TOOKE, T.: *Thoughts and Details on the High and Low Prices of the Last Thirty Years.* 4 vols. London, 1823.

— —: *Considerations on the State of Currency.* London, 1826.

— —: *An Inquiry into the Currency Principle.* London, 1844.

TOOKE, T. and NEWMARCH, W.: *A History of Prices.* 6 vols. London, 1838—57.

TORRENS, R.: *Essay on Money and Paper Currency.* London, 1812.

— —: *The Principles and Practical Operation of Sir Robert Peel's Act.* 2 ed., London, 1857.

VILLARD, H.: *Deficit Spending and the National Income.* New York, 1941.

VINER, J.: *Studies in the Theory of International Trade.* New York, 1937.

VISSERING, W.: *On Chinese Currency, Coins and Paper Money.* Leiden, 1877.

VITI DE MARCO, A. DE: *Moneta e prezzi.* Città di Castella, 1885.

WAGEMANN, E.: *Allgemeine Geldlehre.* Berlin, 1923.

WAGNER, A.: *Theoretische Sozialökonomik.* 2 vols. Leipzig, 1907.

— —: *Die Geld- und Credittheorie der Peel'schen Bankacte.* Wien, 1862.

WAGNER, V. F.: *Geschichte der Kredittheorien; eine dogmenkritische Darstellung.* Wien, 1937.

WAHA, R. DE: *De la théorie quantitative à la théorie psychologique de la monnaie.* Luxembourg, 1933.

WAHLTER, A.: *Geldwert in der Geschichte.* Berlin, 1912.

WALKER, F. A.: *Money.* New York, 1883.

WALRAS, L.: *Théorie de la monnaie.* Paris, 1886.

— —: *Eléments d'économie politique pure ou théorie de la richesse sociale.* Paris, 1896.

WARREN, G. F. and PEARSON, F. A.: *Gold and Prices.* New York and London, 1930.

WESSELS, T.: *Die Geldtheorie Léon Walras.* Köln, 1925.

WHITTAKER, E.: *A History of Economic Ideas.* London, 1940.

WICKSELL, K.: *Interest and Prices.* Transl. by R. F. KAHN. London, 1936.

— —: *Lectures on Political Economy.* Transl. by E. CLASSEN, and edited with an introduction by L. ROBBINS. 2 vols. London, 1935.

WIEBE, G.: *Zur Geschichte der Preisrevolution im 16. und 17. Jahrhundert.* Leipzig, 1895.

WILSON, J.: *Capital, Currency, and Banking.* London, 1847.

WRIGHT, D. MC CORD: *The Creation of Purchasing Power.* Cambridge, Mass., 1942. (Harvard Economic Studies, vol. LXXII.)

XENOPHON: *The Works of Xenophon.* Transl. by H. G. DAKYNS. 4 vols. London, 1892.

ZUCKERKANDL, R.: *Zur Theorie des Preises.* Leipzig, 1889.

ZIJLSTRA, J.: *De omloopssnelheid van het geld en zijn beteknis voor geldwaarde en monetair evenwicht.* (Diss.) Leiden, 1948.

II. ARTICLES

ABBREVATIONS

A. E. R.	*The American Economic Review.*
A. f. S.	*Archiv für Sozialwissenschaft und Sozialpolitik.*
E. J.	*The Economic Journal.*
E. T.	*Ekonomisk tidskrift.*
J. P. E.	*The Journal of Political Economy.*
N. T.	*Nationaløkonomisk Tidsskrift.*
Q. J. E.	*The Quarterly Journal of Economics.*
R. E. p.	*Revue d'Economie politique.*
R. H. D.	*Revue d'Histoire des Doctrines économiques et sociales.*
R. H. é.	*Revue d'Histoire économique et sociale.*
S. E. J.	*The Southern Economic Journal.*
W. A.	*Weltwirtschaftliches Archiv.*
Z. f. N.	*Zeitschrift für Nationalökonomie.*
Z. f. V.	*Zeitschrift für Volkswirtschaft und Sozialpolitik.*

AFTALION, A.: La circulation, les changes et les prix. *Revue économique internationale,* 1924.

ÅKERMAN, G.: Inflation, penningmängd och ränta. *E. T.,* 1921.

ÅKERMAN, J.: Det ekonomiska framåtskridandets problem. (In *Studier i Ekonomi och Historia.* Tillägnade ELI F. HECKSCHER. Stockholm, 1944.)

ALTMANN, S. P.: Die Quantitätstheorie. *Handwörterbuch der Staatswissenschaften,* 3 ed.

AMONN, A.: Cassels System der theoretischen Nationalökonomie. *A. f. S.,* 1924.

ANDERSON, O.: Ist die Quantitätstheorie statistisch nachweisbar? *Z. f. N.,* 1930—31.

ANDREWS, E. B.: The Bimetallist Committee of Boston and New England. *Q. J. E.,* 1894.

ANGELL, J. W.: Money, Prices and Production: Some Fundamental Concepts. *Q. J. E.,* 1933.

— —: The General Dynamics of Money. *J. P. E.,* 1937.

— —: The Components of the Circular Velocity of Money. *Q. J. E.,* 1937.

ARIAS, G.: Les précurseurs de l'économie monétaire en Italie, Davanzati et Montanari. *R. E. p.,* 1922.

BARRAULT, H. E.: Le sens et la portée des théories antiquantitatives de la monnaie. *R. H. D.*, 1910.

BAUDIN, L.: La Théorie quantitative de la monnaie. *L'Actualité économique de Montréal*, 1933.

BERNÁCER, G.: Die Grundgleichung des Geldwertes. *W. A.*, 1942.

— —: Die Geldgleichung unter merkantilistischen Bedingungen. *W. A.*, 1943.

— —: Die Geldgleichung einer kapitalistischen Wirtschaft. *W. A.*, 1944.

BILGRAM, H.: The Quantity Theory Scrutinized. *J. P. E.*, 1921.

BOULDING, K.: A Liquidity Preference Theory of Market Price. *Economica*, 1944.

BRUNNER, K.: Inconsistency and Indeterminacy in Classical Economics. *Econometrica*, 1951.

BURNS, A. P.: The Quantity Theory and Price-Stabilization. *A. E. R.*, 1929.

CANNAN, E.: The Application of the Theoretical Apparatus of Supply and Demand to Units of Currency. *E. J.*, 1921.

CARVER, T. N.: The Value of the Money Unit. *Q. J. E.*, 1897.

CASSEL, G.: Om förändringar i den allmänna prisnivån. *E. T.*, 1904.

CLOW, E.: The Quantity Theory and Its Critics. *J. P. E.*, 1903.

COPELAND, M.: Money, Trade, and Prices — A Test of Causal Primacy. *Q. J. E.*, 1929.

DAVENPORT, H. J.: Velocities, Turnovers and Prices. *A. E. R.*, 1930.

DAVIDSOHN, J.: Bidrag til Liberalismens Historie. Kvantitetsteorin omkring 1. Halvdel af 18. Aarh. *N. T.*, 1928.

DAVIDSON, D.: Guldproduktionen och varuprisen. *E. T.*, 1901.

DAVIES, G. R.: The Quantity Theory and Recent Statistical Studies. *J. P. E.*, 1921.

DECHESNE, L.: Influence de la monnaie et du crédit sur les prix. *R. E. p.*, 1904.

— —: Pour la théorie quantitative de la monnaie et du crédit. *R. E. p.*, 1914.

DEMPSEY, B. W.: The Historical Emergence of Quantity Theory. *Q. J. E.*, 1935.

DIVISIA, F.: L'indice monétaire et la théorie de la monnaie. (Reprinted from *R. E. p.*) Paris, 1926.

DMOCHOWSKI, J.: Nicolas Copernic économiste. *R. E. p.*, 1925.

DUPRIEZ, L.: Central Banking Policy and Long Trends in Prices. (In *Money, Trade, and Economic Growth.* In honor of J. H. WILLIAMS. New York, 1951.)

ELLIS, H. S.: Some Fundamentals in the Theory of Velocity. *Q. J. E.*, 1938.

ELSTER, K.: Die »Grundgleichung« der Geldtheorie. *Hildebrand's Jahrbuch*, 1920.

FISHER, I.: Quantity Theory Approved. (In *The Gold Supply and Prosperity*, ed. by B. W. HOLT, New York, 1907.)

— —: Recent Changes in Price Levels and Their Causes. (In *Bulletin of the American Economic Association*, 4 series, 1911.)

— —: A series of articles on the equation of exchange and the price development in *A. E. R.*, 1911—1917 and 1919.

FISHER, W.: Money and Credit Paper in the Modern Market. *J. P. E.*, 1895.

FOVILLE, A. DE: La théorie quantitative et les prix. *L'Economiste français*, 1895.

— —: La théorie quantitative de la monnaie et du crédit. *R. E. p.*, 1914.

FRASER, L. M.: The Equation of Exchange: a Suggestion. *Economica*. 1939.

FRIEDMAN, M.: A Monetary and Fiscal Framework for Economic Stability. *A. E. R.*, 1948.

GLENDAY, R.: Business Forecasting: a Quantitative Investigation of the Influence of Money on Trade Development. *The Journal of the Royal Statistical Society*, 1932.

GORDON, R. A.: Period and Velocity as Statistical Concepts. *Q. J. E.*, 1940—41.

HABERLER, G.: Kritische Bemerkungen zu Schumpeters Geldtheorie. *Z. f. V.*, 1925.

HAMILTON, E. J.: American Treasure. *The Journal of Economic and Business History*, 1928.

HARDY, S. M.: The Quantity of Money and Prices, 1860—1891. *J. P. E.*, 1895.

HARROD, R. F.: Mr. Keynes on Traditional Theory. *Econometrica*, 1937.

HARSIN, P.: L'afflux des métaux précieux au XVIe siècle et la théorie de la monnaie chez les auteurs français. *R. H. e.*, 1927.

— —: Bodin et la théorie monétaire au XVIe siècle. *Revue belge de Philologie et d'Histoire*, 1928.

— —: Jean Bodin économiste. *Annales de la Société scientifique de Bruxelles*, 1931.

HAUSER, H.: Un précurseur, Jean Bodin, Angevin. *Annales d'Histoire économique et sociale*, 1931.

HAYEK, F. VON: Reflections on the Pure Theory of Money of Mr. J. M. Keynes. *Economica*, 1931.

HAZELL, A. P.: The Quantity Theory of Money from the Marxist Standpoint. *J. P. E.*, 1899.

HICKMAN, W. B.: The Determinacy of Absolute Prices in Classical Economic Theory. *Econometrica*, 1950.

HOLLANDER, J. H.: The Development of the Theory of Money from Adam Smith to David Ricardo. *Q. J. E.*, 1911.

HOLTROP, M. V.: Theories of the Velocity of Circulation of Money in Earlier Economic Literature. *E. J.* (Supplement: *Economic History*), 1929.

HOOVER, C. B.: Keynes and the Economic System. *J. P. E.*, 1948.

JASTROW, J.: Copernicus Münz- und Geldtheorie. *A. f. S.*, 1914.

KEELER, B. C.: The Quantity Theory of Money. (In *The Gold Supply and Prosperity*, ed. by B. W. HOLT, New York, 1907.)

KEILHAU, W.: The Equation of Payments. (In *Economic Essays in Honour of Gustaf Cassel*, London, 1933.)

KERSCHAGL, R.: Überblick über das Schriftum des Geldwesens von 1914 bis 1920. *Z. f. V.*, 1921.

KEYNES, J. M.: Alternative Theories of the Rate of Interest. *E. J.*, 1937.

KREBS, P.: Kritische Studien zur Quantitätstheorie des Geldes. *Technik und Wirtschaft*, 1924.

LANGE, O.: Say's Law: A Restatement and Criticism. (In *Studies in Mathematical Economics and Econometrics*. In memory of HENRY SCHULTZ. Ed. by O. LANGE, F. MCINTYRE and T. O. YNTEMA, Chicago, 1942.)

LAUGHLIN, J. L.: Gold and Prices sine 1873. *Q. J. E.*, 1887.

— —: The Quantity Theory and Its Critics: A Rejoinder. *J. P. E.*, 1903.

— —: Gold and Prices, 1890—1907. *J. P. E.*, 1909.

— —: The Quantity-Theory of Money, *J. P. E.*, 1924.

LE BRANCHU, J. Y.: La théorie quantitative de la monnaie au XVIe siècle. *R. E. p.*, 1934.

LEONTIEFF, W.: The Consistency of the Classical Theory of Money and Prices. *Econometrica*, 1950.

LESCURE, J.: L'accroissement de la production de l'or et la hausse générale des prix. *R. E. p.*, 1911.

— —: Hausse et baisse générale des prix. *R. E. p.*, 1912.

— —: Prix, Monnaie et Credit. (In *Economic Essays in Honour of Gustav Cassel*, London, 1933.)

LESER, C.: The Consumer's Demand for Money. *Econometrica*, 1943.

LEXIS, W.: Papiergeld. *Handwörterbuch der Staatswissenschaften*, 4 ed.

LINDAHL, E.: Om förhållandet mellan penningmängd och prisnivå. Uppsala, 1929. (*Uppsala universitets årsskrift*, 1929.)

LITNER, J.: The Theory of Money and Prices. (In *The New Economics*. Ed. by S. E. HARRIS. New York, 1947.)

MAGEE, J. D.: Money and Prices. *J. P. E.*, 1913.

MARGET, A. W.: Léon Walras and the Cash-Balance Approach. *J. P. E.*, 1931.

— —: A Further Note on Holtrop's Formula for the »Coefficient of Differentiation» and Related Concepts. *J. P. E.*, 1933.

— —: The Monetary Aspects of the Walrasian System. *J. P. E.*, 1935.

MARSCHAK, J.: Die Verkehrsgleichung. *A. f. S.*, 1924.

— —: Money and the Theory of Assets. *Econometrica*, 1938.

— —: The Rationale of the Demand for Money and of Money Illusion. *Metroeconomica*, 1950.

MARTIN, G.: La monnaie et le crédit privé en France aux XVIe—XVIIe siècles; les faits et les théories (1550—1664). *R. H. D.*, 1909.

MATSUOKA, K.: On the Quantity Theory of Gold. *Kyoto University Economic Review*, 1934.

MISES, L. VON: Zur Klassifikation der Geldtheorie. *A. f. S.*, 1917—18.

— —: Die Quantitätstheorie. *Mitteilungen des Verbandes österreichischen Banken und Bankiers.* 1918.

MITCHELL, W. C.: The Quantity Theory of the Value of Money. *J. P. E.*, 1896.

— —: The Real Issues in the Quantity-Theory Controversy. *J. P. E.*, 1904.

MONGIN, M.: Des changements de la valeur de la monnaie. *R. E. p.*, 1887.

MUSGRAVE, R. A.: Money, Liquidity and the Valuation of Assets. (In *Money, Trade, and Economic Growth.* In honor of J. H. WILLIAMS. New York, 1951.)

NICHOLSON, J. S.: Inflation of the Currency and the Rise in Prices. *E. J.*, 1916.

NOGARO, B.: Contribution à une théorie réaliste de la monnaie. *R. E. p.*, 1906.

— —: L'expérience bimétalliste du XIXe siècle et la théorie générale de la monnaie. *R. E. p.*, 1908.

— —: Die Abhängigkeit des Preisniveaus von der Geldmenge. *W. A.*, 1928.

— —: La théorie de l'inflation à la lumière des expériences monétaires contemporaines. *R. E. p.*, 1947.

OHLIN, B.: Kvantitetsteorin i den svenska litteraturen, *E. T.*, 1919.

— —: Some Notes on the Stockholm Theory of Savings and Investment. *E. J.*, 1937.

— —: Stockholmsskolan kontra kvantitetsteorin. *E. T.*, 1943.

PALANDER, T.: Keynes allmänna teori och dess tillämpning inom ränte-, multiplikator- och pristeorien. *E. T.*, 1942.

PALYI, M.: Die Quantitätstheorie. *Handwörterbuch der Staatswissenschaften*, 4 ed.

PARKER, W. S.: An Increase in Gold and the Price-Making Process. *J. P. E.*, 1903.

PATINKIN, D.: Relative Prices, Say's Law and the Demand for Money. *Econometrica*, 1948.

— —: The Indeterminacy of Absolute Prices in Classical Economic Theory. *Econometrica*, 1949.

— —: A Reconsideration of the General Equilibrium Theory of Money. *The Review of Economic Studies*, 1949—50.

PATINKIN, D.: The Invalidity of Classical Monetary Theory. *Econometrica*, 1951.
PEDERSEN, J.: Sedelomløbet i Danmark fra 1882—1913. *Økonomi og Politik*, 1928.
— —: Wicksells Theorie des Zusammenhangs zwichen Zinssatz und Geldwertschwankungen. *A. f. S.*, 1933.
PERSONS, W. M.: The Quantity Theory as Tested by Kemmerer. *Q. J. E.*, 1908.
PETERSEN, E.: Fra kvantitetsteori til elasticitetsteori. *E. T.*, 1944.
PHILLIP, K.: Betragtninger over Kvantitetsligningen. *N. T.*, 1943.
PHINNEY, J. T.: Gold Production and the Price Level: The Cassel Three Per Cent Estimate. *Q. J. E.*, 1933.
PHIPPS, C.: A Note on Patinkin's »Relative Prices». *Econometrica*, 1950.
PIGOU, A. C.: The Value of Money. *Q. J. E.*, 1917—1918.
POSE, A.: Esquisse de l'évolution de la théorie quantitative. *R. H. é.*, 1926.
POSTAN, M.: The Rise of a Money Economy. *Economic History Review*, 1944.
RIST, C.: La circulation monétaire française et le mouvement des prix, *R. E. p.*, 1914.
— —: Hausse des prix, change et signes monétaires en France, Angleterre, Italie, Suisse, Etats-Units, Japan, Canada (in collaboration with A. MARVAS). *R. E. p.*, 1920.
ROBERTSON, D. H.: A Note on the Theory of Money. *Economica*, 1933.
— —: Some Notes on Mr. Keynes' »General Theory of Employment». *Q. J. E.*, 1936.
ROBINSON, J.: The Concept of Hoarding. *E. J.*, 1938.
ROSENSTEIN-RODAN, P. N.: The Coordination of the General Theories of Money and Price. *Economica*, 1936.
SALANT, W. A.: The Demand for Money and the Concept of Income Velocity. *J. P. E.*, 1941.
SCHMAUCH, H.: Nikolaus Copernicus und die preussische Münzreform. (In *Personal- und Vorlesungs-Verzeichnis*. 3. Trimester, 1940. Staatl. Akademie zu Braunsberg.)
SCHÖNFELD, L.: Über Joseph Schumpeters Lösung des ökonomischen Zurechnungsproblems. *Z. f. V.*, 1924.
SCHUMPETER, J.: Das Sozialprodukt und die Rechenpfennige. *A. f. S.*, 1917—18.
SCOTT, W. A.: The Quantity Theory. *Annals of the American Academy of Political and Social Science*, 1897.
SHENOY, B. H.: The Interdependence of the Price-Levels, P, P', and π. *Q. J. E.*, 1933.
SHIBATA, K.: An Examination of Professor Cassel's Quantity Theory of Money. *Kyoto University Economic Review*, 1932.
SIMMONS, E. C.: An Analysis of Factors Affecting the Volume of Currency in Circulation. *Michigan Academy of Science, Arts and Letters*, 1938.
— —: The Relative Liquidity of Money and Other Things. *A. E. R.*, 1947 (Supplement). (Reprinted in *Readings in Monetary Theory*, Philadelphia, 1951.)
— —: The Monetary Mechanism since the War. *J. P. E.*, 1950.
— —: The Structure of the Postwar Money Market. *S. E. J.*, 1951.
SMITHIES, A.: The Quantity of Money and the Rate of Interest. *The Review of Economic Statistics*, 1943.
SNYDER, C.: New Measures in the Equation of Exchange. *A. E. R.*, 1924.
SPENGLER, J. J.: The Physiocrats and Say's Law of Markets. *J. P. E.*, 1945.
— —: The Future of Prices. *S. E. J.*, 1946—47.

SPIETHOFF, A.: Die Quantitätstheorie insbesondere in ihrer Verwertbarkeit als Haussetheorie. (In *Festgaben für Adolf Wagner*, Leipzig, 1905.)

THILBY, G. F.: Demand and Supply of Money. *E. J.*, 1948.

THOMAS, B.: The Monetary Doctrines of Professor Davidson. *E. J.*, 1935.

VILLARD, H.: Monetary Theory. (In *A Survey of Contemporary Economics*. Ed. by H. S. ELLIS. Philadelphia, 1948.)

WAFFENSCHMIDT, W. G.: Studien zu einer quantitativen Geldtheorie. *A. f. S.*, 1924.

WALKER, F. A.: The Value of Money. *Q. J. E.*, 1893.

— —: The Quantity Theory of Money. *Q. J. E.*, 1895.

— —: The Relation of Changes in the Volume of the Currency to Prosperity. (In *Economic Studies of the American Economic Association*, 1896.)

— —: Quantity Theory of Money. (In PALGRAVE's *Dictionary of Political Economy.*)

WALSH, R. M.: Empirical Tests for Price Theories: Fisher, Foster and Catchings, Keynes. *Q. J. E.*, 1934.

WARBURTON, C.: The Volume of Money and the Price Level between the World Wars. *J. P. E.*, 1945.

— —: Quantity and Frequency of Use of Money in the United States, 1919—45. *J. P. E.*, 1946.

— —: The Secular Trend in Monetary Velocity. *Q. J. E.*, 1949.

WARREN, G. F. and PEARSON, F. A.: Relationship of Gold to Prices. *The Journal of the American Statistical Association*, Proceedings, 1933. (Supplement.) See also KEMMERER, E.: Discussion: Gold and Prices. *Ibid.*

WHITELAW, T. N.: Professor Nicholson on »The Causes of Movements in General Prices». *E. J.*, 1904.

WICKSELL, K.: Den dunkla punkten i penningteorien, *E. T.*, 1903.

— —: Mål och medel i nationalekonomien. *E. T.*, 1904.

— —: Ett angrepp på kvantitetsteorin. *E. T.*, 1919.

WIESER, F. VON: Der Geldwert und seine geschichtlichen Veränderungen. *Z. f. V.*, 1904.

— —: Der Geldwert und seine Veränderungen. *Schriften des Vereins für Sozialpolitik*, 1909.

WIJNHOLDS, H.: Geldmenge, Umlaufsgeschwindigkeit und Preisniveau. *W. A.*, 1939.

WILLIAMS, J. H.: The Monetary Doctrines of J. M. Keynes. *Q. J. E.*, 1931.

WILLIS, H. P.: Credit Devices and the Quantity Theory. *J. P. E.*, 1896.

— —: The History and Present Application of the Quantity Theory. *J. P. E.*, 1896.

WORKING, H.: Prices and the Quantity of Circulating Medium 1890—1921. *Q. J. E.*, 1923.

LIST OF NAMES